WHAT GOOD
IS GOD?

WHAT GOOD IS GOD?

IN SEARCH OF A FAITH THAT MATTERS

PHILIP YANCEY

Illustrations by Klaus Ernst

FaithWords

New York Boston Nashville

Scripture taken from the HOLY BIBLE, NEW INTERNATIONAL VERSION®. Copyright © 1973, 1978, 1984 Biblica. Used by permission of Zondervan. All rights reserved.   .

Illustrations by Klaus Ernst. Used by permission.

The illustration of C.S. Lewis on p. 90 is based on a photograph by John S. Murray.

FaithWords
Hachette Book Group
237 Park Avenue
New York, NY 10017

www.faithwords.com   .

Printed in the United States of America

First Edition: October 2010   .
10 9 8 7 6 5 4 3 2 1

FaithWords is a division of Hachette Book Group, Inc.
 · The FaithWords name and logo are trademarks of   ·
Hachette Book Group, Inc.

Library of Congress Cataloging-in-Publication Data

Yancey, Philip.
   What good is God? : in search of a faith that matters / Philip Yancey. — 1st ed.
      p. cm.
   ISBN 978-0-446-55985-0 (regular edition)—ISBN 978-0-446-57416-7
(large print edition)   1. Christianity.   I. Title.
   BR123.Y26 2010
   230—dc22
                              2010011797

Dedication

To the people in ten different parts of the world who shared the experiences—some tragic, some poignant, all illuminating—which gave birth to this book.

Contents

Acknowledgments

Thanks to Kathy Helmers, Joey Paul, Michelle Rapkin, and David Graham, who made valuable contributions to the editing process. Harold Fickett's superb analysis (for which I'm more grateful now than I was at the time) led to an entire rewrite. Veronica Sepe and Andrea Kellner of Hachette and my assistant Melissa Nicholson made sure the facts were accurate and the words and illustrations got to the right place at (almost) the right time. I also thank the artist Klaus Ernst who, with some assistance from Shawn Hogue, conceived and executed the ten illustrations that mark each section. Finally, I thank my wife Janet who accompanied me on almost all these trips, enduring the normal vagaries of travel as well as unplanned adventures along the way.

WHAT GOOD
IS GOD?

The Story
1   Behind the Search

In late November 2008, my wife and I were completing a tour of India sponsored by my publisher. I had spoken on themes from my books in five cities and the last stop involved a public event in India's largest city, Mumbai. As it happened, that was the horrifying night when terrorists attacked tourist sites with grenades and guns, killing 172 people. The city went under lockdown and we had to cancel the scheduled event. Instead I spoke at an impromptu service at a small church in the suburbs on a night shrouded in fear and grief. Later, as we prepared to leave India, shooting erupted in the airport and guards with machine guns searched us and our luggage five separate times before we boarded one of the few international flights still operating.

During the long plane ride home, still rattled by our narrow escape, I thought back to other intense times from my travels. Shuttling interview subjects into dingy hotel rooms in China in order to avoid detection by the secret police. Listening to accounts from the dazed students at Virginia Tech barely a week after their tragedy as I was still recovering from my own life-threatening accident. Interviewing a roomful of prostitutes about their grim life stories. As I get involved in such extreme situations one question looms above all: what good is God? What does religious faith offer peasants undergoing persecution, or students recovering from a campus massacre, or women who have spent years of virtual slavery in the sex trade? If I can find an answer, or even a clue, to the question of what good is God in situations like these, it will help me with the hard questions of faith that confound all of us at times.

At a press conference in the early 1980s a reporter asked the novelist Saul Bellow, "Mr. Bellow, you are a writer and we are writers. What's the difference between us?" Bellow replied, "As journalists, you are concerned with news of the day. As a novelist, I am concerned with news of eternity." Ironically, in my case it was my career as a journalist that pointed me toward the news of eternity. My journalistic adventures have become for me a way to test the truth of what I write. Can "the God of all comfort" truly bring solace to a wounded place like Mumbai or the Virginia Tech campus? Will the scars from racism ever heal in the American South, let alone South Africa? Can a Christian minority have any leavening effect in a sometimes hostile environment such as China or the Middle East? I ask such questions each time I take on a challenging assignment.

I should mention that on personality tests I score off the charts as an introvert. Writing is a lonely act, and I am quite content to hole up in a mountain cabin with a stack of books for a week at a time, speaking to no one but the grocery store clerk. Trips prove exhausting and expensive and the public events in developing countries often feel like "combat speaking." On return I happily settle back into the life of a solitary pilgrim. Nevertheless, I keep leaving home in quest of what happens when the faith I write about in a mountain cabin confronts the real world. Does it work?

✦ ✦ ✦

Every few years a renowned atheist or agnostic comes out with a new book questioning the worth of religion in general and Christianity in particular. Although some of these books resemble the rants of adolescents, others raise important issues. Meanwhile, national polls in the United States show a steady rise in the number of people declaring "no religion" when asked about their religious affiliation (up from 2.7 percent of the population in 1957 to 16 percent in 2009). More Americans now profess "no religion" than all Episcopalians, Presbyterians, Methodists, and Lutherans combined. Their number has nearly doubled since 1990, and in Europe the percentage is far higher.

Strangely, two-thirds of the respondents who claim no religion still believe that God exists. Some of them judge organized religion as hypocritical or irrelevant and others simply question what God is good for. During the years when the West resisted "godless communism," religion seemed an important bulwark. Now our most prominent enemies are religious extremists. Little wonder more and more people have doubts about the value of religious faith.

Defenders of the Christian faith rise up with point by point rebuttals of the skeptics. As a journalist I approach such questions differently. I prefer to go out into the field and examine how faith works itself out, especially under extreme conditions. A faith that matters should produce positive results, thus providing an existential answer to the underlying question, "What good is God?"

Technology manufacturers have a phrase called "the tabletop test." Engineers design wonderful new products: iPhones, netbooks, video game consoles, notebook computers, MP3 players, optical storage devices. But will the shiny new product survive actual use by consumers in the real world? What happens if it gets pushed off a table accidentally or dropped on a sidewalk? Will the device still work?

I look for similar tests in the realm of faith. My travels have taken me to places where Christians face a refiner's fire of oppression, violence, and plague. This book relates stories from places like China, where the church grows spectacularly despite an atheistic government; and the Middle East, where a once-thriving church in the heartland now barely hangs on; and South Africa, where a multicolored church picks through the pieces of its racist past. In the United States I have visited not only Virginia Tech and a convention of prostitutes, but also a group of alcoholics in Chicago and two enclaves in the Bible Belt South.

When I spend time among such people my own faith under-goes a tabletop test. Do I mean what I write about from my home in Colorado? Can I believe that, as the apostle John promised in one of his letters, "the one who is in you is greater than the one who is in the world"? Can I proclaim that truth with confidence to a woman struggling to feed her children without reverting to prostitution, to an alcoholic battling a lifelong addiction, to an inmate in southern Africa's most violent prison?

I must admit, my own faith would be much more perilous if I knew only the U.S. church, which can seem like one more self-perpetuating institution. Not so elsewhere. Almost always I return from my travels encouraged, my faith buoyed. Only a third of the world's Christians now hail from the West, and I have been privileged to see remarkable evidence of God at work: the reconciliation miracle of South Africa, the greatest numerical revival in history breaking out under a repressive Chinese government, Indian Christians turning their attention to the most outcast group of human beings on the planet. As a writer I want to bring that good news to the jaded West, for such stories rarely make the headlines on CNN.

✦   ✦   ✦

In all honesty I must mention one last reason why I accept such assignments: they give me the chance to connect with readers. Writers need the reminder that what we do in isolation may indeed touch people, and so the highlight of all such trips takes place when I meet the readers of my books. In Africa I meet people with biblical names like Shadrach, Meshach, Abednego, Beauty, Precious, Thanks, Witness, Gift, and Fortune. Filipinos have even more exotic names: Bot, Bos, Ronchie, Bing, Peachy, Blessie, Heaven, Cha Cha, Tin Tin ("My friends call me Tin Squared," she laughs). The signing line allows for only a few moment's interaction with my readers, but at least we connect.

"We have an unequal relationship, you and I," I used to joke before a book signing. "You know everything about me because anything I think or do or say ultimately ends up in a book. I know nothing about you. So in the few seconds we have together as I sign your book, tell me the deepest secret of your life, something you've never told anyone." I stopped giving that invitation because some people took me seriously and told me secrets I had no right to know. In the process, I learned how intimate a bond may develop between readers and a writer they have never met.

Such encounters convince me I am not alone in struggling with the issues I write about. Why must I keep circling back to the problem of pain? I sometimes wonder. Then on a book tour I meet an older man with a lush beard who walks to the microphone with a shuffle and mumbles, "God gave me Parkinson's disease. How can I possibly think God listens to what I have to say in prayer?" I hear accounts of suicides, birth defects, terminal diseases, and children hit by trucks. A woman confesses praying in desperation during her nineteen years of an abusive marriage, "Lord, if someone is killed by a drunk driver, let it be my husband." I meet a woman afflicted with multiple sclerosis, shockingly young, who limps over to tell me she is learning all she can about prayer because the disease is progressing so fast soon she will capable of little else.

I speak on the topic of grace and a woman approaches the book table to tell me she needs to work on forgiveness. "Don't we all," I say. "No, I really need to!" she replies, and proceeds to tell me that her father murdered her husband. "First he stole my past by abusing me; now he has stolen my future." Yet she doesn't want her children to grow up hating their grandfather, who is serving time in prison. The man behind her waits patiently as we talk, then tells me of his daughter's rape in the parking garage of the Phoenix airport. "She decided to keep the child, a daughter," he says. "She named her Grace."

After a talk on prayer a teenage girl tells me with a smile that now she has to pray for her sister. Why? "Because you said we should pray for our enemies!" More seriously, a woman in the same line, an ordained pastor, tells of a dark period after her son died when for eighteen months she could not bring herself to pray. She cried out one day,

"God, I don't want to die like this, with all communication cut off!" Even so, another six months passed before she could resume praying.

After each trip I return to my basement office humbled, moved, and also uplifted by my encounters with readers. On a book tour of the East Coast I meet ordinary Christians who devote themselves to causes as disparate as the homeless in Pennsylvania, sex criminals in New Jersey, and Asian students at Harvard. I hear from a soldier who decides to take the admonition "Pray for your enemies" literally: he develops the Web site ATFP.org (Adopt a Terrorist for Prayer) which posts photos of known terrorists. In Australia I meet two ordinary women who put grace into action: they are sending copies of my book on grace to eighty-nine politicians in Northern Ireland, each with a note that Christians halfway around the globe are praying for them in their ongoing search for peace. "We got a deal on the books, just five dollars each, but the postage costs thirteen dollars for every book."

✦   ✦   ✦

This book brings together my two roles, speaker and writer, as I meet with alcoholics and Bible college students, with CEOs in China and Dalits (Untouchables) in India, with C. S. Lewis fans in Cambridge and charismatics in Johannesburg. If Christian faith is true it must have some effect on all these distinct groups, and as I spend time among them my own faith refines. Along the way I find unexpected surprises, such as when I visit the site of Martin Luther King Jr.'s assassination the day after Barack Obama's election, or when a person stalked by the Chinese police suddenly shows up for an interview. In each chapter I tell the story behind the story and then give a version of what I said on that occasion. Writing offers one clear advantage over speaking: I can edit my words. Some of the talks follow very closely what I actually said, while in others I have made changes to avoid repetition and to adapt material relevant only to the original audience. In some cases, I have also changed names to protect privacy.

In my travels I have found certain themes to be universal, regardless of the personal application. The question, "What good is

God?" occurs in some form to every person who experiences pain or death or poverty or unfairness—in other words, to everyone. Indeed, as I look over the last few years' itinerary, it seems clear that I deliberately choose journalistic assignments that contribute to my own search. For a period of time I step into lives of those who have experienced far more oppression, violation, and chaos than I ever will. I hope and pray that something of what I have learned in these ten places will become part of your search, just as they have become part of mine.

When I went to New York to discuss this manuscript with the publisher, on a lark I bought tickets to see Aretha Franklin, the "Queen of Soul," perform at Radio City Music Hall. The climax of the concert came as she rendered the gospel song, "One Night with the King." Spending time in the King's courts could change your course forever, she sang, and then paused to let the words sink in. With renewed breath she belted out the strong promise that a night—or even a moment—in the presence of the King can change everything. Such an encounter leaves no one the same.

Six thousand fans—New Yorkers—rose to their feet applauding wildly and yelling for more. Aretha had tapped in to a deep longing in all of us, the desire for change, the belief that somehow God can wrest permanent good out of this flawed planet and us its flawed inhabitants. Dare we entertain such a hope, such a faith?

PART I

VIRGINIA TECH: CAMPUS MASSACRE

VIRGINIA TECH:
CAMPUS MASSACRE

2   The Cruellest Month

Early one Sunday morning in February 2007, while driving back from a speaking engagement in Los Alamos, New Mexico, I turned down a remote road just across the Colorado border in search of some variety in scenery. Snow had fallen a few days before, and several times slick patches of black ice on the asphalt surprised me. Suddenly, as I headed into one downhill curve my Ford Explorer began to fishtail. I fought it, steering left, then right, then left again until the right rear tire slipped off the pavement and grabbed soft dirt. The Explorer began to tumble sideways down an embankment.

This is it, I thought, instinctively grabbing the steering wheel with both hands to keep my arms from flailing. *It could be over.* There was no time for fear. My heart went into overdrive and I felt a strange mix of dread and helplessness as the vehicle rolled over and over, five times in all. The noise was deafening, a crescendo of glass, plastic, and metal breaking apart all at once. The radio console shot like a projectile out of the dashboard. Every window shattered, spilling skis, boots, ice skates, my laptop computer, a food basket, and luggage across the Colorado countryside. Finally the rolling stopped, with the vehicle in an upright position at the far edge of a cloud of dust.

Get away from the car, I said to myself, recalling movie images of wrecked cars exploding in flames. I unbuckled my seat belt and wedged myself under the collapsed roof to stumble to the ground. My nose was bleeding, I had cuts on my face, legs, and arms, and I felt a searing pain in my upper back, just below the neck. I wandered around in a daze, looking at my belongings lying helter-skelter on the ground. I searched in the dirt for my mobile phone, wondering how long it would take for another car to happen along this desolate road.

Within five minutes a car pulled over and a Mormon wearing a white shirt and tie insisted that I put on a coat and sit in his car while he held my head immobile until an ambulance came. "We're headed to a mission church nearby," he said. "I'm head of the ambulance service for this county. Just do what I say and you'll be OK." It seemed comforting to obey orders. He ran through a list of questions to determine my mental state, asking me the day of the week, the president of the United States, my middle name.

A few hours later, lying strapped to a gurney in a nearby hospital, I learned the source of the pain. "There's no easy way to say this, Mr. Yancey..." the young doctor began, after studying results of my CAT scan. "You have a broken neck, specifically the C3 vertebra, and it's what we call a 'comminuted' or pulverized fracture." The good news: the break had not occurred in the spinal cord canal, in which case I likely would have ended up paralyzed like Christopher Reeve. The bad news: the vertebra had fractured right next to a major artery, which a bone fragment may well have nicked.

"We have a jet standing by to airlift you to Denver if needed," the doctor continued. "We'll do another CAT scan, this time with an iodine dye solution to reveal any leakage from the artery. I must emphasize, this is a life-threatening situation. If the artery is leaking blood, you probably won't make it to Denver. Here's a phone—you may want to contact your loved ones and tell them goodbye, just in case."

In all I lay strapped down seven hours that day as doctors discussed my fate. Did I need surgery? What damage had already been done? What else was injured? The small hospital had a CAT machine but no radiologist, and had outsourced the diagnosis to a radiology group in Australia, which meant several hours of transmission back and forth via satellite. Meanwhile I lay immobile, calling family members, reviewing my life and preparing for death.

As it happened, thank God—oh, yes, thank God—the scans revealed no arterial leakage. The hospital released me that same evening, fitted with a stiff neck brace that would keep my head from moving for the next twelve weeks. "Never go without this brace," the doctor warned. "Wear it around the clock. Here's a backup to use when you shower. One small slip, and you could die."

I doubt I got a full night's sleep during those three months. I read by propping a book up high on a lap desk. I kept splattering toothpaste on the mirror while brushing my teeth, since I couldn't easily bend over the sink. I could not drive a car, ride a bike, or jog. But I was *alive*!

For a few weeks after the accident I walked around in a daze of grace, looking at the sky, trees, grass, my wife, my friends, with fresh eyes. Even as my battered body brought new aches and pains to my attention, each new day also brought fresh promptings to gratitude. I awoke with a profound sense of joy in the simplest things: birds flitting from tree to tree, pillowy morning clouds, the sound of a creek flowing around rocks and ice outside, the ability to move a finger, to dress myself.

I began seeing the world through a different lens. Each time I passed a cross or floral memorial by the side of the road I winced, newly aware of individuals who had gone through an experience like mine but with a far more somber outcome. I felt at once more conscious of the world's suffering, which CNN and the Internet funnel into our homes every day, and more grateful for the sheer joy and beauty of life, which by grace had been restored to me.

✦ ✦ ✦

Six weeks after my accident as I sat in front of my computer screen, now angled to accommodate my neck brace, the telephone rang. A young man named Matt Rogers introduced himself. "You don't know me, but your book *Disappointment with God* meant a lot to me when I was suffering from severe depression," he said. "It helped save my faith. I've always wanted to thank you for that—but that's not the main reason for my call." He paused and swallowed hard.

"I'm sure you've heard about what's happened at Virginia Tech." For a week the massacre of thirty-two university students and faculty by a disturbed Korean student, who then killed himself, had filled the news. "Well, I'm a campus pastor there. You also wrote a book titled *Where Is God When It Hurts?* and that's the question everyone here is asking. Of the thirty-three who died, nine had some connection with our church, which meets on campus. We're planning a special service next Sunday, open to the entire community, and we wonder if you could speak on that topic."

Stalling for time, I asked a few questions about the mood on campus and how the church staff was holding up. "Normally, I would say yes right away," I told him at last. "I'm honored by your invitation. However, there is one complication…" And then I explained about my accident. "The bones in my neck are still healing, and the neurosurgeon warned against any bump or jarring. I'll need to get his clearance to fly. I'll do my best, I promise. What you're doing there is very important, Matt. I'd love to join you."

The doctor had misgivings, especially since getting to the town of Blacksburg would require a change of planes. A rough landing might dislodge an unhealed bone fragment, with dangerous consequences. I nearly picked up the phone to give Matt my regrets until a wild thought occurred to me. I knew a man in Denver who worked as a corporate attorney for a large furniture company owned by a Christian known for his generosity. Greg Ruegsegger had gone through an event eerily similar to Virginia Tech: in 1999 his daughter Kacey was shot at Columbine High School along with thirty-six others, thirteen of whom died. Kacey survived, though permanently disabled, and she and her father had spoken publicly about their experience and what they had learned.

They know exactly what Virginia Tech students are going through, I thought. *They can offer wisdom and practical help like no one else.* I could not suppress a smile as the next thought entered my mind: *Plus, Greg's company has a corporate jet!*

Several dozen phone calls later, everything was arranged for me to fly on a private jet to Virginia, along with my wife, a close friend, and four members of the Ruegsegger family. Private jets are definitely the way to travel, I decided. With departure scheduled for 10:00 AM on Saturday, the pilots asked us to arrive at 9:50, saving several hours of airport parking hassles and security lines. Just because I could, I boarded with a small Swiss Army knife in my pocket. The plane taxied to the end of the runway and took off with a roar at a steep angle of ascent. The pilot banked the small jet to give us a view of the sunlight glistening off the snow-covered mountains to the west, then turned and pointed its needle nose toward our cruising altitude of forty-one thousand feet.

During the flight Kacey Ruegsegger recounted her story. She had transferred to Columbine the year of the shooting. After two friends at her former school killed themselves, Kacey had begun talking ominously of suicide. Her parents removed all locks from inside doors, even the bathroom, and for a time made her sleep in their room so they could keep an eye on her. They also sought out a new environment for her to have a fresh start. Columbine seemed the place.

Kacey was reading a magazine in the library when the shootings began that April day, and when Eric Harris and Dylan Klebold entered the room with weapons she hid under a desk, pulling a chair in front of her. She heard them methodically shooting as they made their way to the west side of the library where she and others had hidden. Looking out from under the desk she saw Eric Harris squat down a few feet away and point his gun at the boy hiding next to her.

In an instant smoke and noise from a shotgun blast filled the space around her.

Then the gunman turned to Kacey. She covered her ears with her hands, which may have saved her life. The shotgun blast at close range mangled her thumb and destroyed her shoulder but missed her head. She cried out. When the gunman yelled, "Quit your bitching!" she feigned death. Of the first six students shot in the library, only Kacey survived.

Though she must have told this story a hundred times, Kacey still broke down in the plane. The rest of us stayed quiet, newly mindful of the horror we would soon hear about on a campus reeling in shock.

"What worries me about Virginia Tech," Kacey said at last, "is that those students are leaving their community of fellow survivors. They're headed back to homes in different states, to be with people who only heard about what happened and didn't really experience it. I felt the support of a grieving community for many months. I'd go to the grocery store with my arm in a sling and strangers would come up to me with a sympathetic and supportive word. We had a monthly dinner with other victims' families. We all shared the tragedy, and healed together. These kids are leaving the only ones who can understand."

✦　✦　✦

The town of Blacksburg nestles in the Blue Ridge Mountains, and spring was ablaze as we drove from the airport. Blossomy redbuds and dogwoods dotted the greening hillsides and pink crab apple trees brightened the town. We checked into a nearby hotel and walked to the campus. Architects had designed the main university buildings with trademark gray-and-yellow "Hokie stones" mined from quarries nearby. I had not expected such traditional buildings at a high-tech college. Yellow crime scene tape surrounded one of the loveliest structures, Norris Hall, where most of the shootings took place, and state troopers stood guard. Seung-Hui Cho had chained the doors of Norris shut and systematically moved from classroom to classroom, firing at least 174 rounds of ammunition at faculty and students until finally turning the semi-automatic handgun on himself.

Virginia Tech has immaculate grounds, and it seemed surreal to walk among the beautiful stone buildings, edged with beds of tulips and daffodils, and come across improvised memorials to those who had died a few days before. The school had tried to control the sprawl of memorials by erecting a striped tent the size of a tennis court in the middle of the central drill field, a tent which now contained tens of thousands of messages from kindergartens, universities, churches, and individuals. Each of the thirty-three who died (yes, including the killer Cho) had a designated space inside the tent where friends and family could leave personal mementos: a baseball, a teddy bear, a copy of *The Great Gatsby*, a Starbucks cup.

As I wandered through the tent I realized what the news media do to our perceptions. I had thought of the thirty-three who died as a group, "the worst mass killing in U.S. history" as television kept repeating. Walking past the individual memorials, I encountered Ryan and Emily and Juan and Waleed and Julia—thirty-three individuals, not a group. The handwritten notes underscored this: *I love you. I knew you. I did not know you. I wish I knew you. I miss you. I am so sorry. You made a difference in my life. Thank you, God, for saving my son; take care of the 32. Rest in peace.*

Across the drill field another memorial site had spontaneously sprung up. This one consisted of thirty-three memorial Hokie stones, along with a placard identifying each person who had died. Visitors had left poems wrapped in plastic, notes on poster board now blurred from weather, photos, American flags, bouquets of cut flowers, Mylar balloons, stuffed animals. The memorials formed a semicircle in front of the main administration building, and at night a ring of candles illuminated the site.

The ambivalence over Seung-Hui Cho showed. No placard marked his name, but people still left notes and flowers. A Hokie stone had appeared at his site, then vanished, then reappeared. I copied down part of a poem that one person had typed up and enclosed in plastic:

> *My innocence is mine on the cross, and you cannot have it.*
> *You will not now nor will you ever have power over me.*
>
> *The truth is I miss you.*
>
> *I wish I could have shown you His love, His passion, His truth.*
> *It has set me free.*
>
> *I missed you. I'm sorry.*

Another read, "To Cho: I hope in your next life you do not have to resort to violence to be heard."

People filed past the memorials mostly in silence, holding on to each other as if in a gale, wiping away tears behind their sunglasses, bending over to read the notes. We stumbled upon even more makeshift memorials in other places on campus: in front of a dorm, by a classroom, on some steps, in a student center. The sweet smell of scented candles hung in the air. Watch the news and you hear reports of one more dreary mass killing on a U.S. campus. Visit in person and you're struck by the incredible outpouring of sympathy and solidarity from every state in the union and many foreign countries.

Campus ministers told us that scores of ministries, some wacky and some healthy, had descended on the campus. Christian musicians flew in from Britain and well-known American evangelists set up tents. Scientologists gave away free copies of L. Ron Hubbard's books. Crisis teams handed out tracts setting forth their beliefs. Ultimately these gestures produced something of a backlash. Living in the South, Virginia Tech students are accustomed to religious talk but they resist what seems confrontational or exploitative. Formulaic answers did not fit the questions stirred up by what had happened on their campus.

✦   ✦   ✦

Saturday evening we met with the staff of New Life Christian Fellowship, our host church. Matt Rogers, who had invited us, said, "As a youth minister, you anticipate weddings, not funerals. We have no playbook for something like this." Actually, no one does. Yet hundreds on campus had turned to the church for guidance and for solace, and the staff had to respond.

A dozen staff members described what they had been going through, both personally and as they counseled students from the dorm and classrooms where the shootings occurred. It was an intense time of questions, tears, and sharing, and the Ruegseggers offered much practical help. As Greg said, "There is a very small fraternity of people who know what you're going through. We know. That's why we came."

Members of the church had already appeared on CNN, Fox, and every major network news program. "The whole world is listening," cautioned the pastors. "Don't respond with hate or bitterness, don't add more pain to a painful situation. Follow Paul's rule in Romans 12: 'Do not be overcome by evil, but overcome evil with good.'"

We also had a gathering with students most affected by the tragedy. The discussion went slowly and tentatively at first until a Korean student opened up. "I was walking in front of Norris Hall as students were jumping out of windows and running. I found out later what happened. As a Korean, I feel shame and guilt. One of my countrymen did this! I have nightmares at night and want to sleep all day. I'm exhausted all the time. What do I do with my guilt?"

Kacey responded immediately. "My heart breaks for you," she said, and didn't try to choke back the tears. She went on to tell of her feelings after Columbine. She too felt "survivor guilt" even though she had had a shoulder blown off. Whenever she met with the families of those classmates who died, she felt embarrassed. "What you're going through is normal. You are living with a different normal than before the shootings. Some of you feel anger. I must say, I didn't feel much anger until recently, eight years after Columbine. I had worked hard to get a nursing degree, but as my shoulder deteriorated further I had to go on disability. Eric Harris took away more than my health that day; he stole my career. I'm still learning what a 'different normal' means for me. Even now, when I see someone wearing an overcoat in a grocery store, I start."

Some students grieved openly. Some did not want to talk at all. Some could talk about nothing else. As I listened to them I realized again how different it is to watch an event like the Virginia Tech tragedy on television compared to living through it. Reporters capture the drama, then summarize, add statistics, interpret, provide an overlay of meaning. In contrast, many of those who live through it wander around in a fog, bewildered, feeling what they've never felt before, having no map of meaning. Emotions shift like the wind.

Later that evening Greg said, "I still worry about what happens next to these kids. Columbine remained at the center of attention where we lived, and we had support all around us. Soon these kids will disperse all over the country, returning to people who don't know how to treat them. It's like soldiers with post-traumatic stress disorder returning to life in suburbia after fighting a war."

On Sunday at a student center on campus we held two services, around twelve hundred people in all, 90 percent of them students. Greg shared something of the Columbine experience, and I spoke on "Where Is God When It Hurts?" My publisher had provided a free copy of my book with that title to every person who attended the services. I doubt I have ever spoken to a quieter, more somber audience.

Wearing a neck brace, though it had no connection to what these students were going through, somehow made me feel more at home. All pain is pain, I have learned. A self-destructive teenager, the recurrence of cancer, a broken neck, a random shooting—they all summon up the same basic questions. What can faith offer at such a time? What good is God?

And what answers could I offer? The students, their faces etched with pain, reminded me of small starving birds with their mouths wide open, desperate for some small morsel of comfort.

3

Where Is God
When It Hurts?

Virginia Tech, April 2007

April is the cruellest month." When T.S. Eliot penned that opening line to his poem "The Waste Land" in 1921, he had no idea how prophetic it would sound in modern America. Oklahoma City, Columbine High School, and now Virginia Tech—on our calendars we remember them all within the span of five days, a week soaked in sorrow.

Along with Greg and Kacey and the others who came from Colorado, I thank you for the honor of joining you today. You have invited us into the most tender and profound moment of your lives, something we don't take lightly.

This morning we gather in an attempt to make sense of what happened on this lovely campus in Blacksburg, still trying to process the un-processable. We come together in church, partly because we know no better place to bring our questions and our pain and partly because we don't know where else to turn. As the apostle Peter once said to Jesus at a moment of confusion and doubt, "Lord, to whom shall we go?"

In thinking through what to say to you, I found myself following two different threads. The first thread is what I would *like* to say, the words I wish I could say. The second thread is the truth.

I wish I could say that the pain you feel will disappear, vanish, never to return. No doubt you've heard comments like these from parents and others: *Things will get better; You'll get past this; This too shall pass.* They mean well, those who offer such comfort, and it's true that what you feel now you will not always feel. Yet it's also true that what happened on April 16, 2007, will stay with you forever. Your life has changed because of that day, because of one troubled young man's actions.

I remember one year when three of my friends died. In my thirties then, I had little experience with death. In the midst of my heartache I came across a two-line couplet from George Herbert that gave me solace: "Grief melts away like snow in May / as if there were no such cold thing." I clung to that hope even as grief smothered me like an avalanche. In fact the grief did melt away, yet like snow it also returned, in fierce and unexpected ways, triggered by a sound, a smell, a photo, some fragment of memory of my friends.

So I cannot say what I want to say, that this too shall pass. Instead I point to the pain you feel, and will continue to feel, as a sign of life and love. I am wearing a neck brace because I broke my neck in an auto accident. As I lay strapped to a body board, for the first few hours the medical staff refused to give me any pain medication while they tested my responses. The doctor kept probing, moving my limbs, pinching me and sticking me with a pin, always asking, "Does this hurt? Do you feel that?" Each time I answered, "Yes! Yes!" and each time he smiled and said, "That's good!" The sensations indicated that my spinal cord had not been damaged. Pain offered proof of life, of union, a vital sign that my body remained whole. Medicine falls helpless before a body that cannot feel.

In grief, love and pain converge. Seung-Hui Cho felt no grief as he gunned down your classmates since he felt no love for them. You feel that grief because you did have a connection. Though some of you had closer ties to the victims than others, all of you belong to the same community, the same *body*, as those who died. When that body suffers, you suffer. Remember that as you cope with the pain. Do not simply try to numb it. Acknowledge it as a sensation of life, of love.

Medical students will tell you that in a deep wound two kinds of tissue must heal: the connective tissue beneath the surface and the outer, protective layer of skin. The reason this church and other ministries on campus offer counseling and hold services like this one is to help that deep, connective tissue heal. Only later will a protective layer grow back in the form of a scar.

✦   ✦   ✦

We gather here as Christians, and as such we aspire to follow one who came from God two thousand years ago. Read through the Gospels and you'll find only one scene in which someone addresses Jesus directly as God: "My Lord and my God!" Do you know who said that? It was doubting Thomas, the disciple stuck in sadness, the last holdout against believing the incredible news of resurrection. Jesus appeared to Thomas in his newly transformed body, obliterating Thomas's doubts. What prompted that outburst of belief, however—"My Lord and my God!"—was the presence of scars. *Feel my hands,* Jesus told him. *Touch my side. Finger my scars.* In a flash of revelation Thomas saw the wonder of Almighty God, the Lord of the Universe, stooping to take on our pain, to complete the union with humanity.

Not even God remained exempt from pain. God joined us and fully shared our human condition, including its distress. Thomas recognized in that pattern the most foundational truth of the universe, that God is love. To love means to hurt, to grieve. Pain manifests life.

The Jews, schooled in Old Testament prophecies, had a saying, "Where Messiah is, there is no misery." After Jesus you could change that saying to, "Where misery is, there is the Messiah." Blessed are the poor, Jesus said, and those who hunger and thirst, and those who mourn—*that's us, today!*—and those who are persecuted. Jesus voluntarily embraced every one of the states he called blessed: he knew poverty and he felt hunger and thirst; he mourned; he was cruelly persecuted.

Where is God when it hurts? We know one answer because

God came to earth and showed us. You need only follow Jesus around and note how he responded to the tragedies of his day: large-scale tragedies such as an act of government terrorism in the temple or a tower collapsing on eighteen innocent bystanders; as well as small tragedies, such as a widow who has lost her only son or even a Roman soldier whose servant has fallen ill. At moments like these Jesus never delivered sermons about judgment or the need to accept God's mysterious providence. Instead, he responded with compassion—a word from Latin which simply means "to suffer with"—and comfort and healing. God stands on the side of those who suffer.

I wish I could answer other questions this morning. I would like to give you an answer to the question, Why? Why this campus rather than Virginia Commonwealth University or William and Mary? Why these thirty-three people instead of you or me? I cannot give you an answer, and I encourage you to resist anyone who offers you one with confidence. God did not answer that question for Job, who deserved an answer as much as anyone who has lived. Nor did Jesus attempt an answer to the "Why?" questions swirling around those who died from accidents and terrorism. We have hints and partial explanations, but no one knows the full answer.

What we do know with certainty is how God feels. We know how God looks on the campus of Virginia Tech right now because God gave us a face, one streaked with tears. Where misery is, there is the Messiah. Three times that we know of, Jesus wept: when his friend Lazarus died, when he looked out over the doomed city of Jerusalem, when he faced his own ordeal of suffering. "The tears of God are the meaning of history," concluded the philosopher Nicholas Wolterstorff, disconsolate after losing his son.

Not everyone will find that answer sufficient. We want a more decisive, satisfying answer. When we hurt, sometimes we want revenge. One of my favorite authors, Frederick Buechner, said, "I am not the Almighty God, but if I were, maybe I would in mercy either heal the unutterable pain of the world or in mercy kick the world to pieces in its pain." God did neither. Rather, God sent Jesus, joining our world with all its unutterable pain in order to set in motion a slower, less dramatic solution—one that crucially involves us.

✦ ✦ ✦

Even though my hair has turned gray, I still remember life as a college student. The future lies ahead of you and you are just awakening to the fact that you are an independent moral being. Until now other people have been running your life. During your childhood, parents tell you what to do and make decisions for you. Then in elementary school, teachers order you around, a pattern that continues through high school and even in college. You inhabit a kind of way station on the road to adulthood, waiting for the real life of career and perhaps marriage and children to begin.

What happened in Blacksburg on April 16 demonstrates beyond all doubt that your life—the decisions you make, what you believe, the kind of person you are—matters *now*. Indeed, we can count on nothing but the present moment. Twenty-eight fellow students and five of your faculty have no future. For them, life has ended.

That reality came starkly home to me exactly two months ago when I was driving on a winding road in Colorado. Suddenly I missed a curve at 60 mph and my Ford Explorer slipped off the pavement and tumbled down a hill. I spent seven hours that day strapped to a body board, with duct tape across my head to keep it from moving. A CAT scan showed that a vertebra high up on my neck had been shattered, and sharp bone fragments were protruding right next to a major artery. I had one arm free, with a cell phone and little battery time left, and I spent those tense hours calling people close to me, knowing it might be the last time for me to hear their voices. It was an odd sensation to lie there helpless, aware that though I was fully conscious, my brain intact, if indeed the artery had been pierced, at any moment I could die.

Samuel Johnson said, "When a man knows he is to be hanged... it concentrates his mind wonderfully." I must tell you that when you're strapped to a body board after a serious accident, that also concentrates the mind. When you survive a massacre at Virginia Tech, it concentrates the mind. As I lay there, I realized how much of my life focused on trivial things. Trust me, during those seven hours I did not think about how many books I had sold, or what kind of car I drove (it was being towed to a junkyard anyway) or how much money I had in my bank account. All that mattered boiled down to a few basic questions. *Who do I love? Who will I miss? What have I done with my life? Am I ready for what's next?* Ever since that day, I've tried to live with those questions more at the forefront.

✦ ✦ ✦

I would like to promise you a long life and a pain-free life, but I cannot do so. God has not made that guarantee and not even Jesus was granted those favors. Rather, the Christian view of the world reduces to a simple formula. The world is good. The world is fallen. The world will be redeemed. Creation, Fall, Redemption—that's the Christian story in a nutshell.

You know that the world is good. Look around you at the glories of spring in the hills of Virginia. Look around you at the friends you love. Though still overwhelmed with sorrow just now, you will learn to laugh again, to play again, to hike up mountains and kayak down their streams, to love, to rear children. Yes, the world is good.

You know, too, that the world is fallen. Here at Virginia Tech in April of 2007 you know that as acutely as anyone on earth. The author and Nobel laureate Elie Wiesel had a conversation with a renowned rabbi and asked him the question that had long been haunting him, "Rabbi, how can you believe in God after Auschwitz?" The rabbi stayed silent for a long moment then replied in a barely audible voice, "How can you not believe in God after Auschwitz?" The shootings here on campus, as well as the mega-evils like Auschwitz, show what humanity on its own can produce. "Apart from God, what was there in a world darkened by Auschwitz?" asks Wiesel.

The final chapter of the Christian story asks us to trust that the world will be redeemed. This is not the world God wants or is satisfied with. God has promised a time when evil will be defeated, when events like the shootings of Amish children at Nickel Mines and of students at Columbine and Virginia Tech will come to an abrupt and stunning end. More, God has promised that even the scars we accumulate on this fallen planet will be redeemed, as Jesus bodily demonstrated to Thomas.

After my own accident I heard immediately from Joni Eareckson Tada, whom I first met almost forty years ago, shortly after the accident that left her paralyzed. "Not knowing how seriously you were injured, we put you on our special quadriplegic prayer list," she wrote. I felt in good company. For a few hours I had contemplated life as a quadriplegic, and I now marvel at the triumphant way, though not without agony, in which Joni and others have redeemed disability. The sufferings of Jesus show us that pain comes to us not as punishment but rather as a testing ground for faith that transcends pain. In truth, pain redeemed impresses me more than pain removed.

I once shared a small group with a Christian leader whose name you would likely recognize. He went through a very hard time as his teenage kids got into trouble, bringing him sleepless nights and expensive legal bills. To make matters worse, my friend himself was diagnosed with a rare form of cancer. Nothing in his life seemed to work out. "I have no problem believing in a good God," he said to us one night. "My question is, What is God good *for?*" We listened to his complaints and suggested various answers, but he batted them away like pesky insects.

A few weeks later I came across a phrase buried on page 300-something in a book by Dallas Willard. It read, "Nothing irredeemable has happened or can happen to us on our way to our destiny in God's full world." I went back to my friend. What about that? I asked. Is God good for that promise—that nothing is irredeemable? "Maybe so," he answered wistfully. "Maybe even this can be redeemed."

I would like to promise you an end to pain and grief, a guarantee that you will never again hurt as you hurt now. More than anything, I wish I could make that promise. Alas, I cannot. I can, however, stand behind the promise that the apostle Paul makes in Romans 8, that *all* things can be redeemed, can work together for our good. Later in that chapter Paul spells out some of the things he has encountered in life, including illness, beatings, imprisonment, shipwreck, and kidnapping. As Paul looks back, he can see that against all odds God has redeemed even those crisis events.

"No, in all these things we are more than conquerors through him that loved us," Paul concludes. "For I am convinced that neither death nor life, neither angels nor demons, neither the present nor the future, nor any powers, neither height nor depth, nor anything else in all creation, will be able to separate us from the love of God that is in Christ Jesus our Lord." Terrible things will happen on this planet, yet we have access to a "peace that passes understanding" that can calm both heart and mind in the midst of tragedy. God's love is the foundational truth of the universe, and I pray that you do not let your grief obscure that fact.

Ten days before the shootings on this campus, Christians around the world remembered the darkest day of all human history, a day in which evil human beings violently rose up against God's own Son and murdered the only truly innocent human being who has ever lived. We remember that day not as Dark Friday, Tragic Friday, Disaster Friday—no, we commemorate *Good* Friday. That awful day made possible the salvation of the world and also Easter, an echo in advance of God's bright promise to make all things new.

Rather than offering false optimism, I hold before you the high challenge of trusting a God who can redeem what now seems irredeemable. Bruno Bettelheim, another survivor of the Holocaust, describes three different responses he observed among his fellow inmates. Some simply felt debilitated. A second group put up a shield of denial, attempting to resume life as before. The third, most healthy group sought instead to reintegrate with life, incorporating into their "different normal" state lessons they had learned from the camps.

✦ ✦ ✦

Once at a book signing a man came up to me and said, "You wrote a book called *Where Is God When It Hurts?*, right?" Yes. "Well, I don't have much time to read. Can you just answer that question for me in a sentence or two." (As an author, you love people like that.) I thought for a minute and said, "I guess I'd have to answer that with another question, 'Where is the church when it hurts?'"

Here is where you the students of Virginia Tech come in. Whether you like it or not, the eyes of the world are trained on this campus. You've seen the satellite trucks parked around town, the reporters prowling the grounds of your school. You've seen your own pastors and this very church featured on CNN. What happened here was so horrible that for many of us everything else stopped. When a disaster happens—Columbine, 9/11, a tsunami or an earthquake, a rampage on a college campus—time slows down. The moment exposes our shallow, celebrity-obsessed, entertainment culture and forces us all to face what matters most. I went on the university Web site and read some of the spontaneous comments that poured in, thirty-eight pages full of e-mails on April 16 alone. The world is watching us here today.

Last fall I visited Amish country in Pennsylvania very near the site of the Nickel Mines school shootings. Just as happened here, reporters from many countries swarmed the hills looking for an angle. They came to report on evil and instead ended up reporting on the church. To the media's surprise the Amish were not asking, "Where is God when it hurts?" They knew where God was. With their long history of persecution, the Amish were not for an instant surprised by another horrifying outbreak of evil. They rallied around, ministered to one another, and even embraced the killer's family. In sum, they healed wounds by relying on a sense of community that had solidified over centuries. The world took notice. One college professor told me he had identified two thousand four hundred articles from around the world that focused on the response of the Amish people, especially on the theme of forgiveness for the killer.

From what I have seen, something similar has taken place among you in Blacksburg. I heard the president of South Korea say that if an American had done something like this in his country, hundreds of thousands of angry protestors would be marching in the streets. Nothing like that has happened on this campus. You have shown outrage against the evil deed, yes, but sympathy and sadness for the family of the one who committed it. As I strolled among the memorials that have sprung up like wildflowers across this campus, I found several for Seung-Hui Cho.

✦ ✦ ✦

I flew in yesterday and will fly out today, accompanied by a family who survived the shootings at Columbine, an event with uncanny parallels to what you have endured. We will be available this afternoon to help you, as best as we can, process what no one your age or any age should have to process. Then we will leave, and you will remain. In a few days you'll go to your homes and try to work out the long, slow process of redemption in a most personal way.

I ask you to honor the grief that you feel, a pain that results from your connection to those who died, your friends and classmates and professors. Grief proves love. The pain will dull over time, but will never fully disappear.

Cling to the hope that nothing that happens, not even this terrible tragedy, is irredeemable. We serve a God who has vowed to make all things new. J. R. R. Tolkien once spoke of "Joy beyond the walls of the world more poignant than grief." You know well the poignancy of grief. As healing progresses, may you know too that joy, a foretaste of a world redeemed.

Finally, do not attempt healing alone. Rely on the people in this room, the staff of this church, other members of Christ's body in your hometown. True healing, of deep connective tissue, takes place in community. Where is God when it hurts? Where God's people are. Where misery is, there is the Messiah, and now on earth the Messiah takes form in the shape of the church. That's what the body of Christ means.

I close with a kind of benediction, from 2 Corinthians 1: "Praise be to the God and Father of our Lord Jesus Christ, the Father of compassion and the God of all comfort, who comforts us in all our troubles, so that we can comfort those in any trouble with the comfort we ourselves have received from God. For just as the sufferings of Christ flow over into our lives, so also through Christ our comfort overflows."

May you students, parents, staff, administrators, pastors, townsfolk—you *Hokies*—know that God of all comfort, and let that transforming knowledge overflow to others.

Part II

CHINA: WINDS OF CHANGE

CHINA:
WINDS OF CHANGE

4 Underground Rumblings

Has any society on earth undergone as much tumult as modern China? Less than one hundred years ago an emperor served by palace eunuchs ruled a nation that practiced slavery, concubinage, and foot binding. Then came occupation by the Japanese, a brutal civil war, Mao Zedong's epic Long March, and the triumph of communism in the world's most populous nation.

Rosy early reports from Western observers told of the new leaders heroically tackling China's gargantuan problems. We must eliminate pests, declared Chairman Mao, now elevated to near-deity, and a peasant throng half a billion strong marched forth to obey. The Four Pests campaign nearly did succeed in eliminating rats, flies, and mosquitoes before turning its attention to sparrows. Whole villages turned out at dusk to beat pots and pans in order to scare the sparrows into the air, where they flapped until exhausted and fell to the earth to die. Too late did the leaders learn that sparrows eat more insects than grain, and soon a locust plague of biblical proportions gobbled up the crops. In all, thirty to fifty million people died from famines during the Great Leap Forward, the Orwellian name for Mao's agricultural policies.

I remember as a child hearing about the starving Chinese, which was supposed to inspire me to eat everything on my plate. In church

I also learned of the missionaries evicted from China and of martyrs tortured and then shot by firing squads. The Red Scare affected me so deeply that in high school I signed up for Chinese classes; perhaps I could work as an American spy, or at least talk the enemy out of killing me. The teacher, a refugee, reminisced about her patrician past before the Communists killed both her parents and confiscated all their family treasures. A million landowners died during the waves of violence in the 1950s, she told us.

The same week I graduated from high school, in May of 1966, Mao launched an even more terrifying campaign, the Great Proletarian Cultural Revolution. The Party had installed a hundred million loudspeakers in villages and homes to broadcast propaganda, and when the Chairman called for volunteers to root out counterrevolutionaries, an army of young people responded to turn the Middle Kingdom upside down. Students beat their teachers with nail-spiked clubs and made them march through town wearing dunce caps. Red Guards invaded houses, took everything of value, and beat or killed anyone accused of hiding money. Merely wearing eyeglasses, a sign of education, made a person suspect; intellectuals had to crawl through crushed glass in front of jeering crowds. Asked about the marauding gangs, the national police chief said nonchalantly, "If people are beaten to death . . . it's none of our business."

With most skilled managers sentenced to labor camps, the economy foundered. There was only one notable business in China then: revolution. Attention next turned to religion. Many Catholic priests and Protestant pastors spent time in re-education camps, often enduring torture until they signed statements renouncing their beliefs. Children were urged to report any parents who prayed or read the Bible at home. Some Christians were crucified, with nails driven through their palms. The Red Guards destroyed thousands of temples, churches, and mosques—six thousand monasteries in Tibet alone—relics of a proud history disappearing in one chaotic decade.

By the time I visited China, in 2004, everything had changed once again. Construction cranes jutted into the sky at all angles and half the world's merchant ships were lined up in harbors to deliver the raw materials needed to complete factories, highways, and buildings (some two thousand new skyscrapers in Beijing alone). China, with its trillion dollars in foreign reserves, was now investing heavily in Africa and propping up Western banks.

Capitalism had returned with a vengeance. At tourist sites Mongolian women in brightly colored costumes chased us with their postcards and trinkets, and on street corners vendors offered Rolex and Tissot watches. "You want genuine or fake?" they asked. The latest fashions from Paris and Milan had replaced drab Mao outfits in the cosmopolitan city center. Every American fast-food chain had outlets in the capital, including a controversial Starbucks in the Forbidden City palace.

One longtime visitor said, "Of all the changes, the most astounding to me is the traffic. I first came here on business in 1981. A limousine met my plane on the tarmac and drove me to an appointment downtown. On that trip I saw a total of three other cars. Bicycles, yes—eight million bicycles in Beijing back then—but no cars. Now look around you." He waved at the parade of Audis, Mercedes, and Buicks stuck in traffic. That day's paper announced the two millionth automobile registration in Beijing, and since my 2004 visit two million more vehicles have joined them.

✦   ✦   ✦

I had come to Beijing not for business, rather to hold a weekend seminar for an international church with seventeen hundred members. The pastors had worked out a compromise with the Communist authorities: congregants meet in a public auditorium, not a church building, and as long as they restrict attendance to internationals the authorities grant them freedom of worship without interference. Bizarrely, church ushers at the door act much like bouncers, checking passports and turning away local Chinese. Sometimes personnel from the Public Security Bureau show up. "How do you recognize them?" I asked my host. "They're the ones in suits frantically trying to record the words of praise songs projected on-screen," he replied.

I spoke six times in all, to a most receptive audience. A place like China offers no social advantage to attending church—quite the opposite—and as a result people gather to worship because they truly believe. The church has members from sixty countries representing many different traditions, and worship services might include a dance troupe from Africa, a European opera singer, or a country-western band.

I had read David Aikman's book *Jesus in Beijing* on the plane trip to China. After more than two decades reporting for *Time* magazine from more than fifty countries, Aikman resigned, primarily to research and write the phenomenal story of the church in China. At the time of the Communist takeover, China was the pearl of the missionary movement, with seven thousand foreign missionaries overseeing seminaries and publishing houses as well as nine hundred hospitals and six thousand schools. Almost overnight Chairman Mao forced them all to leave. Members of the largest agency, the China Inland Mission, met in Australia to consider their fate. Should they disband? Or relocate to other Asian countries? And what about the Christian community left in China? Four hundred years of missionary work had produced a million Protestant and several million Catholic converts, a tiny minority in a country already exceeding a half billion in population. Who would teach them, print their literature, nurse their sick?

For several decades no one knew how the Chinese church was faring, especially in light of the leaked reports of social turmoil. Had Madame Mao succeeded in her vow to destroy Christianity? When China finally began to crack open its borders, some of these same missionaries returned to visit, astonished to find that the church had exploded in size. Aikman estimates the number of Christians in China today may exceed eighty million; others suggest a total of more than a hundred million. No one knows for sure because many of them meet in unregistered (and illegal) house churches of twenty or thirty members. This, the largest religious revival in history by far, took place with little direction and no foreign influence.

The current communist government tolerates Chinese Christians as long as they are tightly regulated, giving official sanction only to churches registered with the Three-Self Patriotic Movement. Since the Party pays pastors' salaries and appoints their leaders, the spiritual quality of such churches varies widely. The author Huston Smith visited one lively Three-Self church in Shanghai in which the pastor pled with the congregation not to attend church more than once each Sunday, for that deprived others of the opportunity; the crowd at each service spilled over into sixteen Sunday school rooms that were wired for sound.

Much of the growth, though, has occurred among the unregistered house churches, which trace back to four remarkable Chinese men known as the four patriarchs. I had asked a Malaysian friend who works with the unregistered churches if she could arrange some meetings for me—not to speak, but to listen to stories of Chinese Christians. She took her assignment seriously, mustering leaders of the house church movement to Beijing for the interviews, and in some cases they traveled ten hours by train.

By now I had spent several days breathing the famously polluted air of China's capital city. That, combined with the strain of speaking six times in one weekend, had given me a severe case of "Beijing throat." My sinuses were draining, my eyes burned, and my throat felt like sandpaper. The following day would involve a twenty-hour trip home in a confined airplane cabin. Physically, the last thing I wanted to do was step into the journalist's role and conduct a series of interviews, yet I suspected these meetings might be the most memorable part of our trip to China.

In order to attract less attention my Malaysian friend had booked a run-down hotel far from the central business district. Furthermore, she had rented several rooms, and had each of the Chinese guests stay in a different room until called. "It's important that they not meet each other," she insisted. "That way, if they're arrested and interrogated they can't incriminate anyone else." When I mentioned I had brought Chinese editions of my books as gifts, she warned, "Good, but please don't sign them! Otherwise, the authorities will know they have met with a foreigner."

For the next five hours I sat in a dingy hotel room that was overheated by a loudly hissing radiator and smelled strongly of insecticide. Even so, my hosts kept the windows closed tight for fear of eavesdroppers. They also searched carefully for recording devices and posted a guard in the lobby. I felt like a character in a James Bond movie, and wondered how necessary these precautions were in modern China.

✦   ✦   ✦

Shortly before the first interview my Malaysian friend's mobile phone rang and she talked excitedly to the caller and then to the translator in Chinese. "Bad news," she said at last in English. "The person we most wanted you to meet, Pastor Yuan, one of the four patriarchs of the Chinese church, cannot come. Because of a Communist Party meeting, the Public Security Bureau has forbidden him to contact foreigners this week. They have guards surrounding his house." Maybe the precautions are necessary after all, I thought.

The interviews began with an old farmer named Joshua. I could have guessed his occupation from his hands and face alone, for his leathery skin showed years of exposure to sun and wind. He had snow-white hair and wore an orange sweater buttoned too tightly across his midriff. Unused to being the object of a journalist's attention, he moved stiffly, rarely looked me in the eye, and gave short answers to my questions. Joshua had spent six months in prison for his faith, followed by four years at a re-education camp. To my surprise, he said he enjoyed the camp: "I met different kinds of people, not just farmers, and we all got along. I learned the value of suffering for Christ." After his release, as the economy loosened, Joshua started a chicken farm. For a time he prospered and built large barns housing thousands of chickens, until the bird flu epidemic wiped out the market. Now he uses the barns to store Bibles.

My Malaysian friend interrupted to explain. "China prints Bibles now, but not all Chinese Christians have access to one. Many of them store their Bibles in an underground hiding place for safekeeping.

We've been bringing in Bibles for years. No one suspects Malaysians of carrying Bibles, so a group of twenty of us will come over with fifty Chinese Bibles in each of our suitcases, and Brother Joshua acts as a distributor. Every year he dispenses five thousand Bibles."

After Joshua left the room a much younger man named Lao San entered. He rubbed his eyes as if he had been napping; he was one who had traveled ten hours on a night train to meet us. Our host introduced Lao San as a scholar with no formal education. He supervises fifty leaders of house churches, many of them young women between the ages of sixteen and twenty. I had read that half of the world's two billion Christians are led by pastors with less than two weeks' formal training; Lao San is trying to change that pattern.

I asked Lao San what he thought the Chinese church needed. "First, we need training. Many of the leaders don't know how to interpret the Bible or preach. China has many strange cults because of this. Also, we need more faith, more courage. Our people still live in fear. Many lost family members in the Cultural Revolution and many spent time in jail. It's OK to cry, they think, but not to laugh. People around us see Christians as good people who pay their rent and taxes, but strange people. Christians get bullied in school. Most are poor, uneducated. We need to show better witness, so people know that we have better life, we have joy."

After Lao San left, Brother Shi entered the room—or, I should say, bounded into the room. Brother Shi had none of the awkwardness of the village people I had just met. Trained as a lawyer, he was bright, sophisticated, witty, and likely to succeed in anything he attempted. I would have pegged his age at twenty-something, but he informed me he had just turned forty-four.

I asked Brother Shi if he had grown up in a Christian home. He laughed. "No, just the opposite. My parents were atheists. I headed up the Communist Youth League in my entire province and served in the Red Guards. The Party leader was grooming me to take over. On my way to the office I would bicycle past a Three-Self church and it always seemed packed with people who were singing and meeting together. That raised my curiosity. I had difficulty getting *anyone* to attend my Youth League meetings. How could this church attract so many people, especially when the rest of us discriminated against Christians?

"One day I parked my bike and went into the church, keeping my head down out of embarrassment. What a shock! I thought only old and lazy people went to church. Instead I heard young people give testimonies with great power. I came back on Sunday and some people recognized me. I could see them pointing me out to their friends. They thought I was spying for the Party. I bought a Bible for eight yuan, which was three days' salary for me, and started reading. I read Genesis through the night, unable to sleep. In a few days I had read the entire Bible."

I broke in, incredulous. "All of it? Leviticus, Numbers, Deuteronomy? Did it make sense to you?"

"I read every word, front to back, like a novel. Of course, much I did not understand. But what it said about human nature made more sense to me than what I had heard in my education by the Communists. I started to believe. I was twenty-seven then, and for a time I felt a war inside me. I knew that declaring myself as a Christian would finish my career. Finally, after several months I could not stand the tension any longer. I went to the top Party leader and resigned. He pleaded with me to come to my senses, but I had made a decision. When I got home that night, my father met me at the door, furious. The Party leader had called him. 'I fought against Christians under Chiang Kai-shek!' my father shouted. 'I fought against Christians in Korea! I will not have Jesus in my own house! If you really want this, then get out!' He threw my belongings in the dirt and the next few weeks I slept in my office. When I saw my father in the street, he would turn his head."

Brother Shi proceeded to relate a series of hair-raising adventures worthy of the Book of Acts. He travels from village to village training leaders in the house church movement. He is constantly on the run, and numerous times has escaped with the Security Bureau in hot pursuit—once just three minutes behind him. Though he has a home, with a wife and child, he can only visit them once or twice a year. Eventually Shi's father also became a Christian, after a miraculous healing of his grandson.

As many as a thousand seminaries and Bible schools are operating in China now, and Brother Shi visits them as he can. He, too, sees proper training as the greatest need in the Chinese church. I asked him, "You work with layers of leaders. If you added up all the church members under them, how many total people are you responsible for as a bishop in the unregistered church?" He thought for a moment, mentally calculating. "Hard to say for sure. My best guess is two hundred sixty thousand." Yet Brother Shi goes by an assumed name, gets no recognition, and does all his work undercover. I could not help comparing his life to that of prominent evangelicals in the celebrity culture of the United States.

✦ ✦ ✦

By now I had been interviewing for four hours. My throat throbbed, my forehead felt feverish. I said to myself, *Philip, nothing you have ever experienced compares to the hardships these people have endured. So toughen up and get through it.* Still, as the afternoon drew to a close I kept glancing at my watch, hoping to leave in time to stop by a pharmacy to find something for my fiery throat. Suddenly the phone rang and we all jumped. It was Pastor Yuan and his wife, downstairs at the hotel desk. They had decided to defy the ban against meeting with a foreigner.

"Give us five minutes!" our hosts told Yuan. Moving frantically, they handed Brother Shi their cameras and incriminating papers and rushed him to another room. No doubt Pastor Yuan had been followed, they explained.

Soon a slender, sprightly senior citizen barely five feet tall stood at the door. "I'm ninety years old and I've spent twenty-two years in prison—what are they going to do to me!" he said with a grin in perfect mission-school English.

Allen Yuan helped found the house church movement back in the days of Japanese occupation. When the Communists took over he refused to cooperate with the Three-Self movement because he did not believe a political party, especially one comprising atheists, should supervise the church. After his arrest, prison guards subjected Yuan to torture and to months of solitary confinement in a windowless cell. "I pulled the blankets over my head and prayed. For ten years no letters from my family got through. I had no Bible, but a few passages and psalms stayed with me, as well as one song. You know the one? 'The Old Rugged Cross.'" He started singing in a loud voice:

> *So I'll cherish the old rugged cross,*
> *Till my trophies at last I lay down;*
> *I will cling to the old rugged cross,*
> *And exchange it some day for a crown.*

Thirteen of those years of confinement Yuan spent in China's northernmost province, above Mongolia. "It was a miracle!" he said with great excitement. "I had only a light jacket and in the freezing winter weather I never caught a cold or the flu. Not sick a single day!" Considering how miserable I felt at that moment, it seemed a most impressive miracle. He kept going. "Plus, they gave me the job of coupling the railroad cars used for carrying coal. The huge cars would bump into each other, very loud, and I would jam a steel rod in the junction to join them together. Many prisoners lost their legs or arms or got crushed in this job, which is probably why they gave it to me. I figure I coupled one million railroad cars, and never once got hurt. Another miracle—God answers prayers!"

Obviously keyed up and anxious to use his English, Pastor Yuan talked for fifteen minutes before I had a chance to ask him a question. It mattered little, as I found out, for he was almost completely deaf, the noise of those railroad cars having taken a toll. I would shout a question about his church and get an answer about the weather.

Pastor Yuan told his story and what he had learned from

persecution. "We live in a time like the apostles," he said. "Christians here are persecuted, yes. But look at Hong Kong and Taiwan—they have prosperity, but they don't seek God. I tell you, I came out of that prison with faith stronger than I went in. Like Joseph, we don't know why we go through hard times until later, looking back. Think of it: we in China may soon have the largest Christian community in the world, and in an atheistic state that tried to stamp us out!"

On Billy Graham's visit to China in 1994, Pastor Yuan entertained the evangelist in his apartment. When President Bill Clinton visited a few years later, the government forbade any foreign reporters from meeting with Yuan—which of course made all two thousand reporters want to do just that. His resulting international renown provided Yuan a shield of protection that he has exploited to the full. Each year he conducts a baptismal service for his converts at a river two hours outside of Beijing, sometimes observed by police through binoculars. He gave me a DVD of his most recent service, a visual record of 453 converts being immersed.*

✦   ✦   ✦

My head was spinning as we prepared to return to the United States, and not just from the sinus infection. Some have called the twenty-first century "the Chinese century," and no wonder. Having been through hell, China is now ascendant, with a can-do spirit reminiscent of earlier days in the United States. Other countries are beginning to look away from the West and toward China for leadership. Meanwhile the Party leaders continue to walk their political tightrope, parceling out economic freedoms while keeping tight control over others.

As the West moves further down the path toward decadence and skepticism, China may be moving in fits and starts in a different direction. David Aikman speculates that once Christians comprise 10 percent of a population, society can reach a cultural tipping point. In Jesus' image, the kingdom of God spreads like yeast in dough,

---

* Allen Yuan died in 2005, eighteen months after my visit.

affecting the whole loaf. I could not help noticing the resemblance between people like Brother Shi and the idealistic early Maoists who were given no chance of converting China to their beliefs.

One last speaking assignment could not have provided a more startling contrast to the stories I heard in the dingy hotel room, and as I later went through my memory bank of China, this scene kept coming to the foreground. An elder in the international church, a highly regarded businessman, booked the Capital Club, a luxurious private club on the fiftieth story of a skyscraper, and invited CEOs of major international corporations for cocktails and a banquet. Large windows framed the glittering lights below: the neon advertisements, the taillights of traffic jams, the floodlit buildings.

"They've come here to make money," the organizer said of those I would be addressing. "They live in gated communities and probably have a very distorted view of China. In your audience you'll have presidents of oil and telecom companies as well as HP and Microsoft China. Every company that matters comes to China. A few foreign diplomats will attend too. To the Chinese, they're all *Christians*, since they're from the West. Yet, as we know, most of them have no clue about the gospel. I'd like you to spend a few minutes talking about it in terms they can understand, especially explaining how it might impact China's future. Is Christianity good or bad for China? How does faith in God affect a whole society?"

The executives, mostly men in power suits, dined on Beijing's finest fare, then retired to a side room to sip vintage Scotch and smoke cigars. In between, I had twenty minutes to talk about faith and the difference it can make in the life of a nation.

5   From the Bottom Up

China, March 2004

Through these windows you can see thousands of skyscrapers, spectacular signs of economic progress since few of them existed a mere forty years ago. From another perspective they also mark the failed dream of the man who founded the People's Republic, Mao Zedong.

Along with other Marxists, Chairman Mao believed that as a result of his revolution a new breed of human being would emerge, the New Socialist Man. As Leon Trotsky described this superior character, "Man will become immeasurably stronger, wiser and subtler; his body will become more harmonized, his movements more rhythmic, his voice more musical. The forms of life will become dynamically dramatic. The average human type will rise to the heights of an Aristotle, a Goethe, or a Marx. And above this ridge new peaks will rise."

My coauthor on three books, Dr. Paul Brand, got a sense of the ideals of this new society in 1985, not long after the Cultural Revolution, when he accepted an invitation to lecture on his specialty, the disease leprosy. Up to that point few Westerners had visited communist China. His host, the Minister of Health, apologized for not having met him at the airport (the plane had been delayed a day) and asked how he had got to the hotel. Brand replied, "No problem. I simply hailed a taxi." How much did they charge you? the health minister asked. "Forty yuan," or the equivalent of ten dollars. The Chinese host seemed shocked at the amount, but Dr. Brand assured him he had paid a reasonable fare by international standards.

The next morning Dr. Brand was summoned to the hotel lobby. There stood the taxi driver, who gave a solemn apology. "Forgive me, sir. The fare should have been three yuan, not forty. In a moment of weakness I gave in to greed and overcharged you. Here is your change, thirty-seven yuan."

Next to him stood a man in a suit. "I am this driver's supervisor. I, too, apologize. This is my fault. I trained this driver in honesty and character, and I failed. I will bring him back for more training." Then the manager for all public transportation in the city spoke in a similar vein. "No, I accept all blame. I set the values of the transportation system. I humbly apologize. We must eliminate this greed and corruption."

Some of you are smiling as I tell this story, and some of you look incredulous. Transparency International currently ranks China well down the list (number seventy-two) of corrupt nations in which to do business, no surprise to most of you. Nowadays the taxi driver's supervisor and the manager of transportation would more likely ask for a cut of the excessive charges. The New Socialist Man did not emerge in China, as it did not emerge in Russia beforehand. After the most exhaustive attempts to change human nature, it turns out the Chinese are just like everybody else.

At the beginning of the Cultural Revolution, China's top general and designated successor to Mao boasted, "Chairman Mao is a genius, everything the Chairman says is truly great; one of the Chairman's words will override the meaning of tens of thousands of ours." As if to underscore that belief, government printing presses pumped out more than five billion copies of *The Little Red Book* of quotations from Chairman Mao, the only book to surpass the Bible in number of copies printed. (I bought one on a street corner for ten cents this morning.) Now, however, biographies by those close to Mao, including his personal physician, paint a very different picture.

The official government line holds that Mao's policies were 70 percent correct while acknowledging that the other 30 percent cost tens of millions of lives. Deng Xiaoping led the move away from ideology toward a more pragmatic approach. "It doesn't matter if the cat is black or white so long as it catches mice," he said as he proposed opening up the economy to free enterprise. He spent seven years in virtual exile during the Cultural Revolution for such counterrevolutionary ideas, but eventually China came around to adopting his policies, which explains why you can do business here today.

In the twentieth century China conducted a human experiment on a grand scale, one unprecedented in history. In large measure it failed, as the government itself admits, and your presence here as foreign businessmen and -women demonstrates that failure, for Mao had insisted on China's self-sufficiency. You have moved here not because of China's past but because of its future. The organizations you serve recognize that what happens here in the next few years may well shape the economy and culture of the twenty-first century. And as a Christian author I have a specific interest in the role that religion will play in that future.

✦ ✦ ✦

Communism's fierce antipathy for Christianity has often puzzled me. Good Christians usually make good citizens: honest, hardworking, charitable, law-abiding. Yet Communists in most countries, including this one, view Christianity as a menace.

When I asked one of the bishops of the unregistered church why the government perceives Christians as such a threat, he gave a clear answer. "Three reasons. First, we have loyalty to God, and the communists want total loyalty to themselves. They are anti-God, and the conflict of loyalties infuriates them. Second, they know about the growth in the church, and fear it as they fear any movement they do not control. They know about the church's role in bringing down communism in Eastern Europe. Third, they have long memories and still think of Christianity as a Western religion. Remember, missionaries gained the right to operate freely in China only after the Opium Wars, which Britain fought to force China to allow them to bring opium into China! We have a lot of history to overcome."

Some years before, I discussed this same issue with the editor in chief of *Pravda*, the largest newspaper in Russia, just as their communist state was collapsing. "We have so much in common with you Christians," he said. "We oppose racism, you oppose racism. We oppose poverty, you oppose poverty. We fight injustice, you fight injustice. Yet somehow we communists have created a monstrosity, killing and imprisoning millions of our citizens." He paused for a moment and then made the remarkable statement, "Residual Christian values may be the only thing to keep our country from falling apart."

The *Pravda* editor rightly saw parallels between two belief systems usually cast in opposition. Some have even called communism a Christian heresy because of its emphasis on equality, sharing, justice, and racial harmony. Communism speaks of a "New Socialist Man"; Christianity speaks of a born-again person. A primary difference between the two, however, lies in their use of power. Communism tends to enforce its beliefs from the top down, at the point of a gun— hence the excesses of Stalin's purges and Mao's Cultural Revolution. Jesus described a movement that grows from the bottom up, with changes taking place internally rather than externally. Whenever his followers have strayed from that principle they've duplicated the errors of the Marxists.

Present-day China, the last large communist state remaining, is pursuing a sort of third way: on the one hand maintaining authoritarian control while on the other hand borrowing from the West whatever might serve its purposes. The Chinese are great copiers, as you know. In this country you can find excellent copies of Western watches, automobiles, airplanes, and nuclear weapons. Increasingly the government rulers have copied the financial system of the West and encouraged entrepreneurship. Other Western values, such as democracy and free speech, they still resist. And what will they do with Christianity?

✦   ✦   ✦

People in other countries tend to see the West through a single lens. They do not distinguish between "real Christians" who truly believe and others who live in a society with Christian roots. They look at Western television and movies and assume these, too, are products of a Christian culture. An atheistic government like China's has trouble understanding the separation of church and state, in which a nation allows groups with conflicting values to flourish without much interference. They are used to dictating policies and beliefs from the top down, rather than letting them grow from the bottom up.

If indeed they equate Christianity with the West then, quite frankly, I understand the reticence of Chinese leaders to embrace freewheeling Western culture. China has a long history of pollution from the West. As the underground church leader reminded me, the "Christian" British Empire fought a war to force opium on the Chinese people in order to help correct the British balance of trade. And before communists took over, one in every fourteen buildings in port cities was a brothel, catering mainly to Western traders. Venereal disease was rampant. Under Mao, China became the first society ever to eradicate venereal disease, finding no new cases in twenty years—a feat quickly undone when it opened again to the West.

Whenever I return to the United States after an international trip I wince at the shallowness of our popular culture. China is dealing with huge issues, such as lifting hundreds of millions of peasants out of poverty. When I turn on American television I'll hear about Angelina Jolie and Brad Pitt and the latest Hollywood gossip. As a society, the United States spends more money on beauty products than on education. While much of the rest of the world copes with hunger and basic diseases, we spend billions on cosmetic surgery and weight-loss programs.

Sadly, our shallow values are beginning to penetrate China. On the magazine racks I see the same images that we see in the West: beautiful supermodels, the newest millionaires, famous athletes. Yet when I walk the streets, especially outside the main cities, I see mostly poor and ordinary-looking people with crooked teeth and shabby clothes. Modern celebrity cultures, whether in the United States or China, idolize what is unattainable to most people.

I hope that you business leaders give some thought to the long-range impact you may be having on China. In addition to the products you are importing, you are also importing values. Nike, for example, has run one of the most successful marketing campaigns in China, and they've done so by mocking traditional Asian values in favor of American iconoclasm. On a recent tour, a streetball team performed as the rapper 50 Cent blasted the audience with lyrics boasting that he is a P-I-M-P with their mothers in his sights. Chinese teenagers soaked up the ballplayers' trash talk, like "Shanghai rubbish, you lose again!" Do we really want to teach more than a billion Chinese to mimic the worst aspects of the decadent West?

✦   ✦   ✦

Despite the risk of such cultural pollution, the leaders of China continue to dismantle the Bamboo Curtain that once sealed off their nation. Why do they do so? Of particular interest to me, why do those leaders seem increasingly tolerant of Christianity?

On this trip I visited friends outside Beijing, where I got a better taste of the real China. We shopped for souvenirs at a dirt-street market and ate a fine meal at a local restaurant for less than two dollars. Many American Christians voluntarily move to places like China to teach English, and on the side they share their faith. I met single young men and women whose friends back in the United States get married, have children, and settle down to a comfortable life in the suburbs. Instead these adventurers live in grungy apartment buildings with few amenities, yet they make the most of it. They run the Beijing marathon, take train trips into the countryside, and befriend Chinese nationals at coffee shops. Their impact on a rapidly changing society is incalculable.

David Aikman, former Beijing bureau chief for *Time* magazine, estimates that up to three thousand Western Christians work in China as English teachers, many of them vocal about their faith. "This often annoys Public Security Bureau officials monitoring the foreign presence across Chinese campuses. But over the years, China's higher education system has learned to appreciate the quality of the Christian teachers. They behave well, they don't get drunk, they don't flirt with the local girls, they don't have romantic relationships even with other foreigners, they are diligent, and they don't complain a lot." Aikman adds, "The steady drip-drip-drip of one-on-one Christian evangelism by these earnest foreign teachers has had a deep impact among young Chinese intellectuals. Almost every urban young Christian I met in China had come to the Christian faith through a foreign, English-speaking teacher."

Because of their ambivalence about the West, Chinese bureaucrats face a constant dilemma: whether to crack down on or encourage the growth of Christianity in China. Is faith in God good or bad for society? Sometimes they launch campaigns against the Chinese church and sometimes they openly tolerate it. Remember Deng Xiaoping's proverb, "It doesn't matter if the cat is black or white so long as it catches mice." Chinese leaders know that the top fifteen countries ranked on a respected Prosperity Index have a Christian heritage. Indexes that rank nations by corruption and economic freedom show exactly the same trend. Even die-hard atheists have to recognize that religious faith can have positive effects on society.*

Aikman records a statement from a Chinese social scientist indoctrinated in Maoism who had carefully studied the west. "One of the things we were asked to look into was what accounted for the success, in fact, the pre-eminence of the West all over the world. We studied everything we could from the historical, political, economic, and cultural perspective. At first, we thought it was because you had

---

* From the Communist Party's perspective, it can have a dangerous effect too. In 2009, the human rights organization Freedom Watch certified eighty-nine countries as "free"; eighty-one of them were predominantly or historically Christian.

more powerful guns than we had. Then we thought it was because you had the best political system. Next we focused on your economic system. But in the past twenty years, we have realized that the heart of your culture is your religion: Christianity. That is why the West has been so powerful. The Christian moral foundation of social and cultural life was what made possible the emergence of capitalism and then the successful transition to democratic politics. We don't have any doubt about this."

I should clarify that for the Christian these benefits are side-effects of following Jesus. I am a Christian not because Jesus' way benefits society but because I believe it is true. If true, it *should* create the conditions in which human life works best. Studies by Chinese sociologists reveal that, in rural areas where traveling evangelists introduce the Christian faith, opium addiction goes down, crime drops, and Christian families grow wealthier than their neighbors. China's leaders, who are pragmatic politicians and not believers, are looking more favorably on religion for the simple reason that it can serve their ends by improving social behavior.

The leaders must also recognize that the turmoil in China, combined with the lightning pace of change, has stirred up a latent spiritual hunger. I have heard first-person accounts from the village level, where peasants gather together and worship despite the real threat of persecution. Maoist ideology has failed them, and they now place their faith on a different foundation. As the New Testament Book of Hebrews exhorts its readers, who also faced government oppression:

> Keep your lives free from the love of money and be content with what you have, because God has said, "Never will I leave you; never will I forsake you." So we say with confidence, "The Lord is my helper; I will not be afraid. What can man do to me?" *(Hebrews 13:4–6)*

That same spiritual hunger crops up among the educated elite in China. Several years ago Allen Hertzke, a professor at the University of

Oklahoma, gave a lecture tour to Chinese university students. To his surprise, most of their questions to him centered on religion: "Do *you* believe in God?" "Can't people be moral without religion?" "If the Bible is the word of God, how come God didn't know about China?" Hertzke sensed a moral and intellectual vacuum in China's next generation.

China knows all too well the effect of an arbitrary, yo-yo morality imposed from the top down. Beauty was bad, now it's good. Wealth was bad, now good. Religion? Once all bad, now not-so-bad. The Chinese experience reminds me of a skeptical friend of mine who used to ask himself, "What would an atheist do?" in deliberate mockery of the What Would Jesus Do (WWJD) slogan. He finally stopped asking because he found no reliable answers. China has shown the world the incalculable human cost of a morality untethered to absolutes, arbitrated by a cadre of flawed leaders, and enforced by a gang of radicals. Some, at least, are looking for a more reliable basis of right and wrong.

A Romanian pastor named Josif Ton once wrote about the confusion that results from the Marxist view of humanity. "[They teach] their pupils that life is the product of chance combinations of matter, that it is governed by Darwinian laws of adaptation and survival, and that it is man's only chance. There is no after-life, no 'savior' to reward self-sacrifice or to punish egoism or rapacity. After the pupils have been thus taught, I am sent in to teach them to be noble and honorable men and women, expending all their energies on doing good for the benefit of society, even to the point of self-sacrifice. They must be courteous, tell only the truth, and live a morally pure life. But they lack motivation for goodness. They see that in a purely material world only he who hurries and grabs for himself possesses anything. Why should they be self-denying and honest?"*

---

* In *The Abolition of Man*, C. S. Lewis gave the same warning to post-Christian societies that debunk the roots of their morality. "We continue to clamour for those very qualities we are rendering impossible...We make men without chests and expect of them virtue and enterprise. We laugh at honour and are shocked to find traitors in our midst. We castrate and bid the geldings be fruitful."

Is materialism enough? What is the basis for moral behavior? Can we be good without God? These are the questions facing China in the immediate future. The answers will have a major influence on how the managers and workers in your companies perform, as well as on how China projects itself in its new global leadership role.

✦   ✦   ✦

The world has well noted the dramatic growth in China's economy, which has catapulted the country in one generation from a peasant society to an economic powerhouse. In my brief time here I have also seen signs of the dramatic growth in the Christian church. In the 1950s many wondered whether Christianity would even survive in China, given the expulsion of all foreign workers and the government's persecution of the church. Now, according to some estimates, twenty thousand Chinese convert to Christianity every single day. In the Back to Jerusalem movement, the Chinese church is mobilizing to send one hundred thousand missionaries along the Silk Road, hoping to evangelize the fifty-one countries located between China and Jerusalem.

As I travel internationally and study history, I am struck by the phenomenon of God "moving"—not in some mystical sense but geographically, moving from one part of the world to another. The apostle Paul addressed his New Testament letters to churches in the Middle East; today, only vestiges of those churches survive and to find them you'd best hire a Muslim archeologist as a guide. Soon the faith spread to Europe, taming the wild Germanic and Viking tribes as well as those of Britain and Ireland. It ruled there for well over a millennium. Much evidence of Christianity still stands, of course, yet in the great cathedrals you're now more likely to find Japanese tour groups than worshipers.

Eventually the faith established a foothold in the Americas, where it still maintains a lively presence. In recent years, however, it has spread most strikingly in places like Africa and parts of Asia, so that now less than a third of Christians hail from Europe and North

America. What can account for this hopscotch pattern? And why are there so many "formerly Christian countries"? (You hear of few formerly Muslim countries.)

I go back to the principle I mentioned earlier, Jesus' teaching that the kingdom of God grows from the bottom up rather than being imposed from the top down. I've concluded that God goes where he's wanted. As the corruption and economic indexes prove, Christianity can be good for a society. But as that society achieves a level of comfort and prosperity, its citizens feel less need for religious faith. They live off the moral capital of the past. Meanwhile God quietly moves on, to a place that senses more need.

One in five people on this planet lives in China. As the explosive religious growth continues to permeate this society, what will happen? Could China emerge not just as a global economic leader but as the next major center of Christian faith? We can only wait and see.

I have met few Chinese who still believe the idealistic rhetoric of the early Maoists. But in my meetings with "underground Christians" I sense some of the same fervor of the Chinese revolutionaries who against all odds conquered this the most populous nation on earth. With their coercive, top-down approach, the Red Guards inflicted wounds from which this society is still recovering. With a different approach centered on Christian qualities of love, justice, and compassion, these new revolutionaries are seeking to change society from the bottom up.

C. S. Lewis said, "If you read history you will find out that the Christians who did most for the present world were precisely those who thought most of the next...Aim at heaven and you will get earth thrown in. Aim at earth and you get neither."

PART III

GREEN LAKE: PROFESSIONAL SEX WORKERS

GREEN LAKE:
PROFESSIONAL SEX WORKERS

6   At the Low, You Cry for Help

I never thought I would be sitting next to prostitutes comparing their daily quotas. Linda, a former top madam in Australia whose business used to gross $30,000 per week, remarked that in her day the "girls" serviced around five clients per day; now they have to accommodate ten to fifteen. Hilda from Costa Rica reacted with shock: "Fifteen? I did up to a hundred a day, on a double shift! The men lined up outside the door and we had only ten minutes with each one."

I shifted uncomfortably in my seat. The only man in a roomful of women, I was hearing horrifying stories of male cruelty and exploitation. Before today I had never met a prostitute and now dozens surrounded me. Some were gorgeous, the kind you see glamorized on television shows set in Las Vegas. Some were plain-looking, and some showed signs of a rough life on the streets: missing teeth, scars, bad complexion. They talked about sex acts matter-of-factly, as a car salesman might talk about tires or sunroofs. What had I got myself into?

I was attending a conference in Green Lake, Wisconsin, on ministry to women in prostitution, with forty-five organizations and thirty countries represented. When the invitation to speak first came, several months before, I told the caller that my calendar had been booked for some time. "We figured that," the organizer said, "but as a journalist you might want to make an exception for this conference. You see, we'll have as many as a hundred women, all former prostitutes, attending...." He definitely got my attention—and also my wife's. Unable to accompany me on this trip, she wanted more information before turning her husband loose in such a gathering.

After some discussion my wife, Janet, and I agreed that I would accept this most unusual assignment as long as I could have an afternoon session with the women to hear their stories. We came up with a list of questions to ask them, including one Janet wondered about: "After all you've been through, how do you keep from hating men?"

Now in Green Lake I was leading that session in a conference room crowded with former prostitutes, or "professional sex workers," the label they prefer. For three hours I listened to heartbreaking accounts of degradation and transformation. Their stories shattered all my preconceptions about life in the sex trade.

Hilda,* the woman from Costa Rica, told her story in rapid-fire Spanish, the translator barely able to keep up. Several times Hilda had to stop and regain control of her emotions. "I am sorry," she said with a sob. "I have never told anyone about my mother." She collected herself. "My family had no money and so when I was four years old my mother sold me into sexual slavery. While other kids my age went to school I worked in a brothel, earning the high rates paid for young girls. Oh, it was so hard! Every night I cried myself to sleep. And my mother took all the money I earned.

"As a teenager I got pregnant, not once but twice, and each time my mother took my child from me. 'A filthy girl like you cannot raise a child,' she said. She made me go back to the brothel. From then on I worked harder, often double shifts, to earn money to support my children. It was the only way I could show my love for them. All my life I felt ugly and dirty, ashamed. I relied on alcohol and cocaine to dull the pain. I had no reason to live except for my children.

"One day a customer got furious when I wouldn't do the kinky thing he asked. He worked me over with a baseball bat, splitting my

---

* Names have been changed.

head open. See?" She pulled her hair back to show us the scar. "As I lay in the hospital bed, I plotted to kill myself. I was desperate. Maybe if I just pulled out all the tubes they had attached to me...Instead, I got on my knees and pleaded with God. I wanted somehow to escape prostitution, to become a real mother to my children. And then God gave me a miracle, a vision. He said, 'Look for Rahab Foundation.' I could barely read and didn't know the word Rahab. It's not a Spanish word. One of the nurses helped me find their phone number, though, and I called."

A few days later Hilda left the hospital and showed up, bruised and hemorrhaging, at Rahab Foundation's door. "I need help," she said. "I'm dying. I can't take it anymore." A kindly woman named Mariliana took her in, cared for her, and told her about God's love.

"I couldn't believe the hope on Mariliana's face," Hilda said, and she reached over to put her arm around Mariliana, who all the while had been translating. Now Mariliana had to pause and fight back tears. "She smiled and hugged me. She gave me a clean bed, flowers in the room, and a promise that no men would harass me. She would help me get away from prostitution and start a new life. 'You're safe here, Hilda,' she said, over and over. She told me the home was named for a prostitute in the Bible, Rahab, who became a heroine. She taught me how to be a real mother, and now I am studying a trade to live for the glory of God."

✦   ✦   ✦

Earlier that day I had roamed through an exhibit hall in which some of the ministries had booths presenting their work. I looked at the homemade displays, so different from the glitzy exhibits I knew from publishing conventions. I read brochures and talked to people involved in this challenging field.

Of the estimated twenty-five million women who work in prostitution, I learned, the vast majority, like Hilda, come from relatively poor countries. Traffickers purchase young women and children in places like Thailand, the Philippines, and the former Soviet Union, promise them glamorous jobs, then install them in strip clubs and brothels in Asia and Western Europe. As many as eight million prostitutes work in India alone, creating a major health crisis with HIV/AIDS and sexually transmitted diseases. The city of Mumbai has a red-light district where thousands of prostitutes kidnapped from the villages work as virtual slaves in four-story slum brothels. The United Nations estimates that three million women are trafficked worldwide each year, and more than a million children. The demand for children has grown because some brothel customers mistakenly believe that sex with a virgin can cure the disease AIDS—which of course only spreads the disease further.

As the exhibits made clear, ministries to women in prostitution use a variety of approaches. After sixty-three women, most of them prostitutes, vanished from Vancouver's poorest neighborhood—a pig farmer was later charged with twenty-seven of their murders—organizations set up safe houses and began offering street women free manicures and hairstyles and foot massages. "Men treat them as garbage," said a volunteer known as "The Feet Lady" for her massages; "I do the opposite." In Prague, volunteers invite sex workers for meals or coffee and give them flowers. International Justice Mission dispatches lawyers to pressure local law enforcement to break up trafficking rings in countries like Thailand and India. Shared Hope International shelters about five hundred young women freed from sex slavery in the Mumbai brothels.

A woman from New Zealand told me of her work among Thai women trafficked into Germany, twelve thousand Thai prostitutes in Berlin alone. She gives them music tapes, flowers, small expressions of friendship. "These women feel so degraded and alone in a strange, cold place. They have a hard time trusting anyone because most of them have been abused by their fathers, their brothers, and then by a succession of men interested only in their bodies. I offer love, not religion, but if they do express an interest in God I give them Christian literature. I've seen them in strip clubs, balancing in the midst of a pole dance in such a way that they can read one of my booklets as the men around them ogle their bodies." It was an image I could not easily chase from my mind.

Back in the conference room, a woman from Kyrgyzstan told of her rape at the age of three. "I know what these girls go through," she said. "And I know why they became sex workers. You have no idea how hard it is in a country like ours. We have no work. I've begun taking in young girls, fifteen or sixteen years old, who live on the streets. Together with God's help we are trying to change, to find a new way to live."

As the women told me, conditions for sex workers vary dramatically from place to place. A prostitute working in Costa Rica, or even the streets of Detroit, lives in a different world from one in Las Vegas or Dubai. After hearing several tragic stories from the developing world, I asked the question my wife had suggested, "Tell me, after all you go through, how do you keep from hating men?"

I had noticed Sandra, a blue-eyed Australian blonde with a spectacular figure, sitting in front of me, just to my left. What man wouldn't? When I asked the question, she jumped in: "Hate men? I love men! They're so easy to manipulate."

Sandra had a history more typical of sex workers in wealthy countries. "I knew I was beautiful because in school guys always wanted to sleep with me. I would walk into a room and all the men would turn and look. So why not charge for their attention? I signed on with a pimp, and for six months it was wonderful. He put me in a nice hotel suite, I ordered room service whenever I wanted, and I had more money than I could imagine.

"Then I got addicted to drugs and alcohol. The sex got kinkier as men would watch hard-core pornography and want me to do the same things. I cannot tell you how unutterably *lonely* I began to feel. I sat on my bed and watched TV all day until the men came in at night. I had no friends, no family, no life outside that room. I lived under a constant cloud of shame. For a solid year I never got out of bed, I was so depressed."

Sandra eventually found her way to Linda's House of Hope, a

Christian shelter run by the former top madam of Perth. "I admit that I'm still struggling, even after six months away from the business. I got addicted to the power and money as well as to the drugs. Because I dropped out of school, I have few career options, certainly none that would pay as well. Yet I know what God wants for me. I need to be healed."

I thought of Hilda from Costa Rica, who had spoken earlier. Her need for healing—from physical abuse, family rejection, poverty—was far more obvious. Sandra needed healing of a different kind: from the lies of a sex-saturated, money-obsessed culture of indulgence. In some ways her path seemed even harder.

Linda, the former madam Sandra had referred to, spoke next. "You hear that prostitution is a victimless crime. Listen to these stories and judge for yourself. To me, it's the number one evil in the world. I know prostitutes as young as nine working in Perth. Every sex worker I know was abused as a child. My Christian mother prayed for twenty years that I get out, but like Sandra here I was addicted to the money. When I finally left the business, I feared for my life. Eight times my former pimp has tried to murder me. I meet with religious leaders, only to find they don't want to get involved with this cause. Politicians—some of them my former clients!—simply want to legalize the trade. Things are tight for me financially, but I would rather eat grubs the rest of my life than go back."

✦ ✦ ✦

It seemed a good time to ask the group another of my prepared questions: "Of the women in prostitution you know, how many want to get out?" Everyone who spoke agreed: all of them. For the first few months the profession has appeal because it brings in easy money and you're treated like a queen. Over time, though, pimps demand more and more, customers get abusive, and drugs and alcohol are the only recourse.

I could not help thinking of the ads that show up in my e-mail in-box when the spam filter doesn't do its job. Good-time-girls with exotic names promise to do anything I want if I just click on this easy link. The sex industry presents itself as a fun transaction between adults, one in which no one gets hurt and there are no consequences. For several hours I had been hearing just the opposite. Some of the women, like Hilda, suffered physical harm. All suffered emotional harm. All felt like victims.

I had time for just one more question. "Did you know that Jesus referred to your profession? Let me read you what he said: 'I tell you the truth, the tax collectors and the prostitutes are entering the king-dom of God ahead of you.' He was speaking to the religious authori-ties of his day. What do you think Jesus meant? Why did he single out prostitutes?"

After several minutes of silence a young woman from Eastern Europe spoke up in her broken English. "Everyone, she has some-one to look down on. Not us. We are at the low. Our families, they feel shame of us. No mother nowhere looks at her little girl and says, 'Honey, when you grow up I want you be good prostitute.' Most places, we are breaking the law. Believe me, we know how people feel about us. People call us names: whore, slut, hooker, harlot. We feel it too. We are the bottom. And sometimes when you are at the low, you cry for help. So when Jesus comes, we respond. Maybe Jesus meant that."

Maybe so.

A few hours later I had to address the full conference. Alone in my room I worked on my talk right up to the meeting time. In light of what I had heard, what could I say that might bring comfort and challenge to both groups, the sex workers I had interviewed and also those who minister to them? Conference organizers had assigned me the theme of grace, the subject of one of my books. When you are at the bottom, can God's grace reach that low? Can faith make a difference?

I noticed a few other men, probably employees of the conference grounds, scattered through the audience, but once again I felt badly outnumbered. I faced a roomful of women, and this time they were the ones listening.

7   Grace, Like Water, Flows Downward

Green Lake, August 2004

Several times in my writing I have mentioned a friend of mine in Chicago, always using a pseudonym to protect his privacy, though he would laugh and say that anyone who knew him would recognize him at once. Not long ago George suffered a massive stroke that destroyed much of his brain, and never again will we share the long, formless conversations that ranged over Chicago politics, gender theory, theology, and his memories of Vietnam.

For years George ran a bookstore, more out of a desire to stay abreast of new books than from any profit motive—a good thing, since the bookstore rarely made money and eventually folded. If a customer piqued his curiosity, George would issue an invitation down the block to the greasy-spoon diner where he held court. He spent much of every day there, drinking endless cups of coffee and chain-smoking (in the days when restaurants allowed it). None of us scolded him about his addictions to caffeine and tobacco because we knew they deterred him from a worse addiction, alcohol, and a doctor had warned him that one more alcoholic binge would likely kill him. George threw an annual party to celebrate each new year of sobriety.

George broke the mold. Reared Mennonite pacifist on a farm in Kansas, he rebelled by joining the Army and serving in Vietnam, then settled in the big city of Chicago. A bisexual, he had liaisons both male and female. Yet my chain-smoking-bisexual-alcoholic friend George knew as much theology as a seminary professor. He told me he had made the first tentative steps back to God by acknowledging a Higher Power in A.A. Then one day while surfing the channels on cable television he inexplicably stopped at a religious program. A choir was singing the invitation hymn, "Just as I Am." George put down the remote control and listened to the first verse, and then the second:

> *Just as I am, and waiting not*
> *To rid my soul of one dark blot,*
> *To Thee whose blood can cleanse each spot,*
> *O Lamb of God, I come, I come.*

He watched as people came forward, edging sideways through the narrow rows of seats and weaving their way down front, where counselors greeted them and guided them aside for prayer. It was a familiar sight to George, a throwback to his childhood, but for some reason he kept watching and much to his surprise a film of tears soon covered his eyes.

> *Just as I am, Thou wilt receive,*
> *Wilt welcome, pardon, cleanse, relieve,*
> *Because Thy promise I believe,*
> *O Lamb of God, I come! I come!*

George said, "That night I fathomed for the first time the truth that God loves me just as I am. Everyone else loves me with strings attached. I disappoint my family because I have never realized my potential—in school, in career, whatever. I disappoint my church in my decision to fight in a war and in my personal behavior. I disappoint my friends and doctors in the way I treat my health, with the cigarettes and drinking and poor diet. I'm poor, fat, ugly, and soon old. Only God loves me just as I am."

✦   ✦   ✦

Some of you in this room know not only the feeling of disappointment from family and friends; you know rejection and shame and even banishment. You know the self-hatred that comes from constantly letting down other people's expectations, as well as your own. And those of you who represent various ministries around the world listen to such stories every day as you work in the shadowy margins that "good people" avoid.

From my friend George I learned that grace, like water, flows downward. When I climb mountains in my home state of Colorado, I see the power of that downward force. What begins as a tiny rivulet high up in a snowfield gathers strength as it trickles down to join other streamlets to cut channels through dirt and grass and even rock. Over time that force can alter the landscape, can carve a canyon like the Grand, all because it relentlessly seeks the lowest part.

This afternoon I heard stories of desolation and of redemption that easily match George's story, gripping accounts of what happens when a woman rejected by everyone else suddenly grasps that she is not rejected by God. No matter how low we sink, grace flows to that lowest part.

I once interviewed Robert Coles, a psychiatrist and Harvard professor who devoted much of his career to shining a spotlight on people on the margins: in his case, sharecroppers, migrant workers, children of the Appalachian poor. He told me he begins each class at Harvard by quoting James Agee, a writer who documented the plight of the poor in rural America. "Not one of these . . . persons is ever quite to be duplicated, nor replaced, nor has it ever quite had precedent: but each is a new and incommunicably tender life, wounded in every breath and almost as hardly killed as easily wounded: sustaining, for a while, without defense, the enormous assaults of the universe."

Here in Green Lake I have heard gritty details of those "enormous assaults" as well as poignant reminders of the tenderness of life. I have also heard living proof of the power of grace which first flows downward and then buoys a person to unimagined heights. The Salvation Army uses the term "trophies of grace" to describe what can happen among the down-and-out. The women in this room present a trophy case of God's grace.

Those of you who minister to professional sex workers face unique challenges. Potential donors may balk at pouring resources into women who, to their way of thinking, belong in prison and not church. You are, of course, following the pattern of Jesus, a pattern misunderstood in his time as well. I would add that the work you do has value not just for the women to whom you minister but also for the rest of us who stand on the sidelines. You remind us of the mystery of each individual person, a message that modern society and also we in the church surely need.

My friend George embodied mystery for me. I could never draw borders around George; he kept breaking through the lines. A pacifist who wielded a gun in Vietnam, an armchair theologian who enjoyed sexual experimentation, a brilliant mind who barely earned the minimum wage, an addict who conquered one substance but not others— George always remained a mystery.

On a trip to Russia I bought one of those Matryoshka "nested dolls" that break apart at the waist to reveal smaller and smaller dolls inside. The political scene was changing almost hourly in 1991 and I guessed wrong, choosing one with Mikhail Gorbachev on the outside. Twist the doll apart and you find Boris Yeltsin (who soon replaced Gorbachev in the prime position). Twist apart Yeltsin and you uncover other dolls of decreasing size: Khrushchev, Stalin, Lenin. It occurred to me later that each one of us, like the nested dolls, contains multiple selves, making us a mysterious combination of good and evil, wisdom and folly, reason and instinct.

In modern times, mystery has little place. We like to break things down, analyze them. Sociologists identify what conditions create criminals and evolutionary biologists look to the animal kingdom for clues into why humans behave the way we do. Yet individual human beings keep breaking through the lines in mysterious ways.

Two spoiled teenagers in Colorado, with all the privileges of wealth, walk into a classroom at Columbine High School and murder twelve of their classmates and a teacher. An Albanian nun named Teresa finds little happiness teaching geography to wealthy children but much happiness tending to the dying beggars of Calcutta. Mystery rules.

✦   ✦   ✦

All of us have within ourselves the potential for despair and also triumph, sin and salvation, cruelty and compassion, loyalty and betrayal, love and hate. The choices we make and the people we become do not reduce to a predictable graph. Does a woman take up prostitution because of childhood abuse? Economic reasons? Deep-seated loneliness? Chemical imbalance? Poor self-image? Even after all the factors are known, mystery remains.

Like most human behavior, sexuality defies reduction. The rock group Bloodhound Gang urges humans, who "ain't nothin' but mammals," to act like it, having sex the same way other animals do it on the Discovery Channel. The lyrics capture well the philosophy of a sex-saturated society that offers video clips of every conceivable human act to anyone with access to a computer and the Internet. The problem with that philosophy is that we humans *don't* do it like other mammals.

In Colorado I live among a variety of mammals, and I've observed that for them sex holds little mystery. For three weeks each September bull elk bugle and clash antlers and then the winner frenziedly mates with a harem of fifty to a hundred cows. Elk take no precautions of privacy, acting out their instincts on a local golf course or even in my backyard. Apparently they don't give sex a single thought the other forty-nine weeks of the year. For them it is a seasonal, physical act and nothing more.

Is sex merely a physical act for humans? Tune your radio to a country-western station and listen to the lyrics of infidelity. Or check out the murders reported in the daily newspaper, a large proportion of which trace back to a fight with an estranged lover. Of course, you don't need those clues. I heard compelling proof this afternoon that sex involves far more than the physical body. It touches the soul. Every woman who spoke told of the scars that result from pretending otherwise. Scars from childhood led many of you into the sex trade. Scars from that trade stirred you to seek a way of escape, especially as you came in contact with the healing salve of grace.

Our desires, including sexual desires, are not wrong. They are, rather, like the rungs of a ladder that lead us toward beauty, toward relationship and intimacy, and ultimately toward God who granted us these gifts. Remove the rungs from the ladder, though, and you are left with scattered sticks of wood leading nowhere. The path to health for those of you leaving the sex trade will mean neither quenching nor exploiting desire but rather restoring it to its proper place.

Those of you who work with children and young women in places like India, Brazil, Thailand, Australia, and the Czech Republic understand our culture's failure to explain away and demystify the human person. The moment we become convinced we have figured out an individual, that moment we open ourselves up to surprise and error. Human life is irreducible, and plays out much more like a Dostoevsky novel than a manual of computer software. Some of your prime converts, women sitting near you in this room, will likely fall away, even as some of your harshest opponents will one day embrace you, repentant.*

"It is a serious thing," wrote C. S. Lewis, "to live in a society of possible gods and goddesses, to remember that the dullest and most uninteresting person you talk to may one day be a creature which, if you saw it now, you would be strongly tempted to worship, or else

---

* I heard from those who minister to sex workers that many of their converts eventually slide back into their former way of life. As I would later learn, Sandra, the blonde from Australia, was one of them. After moving to Europe and enrolling in a seminary, she began to miss the perks of her former life. With no formal education, she felt successful at one thing only: pleasing men with her body. So she returned to Australia to resume her profession.

a horror and a corruption such as you now meet, if at all, only in a nightmare. All day long we are, in some degree, helping each other to one or other of these destinations."

✦ ✦ ✦

The mystery of the person includes our fallibility, and this conference also reminds me of that important truth. From the earliest days of the faith some Christians have resisted facing the simple fact that all of us fall short. The apostle Paul battled against Gnostics who alleged a higher plane of enlightenment, against Pharisaic Christians who required strict adherence to religious laws, against the "righteous" who scorned certain categories of sinners.

We have modern-day equivalents for each of these tendencies. I grew up among perfectionistic Christians who claimed to have attained a higher plane of living. They attended "deeper life" conferences and competed with one another to avoid questionable activities. One woman in my church insisted she had not sinned for twelve years. Yet these same people felt no qualms about telling racist jokes or opposing civil rights. And they felt a sweet and toxic pride in looking down on those less spiritual, especially notorious sinners. Homosexuals fell into that last category, as did prostitutes.

Paul attacks these ranking tendencies head-on in Romans 1 and 2. He begins his catalog of sinners by listing flagrant violators: depraved perverts, murderers, God-haters (though, curiously, he also mentions such everyday sins as greed, envy, gossip, and disobeying parents).

Just as his good-citizen readers nod knowingly, smug in their moral superiority, Paul turns the tables in chapter 2: "You, therefore, have no excuse, you who pass judgment on someone else, for at whatever point you judge the other, you are condemning yourself, because you who pass judgment do the same things." I may never have robbed a bank, but have I ever fudged on my income tax? Or ignored a pressing need because of compassion fatigue? Paul follows Jesus' logic in the Sermon on the Mount: murder and adultery differ from hatred and lust only by a matter of degree. Indeed, the flagrantly evil person has a peculiar advantage of sorts: an inner gyroscope of conscience that registers a sense of being off course.

Paul reserves his most scathing comments for a third category, self-righteous people, which in his day comprised the Jews who scrupulously observed the law. A Pharisee of the Pharisees, he knew the syndrome well, as his pronouns attest. He refers to the wicked as "they" and the good-citizen types as "you." But when he discusses the self-righteous, Paul shifts to the first person. "What shall *we* conclude then? Are we any better? Not at all!" He knew the danger that accompanies a feeling of moral superiority. In his most self-righteous days, after all, Paul had persecuted Christians and assisted in at least one torturous death. In another letter Paul said, "Christ Jesus came into the world to save sinners—of whom I am the worst." Note that Paul, a master of language, said I *am* the worst, not I *was* the worst. He understood fallibility.

Just as denial may keep a person from seeing a doctor about a lump or skin lesion, endangering life, denial of sin may lead to far worse consequences. Unless we accept the grim diagnosis, we will not seek a cure. Paul concludes, "There is no one righteous, not even one." And that sweeping statement sets up his magnificent presentation of the gospel in Romans 3. God's grace, the only possible solution to human fallibility, comes free of charge, apart from law, apart from any human efforts toward self-improvement. For a free gift, we need only hold out open, needy hands—the most difficult gesture of all for a self-righteously evil person.

My friend George once said to me, "I feel caught somewhere between 'Just as I Am' and 'Just as I Should Be.'" In fact, we're all caught there. In my teenage and college years I branded the uptight, perfectionistic people in my church as hypocrites, and perhaps they were. Now I look on them with sympathy and self-recognition. If we compare who we are to who we claim to be, we are all hypocrites, and the church provides a place where we can openly confess our failures and receive the cleansing power of grace.

One of the most moving stories I heard this afternoon came

from the young Thai woman who spoke with searing honesty of her sexual addiction. She even wanted to rape her own young sons, she said, her hands covering her face. She went on to say that God's grace can heal, and after a moment of reflection added, "It isn't easy to be healed."

How right she is. Each of us can tell of forces inside us that fight against healing. My friend George never tried to water down his struggles. The apostle Paul detailed his in the eloquently chaotic chapter of Romans 7. It isn't easy to be healed. One thing is harder, though: staying unhealed.

The author and pastor John Piper insists that the worst tragedy in sexual sins is not fornication or pornography or other acts of moral failure. The tragedy is that a gnawing sense of guilt and unworthiness over sexual failure can overtake us, causing us to feel cast aside from God's use and even God's love. Wallowing in guilt, we shrink from the forgiveness God freely offers.

King David, who became a public emblem of fallibility for an entire nation, wrote these words in Psalm 51 after his greatest failure: "You do not delight in sacrifice, or I would bring it; you do not take pleasure in burnt offerings. The sacrifices of God are a broken spirit; a broken and contrite heart, O God, you will not despise." A thousand years later, Paul said something similar to the Romans, summarizing our Christian hope in a simple formula, "Where sin increased, grace increased all the more."

✦   ✦   ✦

This conference celebrates the rousing truth that grace increases all the more. If we had come together merely to offer more dreary proofs of human mystery and fallibility, we would have no hope to offer the world. Rather, people have convened from thirty countries to proclaim one more quality: redeemability. Like the high, clear note of a trumpet, the Bible heralds the sure promise that no matter who I am and what I have done, the door to transformation swings open before me.

The first Gospel, Matthew, begins with a list of names that represent a selection of Jesus' ancestors. The peasant family of Joseph and Mary could trace their lineage back to noteworthy people, including Israel's greatest king and its original founder. Yet Matthew's list of names also lets skeletons out of the closet. Take the women mentioned, a rarity in Jewish genealogies. Tamar, a childless widow, had to dress like a prostitute and seduce her father-in-law in order to produce her contribution to Jesus' line. Rahab did not merely pretend, but actually made her living as a prostitute. And Bathsheba was the object of David's lust, leading to the most famous royal scandal of the Old Testament. These shady ancestors show that Jesus entered human history in the raw, a willing descendant of its shame. They also show the power of redemption that welcomed such women into the history of one who brought salvation to the world.

A biblical gathering of murderers would include some of its most prominent names: Moses, David, Paul. A gathering of traitors would include not only Judas but also Peter and the other disciples. And a gathering of the sexually promiscuous would include two nameless women who had a life-changing encounter with Jesus.

In John 8 we meet a woman who has been caught in the very act of adultery. Most likely stripped to the waist as a token of her shame, she is dragged before a group of religious professionals who call for her death by stoning. Predictably, no one accuses the male partner in her adultery (though she was caught in the act), and it soon becomes clear that her accusers have little interest in the woman's welfare and much interest in trapping Jesus.

For his part, Jesus lets the tension of the scene play out for a while as he writes on the ground in silence. Then he straightens up and addresses the buzzing mob: "If any one of you is without sin, let him be the first to throw a stone at her." With that comment, he abolishes their artificial distinction between "good people" *like us religious leaders* and "bad people" *like that slut*. Jesus views the crowd through a different set of lenses. He sees people in need of God's grace who deny it, like the teachers of the law and the Pharisees, and people in need of God's grace who accept it, like the woman who cowers before him awaiting the thud of the first stone.

After all the rest have filed away, the one person in that scene who indeed has no sin dismisses the guilty woman. "Neither do I condemn you," Jesus says. "Go now and leave your life of sin." She too faces the stunning prospect of being judged by her future and not her past.

Luke 7 tells of another encounter, featuring not just an adulteress but a working prostitute, a woman who makes her living by selling her body. In an act of incredible daring, she bursts into the home of a Pharisee, defying all rules of ritual purity, and pours expensive perfume on Jesus' feet, provocatively wiping off the mixture of tears and perfume with her loosened hair. Perfume was a prized asset for a prostitute in a desert environment, which explains why her offering may have equaled a year's wages. By pouring her most valuable possession on Jesus' feet, this woman abandons her career and entrusts her entire future to Jesus.

The Pharisee host, who has already treated Jesus rudely, responds with indignation. *Doesn't he know who this woman is—she's a sinner!* To him, Jesus' tolerance of such a scandalous display proves he could not be a true prophet. Yet the very act that makes Jesus unfit in the Pharisee's eyes establishes Jesus' fitness as a dispenser of God's abundant grace. "I tell you, her many sins have been forgiven—for she loved much. But he who has been forgiven little loves little."

Pharisees, the most respected religious leaders of their day, had an airtight system of morality and every professional advantage. In contrast, Jesus' followers began with the odds stacked against them. They included women of dubious virtue like these two as well as traitorous disciples, slaves and slave owners both, and a zealot who tortured Christians. Among them, these glaring examples of human fallibility had broken all Ten Commandments. Yet that motley band, fired by the Spirit of Jesus, went out to change the world. Meanwhile, Pharisees soon disappeared from the scene even as the Jesus movement kept growing, and grows to this day. Grace triumphs.

At this conference I have heard new chapters in the ongoing saga of redemption. I have heard from a top madam in Australia who now devotes herself to sheltering other women who seek liberation from sexual slavery. I have heard from a woman sold into prostitution as a child who lived with daily abuse that nearly killed her until God answered her prayer in a miraculous way. The very names of the ministries that have come together in Green Lake hold out a promise of hope: New Life Center, Scarlet Cord, Project Rescue, Lost Coin, the Hagar Project.

We are all trophies of God's grace, some more dramatically than others. Jesus came for the sick and not the well, for the sinner and not the righteous. He came to redeem and transform, to make all things new. May you go forth more committed than ever to nourish the souls whom you touch, those tender lives who have sustained the enormous assaults of the universe.

Part IV

CAMBRIDGE: REMEMBERING C. S. LEWIS

CAMBRIDGE:
REMEMBERING C. S. LEWIS

8   Apostle to the Skeptics

I first encountered C. S. Lewis while attending a Bible college in the American South at a time when neither the college nor I was in very healthy shape. Drifting along between presidents, the school had filled faculty rosters with furloughing missionaries and other temporary professors who trod in waters all too deep. For my part, seared by a fundamentalist church upbringing and with the arrogance of immaturity, I soon came to look on the school with disdain. *How did I end up in this place?* I asked myself over and over. I took a devilish delight in pricking holes in the faith of classmates and stumping professors with questions they could not answer.

As I recall, I read Lewis's space trilogy first. Though perhaps not his best work, it had an undermining effect on me for he made the supernatural so believable that I could not help wondering, *What if it's true?* What if there is a world beyond and what if supernatural forces are indeed operating behind the scenes on this planet and in my life? The tremors strengthened into an earthquake as I went on to read *Mere Christianity, Miracles,* and *The Problem of Pain,* books which demolished my defenses even as they exposed my underlying sin of pride.

I was attending the school a few years after Lewis's death in 1963, and I ordered his more obscure books, which had not yet made it across the Atlantic, from secondhand bookshops in England. After wrestling with them as with a debate opponent, I felt myself drawn, as Lewis himself had, kicking and screaming all the way into the kingdom of God. Since then he has been a constant companion, a shadow mentor who sits beside me urging me to improve my writing style, my thinking, my vision, and also my life.

Lewis came to faith step by step, edging first into theism and only gradually toward belief in the Incarnation and Christian orthodoxy. "I felt as if I were a man of snow at long last beginning to melt," he later reflected. A convert from atheism, he maintained a lifelong compassion for those who likewise found belief difficult. The American poet Chad Walsh, in the first book written about Lewis, in 1948, gave him the apt title "Apostle to the Skeptics," and decades later Lewis's writing continues to challenge and guide skeptics. Plank by plank he dismantles intellectual barriers to faith and opens the mind and imagination to another way of seeing.

C. S. Lewis suggested that moderns in the post-Christian age are to pagans as a divorcée is to a virgin. Some parts of the world, such as rural China, may receive the gospel as fresh good news, but the West has a cynical, "been there, done that" spirit of resistance. To reach such readers, the writer must use a more subtle, even subversive approach. As he told a group of Anglican priests, "What we want is not more little books about Christianity, but more little books by Christians on other subjects—with their Christianity *latent*."

By example, Lewis taught me a style of approach that I try to follow in my own writing. Most of us rarely accept a logical argument unless it fits our sense of reality, and the persuasive writer must cultivate that intuitive sense—much as Lewis did for me with his space trilogy before I encountered his apologetics. I came to believe in the invisible world only after tracing its clues in the visible world. Lewis himself converted to Christianity only after sensing that it corresponded to his deepest longings, his *Sehnsucht*.

Though in person a powerful apologist who intimidated his students and relished public debate, in his writings Lewis romanced rather than browbeat readers. He did not impose faith on a line of reasoning as a preacher might, but drew it out as a natural by-product. He had engaged in a gallant tug of war with God, only to find at the end of the rope a God entirely different from what he had imagined as a young boy in strict Protestant Belfast. Likewise, I fought hard against a cosmic bully only to confront a God of grace and mercy.

Along the way, I discovered my own writing platform. Having been burned by the church, I remained suspicious of preachers and theologians who spoke from an elevated platform of authority. From Lewis I learned to try to adopt the stance of the reader, first establishing trust and then inviting the reader to accompany me as I explore questions and doubts. That style suits both my profession as a journalist and my personal pilgrimage.

Yet Lewis was no journalist but a scholar in medieval literature. His willingness to "con-descend" to the level of popular writing may stand as his most impressive achievement, one not always celebrated by his Oxford colleagues. Using homey metaphors and illustrations—poached eggs, mud pies, mousetraps—he leads readers through a maze of complex issues so deftly that the route seems clear and the destination unavoidable. For Lewis, a faith that matters must permeate all of life, not just the academic life.

When he heard criticism from other Oxford scholars who contemned such works as *The Screwtape Letters*, the space trilogy, and *The Chronicles of Narnia*, Lewis used to quote Salvation Army General William Booth's comment to Rudyard Kipling, "Young man, if I could win one soul for God by—by playing the tambourine with my toes, I'd do it." The tambourine-playing cost Lewis: other dons jealous of his success and resentful of his outspoken faith denied him a full professorship at Oxford (an injustice that rival Cambridge University later rectified).*

---

* J. R. R. Tolkien explained the hostility toward Lewis, "In Oxford, you are forgiven for writing only two kinds of books. You may write books on your own subject whatever that is, literature, or science, or history. And you may write detective stories because all dons at some time get the flu, and they have to have something to read in bed. But what you are not forgiven is writing popular works, such as Jack did on theology, and especially if they win international success as his did."

In short, C. S. Lewis affirmed my calling as a writer who works out my faith in print. We live sequestered lives, those of us who make a living by herding words. I can hardly write if someone shares the same room with me. And the results of my work are both slippery and vicarious: when I write I am not actively caring for the poor, ministering to AIDS victims, feeding the hungry, or even conversing about spiritual matters. Lewis proved to me that this most isolated act can still make a difference. As one who was changed—literally, dramatically, permanently—by an Oxford don who often felt more at home with books than people, I trust that God may use my own feeble efforts to connect with readers out there somewhere, most of whom I will never meet.

✦   ✦   ✦

Sitting in a chair staring at words all day makes for an unnatural existence and at the same time opens the gate to some unique temptations. In a letter to his friend Arthur Greeves, Lewis discussed the fertile soil in which a writer's pride first begins to grow:

> I have found out ludicrous and terrible things about my own character. Sitting by, watching the rising thoughts to break their necks as they pop up, one learns to know the sort of thoughts that do come. And, will you believe it, one out of every three is a thought of self-admiration: when everything else fails, having had its neck broken, up comes the thought "What an admirable fellow I am to have broken their necks!" I catch myself posturing before the mirror, so to speak, all day long....It's like fighting the hydra....*Pride*...is the mother of *all* sins, and the original sin of Lucifer....I am an instrument strung but preferring to play itself because it thinks it knows the tune better than the Musician.

The writing profession daily invites a struggle with pride. I have to assume that my words are worth your time, worth your putting aside your to-do list and sitting in quiet scrutiny of the marks I leave on paper. If I did not believe that, I would look for another career.

Paradoxically, an act that begins in lonely self-absorption may transform into public exhibitionism. The unexpected success that followed Lewis's string of best-selling books in the 1940s introduced new occasions for pride. Royalties and fan mail started flooding in and he soon received far more speaking and writing invitations than he could fulfill. *Time* magazine featured him on its cover in 1947. A writer in the public spotlight can respond in several unhealthy ways: by basking in the attention, like Norman Mailer, or by resentfully withdrawing, like J. D. Salinger. Lewis modeled a different way.

Knowing well the wiles of Screwtape, Lewis sought to counter them on all fronts. He gave away two-thirds of the money that came in. He treated his own writings and books casually, giving little thought to his literary legacy. He absorbed the slights and insults at Oxford without rebuttal. He answered every personal letter that came to him. Perhaps most important, he resisted the lure of celebrity by maintaining an ordinary life of walks, tutoring, lectures, writing, and meetings with friends.

By most measures C. S. Lewis lived a boring existence. He rarely traveled and never learned to drive a car. He described himself as a kind of extant dinosaur, a committed Christian in a secular age, nourished by centuries-old music and literature. Yet his friends knew him as a man fully, even exuberantly alive. "The quiet fulness of ordinary nature," a phrase used as a chapter epigraph in his book *The Allegory of Love,* yields a clue. Lewis was finely attuned to the beauty of the ordinary, in which he saw signs of God's own hand.

After a trip to his native Ireland he returned "drunk with blue mountains, yellow beaches, dark fuchsia, breaking waves, braying donkeys, peat smell, and the heather just beginning to bloom." To sit by a stream eating sandwiches with feet dangling in the water, to watch spring announce itself in the plantings along Addison's Walk at his college, to listen to Wagner in the open air—these simple pleasures seemed fullness enough. Nothing satisfied him more than a quiet day with friends. "These are the golden sessions: when four or five of us after a hard day's walking have come to our inn; when our slippers are on, our feet spread out towards the blaze and our drinks at our elbows; when the whole world, and something beyond the world, opens itself to our minds as we talk....Life—natural life—has no better gift to give."

Lewis had described the transcendent effect of such pleasures in his autobiography, *Surprised by Joy*, and then at the ripe age of fifty-three the confirmed bachelor met a woman ironically named Joy. Suddenly the repressed, clubby Oxford don, accustomed to winning all arguments and ordering his private (masculine) world, found that airtight world invaded by a brash Noo Yawker, Joy Davidman Gresham, who embodied Lewis's opposite: sassy, divorced, Jewish, and a former communist. Somehow the two fell in love and married—although in reverse order, as Lewis initially agreed to a civil marriage simply to help her with visa problems.

The next year, as Joy lay suffering from bone cancer, they consecrated the marriage. The play and movie *Shadowlands* depict this most improbable romance, a season of unplanned bliss clouded by Joy's terminal illness. "I never expected to have, in my sixties, the happiness that passed me by in my twenties," Lewis told a friend. Joy lived just over three years after the bedside marriage—including a period of remission that seemed at first a miracle of healing—forty months of exquisite rapture and crushing grief for C. S. Lewis.

Lewis wrote a friend that he most desired death during joyful moments, not when life seemed harshest. For him the pleasures of this world always pointed to another, with good things serving as indirect proofs of a good God. "All joy (as distinct from mere pleasure, still more amusement) emphasizes our pilgrim status; always reminds, beckons, awakens desire. Our best havings are wantings."

✦ ✦ ✦

Three years after Joy's death C. S. Lewis himself died, on November 22, 1963, a loss that got scant attention because of another famous death. On that Friday evening the British playwright David Lodge was watching a local performance of one of his own satirical creations. The audience chuckled as an actor in the play showed up for a job interview carrying a portable radio. He set down the radio and let live music play in the background while the play went on. Within a few minutes a voice came over the radio with a news bulletin: "We interrupt this program to inform you that today the American president John F. Kennedy was assassinated in Dallas, Texas..." The audience gasped and the actor alertly switched off the radio, but too late. In one sentence, the reality of the outside world had shattered the artificial world of the theater production. Suddenly, whatever action took place onstage seemed superficial and irrelevant.

That is what C. S. Lewis did for me and many others. He interrupted my own small world of selfish ambition, materiality, pride, and pain with news from another world—in this case news not tragic but unimaginably good: a sure promise that God has not given up on this planet. Lewis saw this life as a rehearsal for the next, with inbuilt clues both positive and negative. Our sweet longings are intimations of a redeemed creation to come, "the scent of a flower we have not found, the echo of a tune we have not heard, news from a country we have never yet visited." For Lewis even pain serves a kindred purpose, as a sort of megaphone reminding us that we live on a fallen planet in desperate need of reconstruction. Pain keeps us from viewing this present earth as a final home.

Not long ago I was asked to contribute to a volume titled *Mere Christians: Inspiring Stories of Encounters with C. S. Lewis.* It includes fifty-five chapters, some by famous people such as Francis Collins, Charles Colson, George Gallup Jr., and Anne Rice. Other contributors comprise a diverse group: an Iranian-born female pastor, a missionary doctor, a real estate appraiser, a grandmother, a professional football player, a country music singer, a Yale University bioresearcher, the founder of Domino's Pizza. All of them credit Lewis with helping to shore up their faith by pointing to, and making believable, that world beyond.

I doubt C. S. Lewis ever anticipated that nearly half a century after his death his words would still be having such an effect. Surely he did not foresee that several million people annually would buy one of his dozens of books still in print, and that Disney Studios and Fox would release movies based on Narnia with spin-off products displayed in suburban shopping malls and advertised on Japanese subways. If informed of that fact during his life, he likely would have shrunk back in alarm. We writers are not Nouns, he used to say. We are mere adjectives serving the great Noun of truth. Lewis filled that role faithfully and masterfully, and because he did so many thousands have come to know and love that Noun. Including me.

Every few years the C. S. Lewis Foundation sponsors an Oxbridge conference on C. S. Lewis, convening one full week at Oxford and another week at Cambridge. I first spoke in 1998 at the Sheldonian Theatre, an elegant hall in Oxford designed by Sir Christopher Wren. Tradition requires the speaker to wear an academic gown and mortarboard (the latter, however, proved impossible to keep on my curly hair). My book *The Jesus I Never Knew* had recently been published, and conference organizers asked me to speak on that theme. As I do before beginning any book, I had laboriously gone through my stack of books by Lewis to review what he had written on the subject. Participants in the Jesus Seminar were attracting press coverage, and I found myself wishing Lewis were alive to respond to some of their fantastic theories about Jesus and the Gospels.

At the conference I heard an actor deliver Lewis's magnificent sermon "The Weight of Glory" from the very pulpit where Lewis had first preached it. I toured Lewis's home the Kilns and visited his grave, walked the towpath along the Thames, lingered in formal gardens, and attended evening concerts. Oxford has managed to preserve the best aspects of Western civilization (which, oddly, tends to attract hordes of rowdy tourists in sloppy dress). I found myself envying Lewis's quietly ordered life before the intrusion of computers, e-mail, and mobile phones.

Ten years later I returned to speak at the same conference, this time in Cambridge. The speakers' lineup shows the breadth of Lewis's appeal: DNA expert Francis Collins and physicist John Polkinghorne, the poet Dana Gioia, the philosophers Richard Swinburne and Nancey Murphy, the psychologist Paul Vitz, as well as a former White House speechwriter, a film critic, and sundry artists and musicians.

Readers of *Christianity Today* rate Lewis the most influential Christian writer of our time even though he hardly fits the evangelical profile. A conference in his memory brings together men and women from all denominations and backgrounds because he focused on *mere* Christianity, avoiding such divisive issues as universalism, baptism, the sacraments, inerrancy, and eschatology. "Ever since I became a Christian," he wrote in 1952, "I have thought that the best, perhaps the only service I could do for my unbelieving neighbors was to explain and defend the belief that has been common to nearly all Christians at all times." Even a presumed critic like the fundamentalist Bob Jones Jr. had to admit, "That man smokes a pipe, and that man drinks liquor—but I *do* believe he is a Christian!"

Moreover, Lewis's appreciation of pleasures as the "drippings of grace" brings together the visible and invisible worlds. Unlike hermits of the Middle Ages and legalists of modern times, Lewis saw no need to withdraw from the world and shun pleasure. He loved a stiff drink, a puff on the pipe, a gathering of friends, a Shakespeare play, a witty joke. As the diabolical Screwtape had to admit, pleasure "is His invention, not ours." Life's delights are indeed good, just not good enough; our desires are too small, our vision too limited.

I find in Lewis something rarely seen in either secular or sacred society: a delicate balance of embracing the world while not idolizing it. For all its defects, this planet bears marks of the original design, traces of beauty and joy that both recall and anticipate the Creator's intent. If moderns approach Christianity like divorcées, perhaps C. S. Lewis serves as a reconciler who fans to life the dying embers of faith.

To the question "What good is God?" Lewis offers a different kind of answer than I had found among prostitutes, the underground church in China, and the survivors of Virginia Tech: the example of a transformed atheist who lived out his faith in the midst of an aggressively secular scholastic environment. It occurred to me that Lewis is, above all, a unifier, a theme I decided to address in my talk.

9 Straddling Two Worlds

Cambridge, August 2008

Some friends of mine went on a walking tour of Italy, visiting churches and art museums during the day and attending concerts at night. None of the other tour members shared my friends' interest in matters of faith, and in fact a blustery Englishman opined during one day's hike, "Europe would have been so much better off if Christianity had never happened!" He failed to see the irony in paying for an expensive tour of cultural artifacts all of which sprang from Christianity.

Religion gets bad press these days, understandably so. Much of the world views religious faith as the great divider: between Muslim and Christian, Hindu and Muslim, Tibetan Buddhist and Chinese Communist, Catholic and Protestant, Shiite and Sunni, Muslim and Jew. Suicide bombers, counting on rewards in an afterlife, destroy the present lives of themselves and others. The average secular person, who sees fanatics hurling insults and bombs at each other, turns from religion in disgust. Americans once viewed their enemies as godless communists; now that they face attacks from Islamic extremists, more and more are rejecting religious affiliation.

As a Christian I must admit that my faith does draw dividing lines: the children of light and the children of darkness, good and evil, life of the spirit and life of the flesh, the natural world and the spiritual world. In his paradoxical style, G. K. Chesterton saw no problem with this duality. He said, "Christianity got over the difficulty of combining furious opposites, by keeping them both, and keeping them both furious." I would suggest that C. S. Lewis, who looked upon Chesterton as a spiritual father, nevertheless presents a healthier approach, one that a divided world urgently needs. Lewis found a way to bring together, to *unify*, apparent opposites.

One apparent opposite leaps immediately to mind. "Do not love the world or anything in the world," warned the apostle John. Yet clearly some of us do love the world. We are, after all, sitting in Great St. Mary's Church, an English Gothic building that pleases the eye and a venue in which we have heard fine music and poetry. Yesterday I took a walk in the fragrant, blossom-laden gardens of Clare College. I sampled excellent international cuisine. By doing these things, have I disobeyed the apostle John?

An ambivalence about pleasure has marked all religions, including Christianity. The novelist Salman Rushdie observes that the true battle of history is fought not between rich and poor, socialist and capitalist, or black and white, but between the epicure and the puritan. He sees evidence in the struggle between strict and secular Muslims; the same tension appears within the more legalistic denominations within Christianity. The church of my upbringing judged movies, coed swimming, and rock music as "worldly" and thus sinful. Taking the apostle John to a literalistic extreme, hermits once sat naked on poles or hid in caves in the Egyptian desert, refusing all nourishment save bread and water.

In a church architecturally similar to this one, in the sister city of Oxford, C. S. Lewis addressed this issue head-on. He sought to explore how Christianity relates to culture for the arts, especially poetry and music, had given Lewis much pleasure. The year was 1939 and, as the United States had not yet entered the war, Britain was fighting Hitler's Germany virtually alone. Lewis addressed the sermon "Learning in Wartime" to students who were trying to concentrate on academics before joining their friends on the front lines in North Africa and Europe. How, asked Lewis, can young men soon to face mortal danger, with the future of civilization hanging in the balance, spend time on history and philosophy, let alone Lewis's field of medieval literature? "Is it not like fiddling while Rome burns?"

To begin, Lewis pointed out that none of us knows when life will come to an abrupt end; war merely increases the immediate odds. The question is not whether literature is worth studying in wartime but whether literature is worth studying at all. For creatures who are every moment advancing either to heaven or hell, is the pursuit of good culture ever a worthy pursuit?

Evidently, yes. God created the natural world, after all, and called it good. Furthermore, in the Old Testament God inspired sacred craftsmanship and a written revelation still regarded as a masterpiece. The New Testament shows more ambivalence toward culture, perhaps because early Christians lived under the shadow of cultured but pagan Rome. Lewis thought it necessary to put culture in its proper place. "The work of a Beethoven, and the work of a char-woman," he said, "become spiritual on precisely the same condition, that of being offered to God, of being done humbly 'as to the Lord.'" The salvation of a single soul, he said elsewhere, is worth more than all the epics and tragedies ever written—quite an admission for a man who taught literature for a living.

C. S. Lewis recognized human creativity as a good, but not an ultimate good. The glory of God represents the ultimate good, which culture may well serve. (We know, of course, that popular culture may also glorify evil.) This very conference, set amid the spires of two univer-sities with Christian roots, celebrates a man who sought to glorify God in his writing, his teaching, and his life. As Lewis told the students, "The intellectual life is not the only road to God, nor the safest, but we find it to be a road, and it may be the appointed road for us. Of course it will be so only so long as we keep the impulse pure and disinterested."

✦ ✦ ✦

Recall my friends on the walking tour of Italy: in Europe the culture that resulted from Christianity has survived with a better reputation than the Christians themselves. In St. Petersburg, Russia, I visited the Hermitage Museum, where one stunning room displays twenty-four paintings by Rembrandt, including "The Return of the Prodigal Son." Groups of Russian schoolchildren happened to be touring the museum that day and they would stop at key paintings—Abraham's sacrifice of Isaac, the Annunciation—which their teachers would attempt to explain.

Watching the interaction, I thought of another of Rembrandt's subjects, the scene from Acts 8 of Philip climbing into the chariot of an Ethiopian who was reading from a scroll of the prophet Isaiah. "Do you understand what you are reading?" Philip asked. In post-Christian Europe, those of us conversant in the faith have a similar task. The vocabulary already exists in a nation like Russia: in the novels of Tolstoy and Dostoevsky, so influential in my own faith, in the great artwork hanging on the walls of the Hermitage, and in the icons prominent in every church. Someone simply needs to climb in the chariot and explain the open scroll.

Culture can serve as a pointer to God: C. S. Lewis left us this strong legacy, for it mirrors his own conversion path of tracking longings to their source. For him the good things of life, whether the beauties of nature or of human creativity, sound as advance echoes of a perfected world to come. "The hills and valleys of Heaven will be to those you now experience not as a copy is to an original, nor as a substitute to the genuine article, but as the flower to the root, or the diamond to the coal."

A friend of mine in Manhattan, a Japanese-American by the name of Makoto Fujimura, faced an unusual opportunity in the wake of 9/11. Mako is a world-class artist and also a thoughtful Christian. His concern that Christians have abandoned the arts led him to form an organization, the International Arts Movement, to encourage Christians involved in culture-making. Mako happens to live a few blocks from Ground Zero in a neighborhood popular with artists. After the World Trade Center disaster, with many of these artists shut out of their homes and studios, Mako opened a communal studio to allow them to continue working. He dedicated it as "an oasis of collaboration by Ground Zero artists."

At that time, Mako told me, many of these artists were producing works intended to shock, most of them portraying obscenity and violence. On September 11 reality trumped creativity: what happened in their own neighborhood was more obscene and violent by far than anything they had imagined. In the safety of Mako's studio, these artists rediscovered other values—beauty, humaneness, courage, gentleness—and their works began to reflect this new outlook. One avant-garde artist who had worked to "decode gender and sexuality" made a different kind of creation, folding hundreds of white origami butterflies and arranging them in a beautiful pattern.

For six months the artists held exhibitions, performances, poetry readings, and prayer gatherings in this safe place, this oasis. As Mako later commented, "our imaginative capacities carry a responsibility to heal, every bit as much as they carry a responsibility to depict angst." For C. S. Lewis the works of imagination did just that, offering consolation to a wounded planet even while awakening a desire for ultimate healing.

✦ ✦ ✦

A conference like this one strives for artistic excellence. The organizers sought to have the *best* musicians and artists, and they have succeeded admirably. The worship services, concerts, dramatic performances, and poetry readings all reflect a commitment to high quality—which inadvertently brings up another area of tension. In the Beatitudes, in his parables, in his social contacts, Jesus tended to honor the losers of this world, not the winners. Our modern culture extravagantly rewards beauty, athletic skill, wealth, and artistic achievement, qualities which seemed to impress Jesus not at all. How can we combine a commitment to excellence with compassion for those who may never attain it?

Let me express the tension bluntly. How can we admire Miss Universe without devaluing the fifteen-year-old high school girl who wears glasses, has pimples, and whose figure resembles a lamppost? Or how can we honor Bill Gates and also the man who empties Bill Gates's garbage?

C. S. Lewis showed us the way. In his books, which span diverse genres, he strove for an ideal of excellence, which explains why a half-century after his death so many of them remain in print. As one who writes for a living, I marvel that when I read Lewis he always seems to know precisely what thought, even what word, must come next. Whether speaking to the nation on a radio broadcast, analyzing Milton's *Paradise Lost*, expressing waves of sorrow over his wife's death, or writing stories for children, Lewis achieved a high standard. And woe upon any student who showed up at his tutorials unprepared or with sloppy work.

Yet the same scholar who loved nothing more than an articulate debate with fellow dons at his favorite pub employed a beloved caretaker who regularly abused the English language. "Them's nawt ready," Fred Paxford would say if a cook asked for a certain vegetable from the garden. For three decades Lewis lived with a dominating woman who often treated him like a maid and errand boy, in part to fulfill a vow he had made to her son who had died in World War I. When Mrs. Moore at last had to move into a nursing home, Lewis visited her daily. The poor and hungry frequently showed up as guests for meals at his home, and during World War II the Kilns housed children evacuated from London because of the bombings. Lewis married Joy, a woman not known for her beauty, in a hospital room where she lay suffering from cancer, and cared for her tenderly ever after.

I have yet to find a rationale in evolutionary naturalism—the survival of the *fittest*—that suggests why we ought to care for the weak and suffering. Nature is stern: the herd advances by abandoning those who would hinder it. Lewis, however, understood that Christianity includes both an appreciation for quality (all good things are gifts of the Father in heaven) and compassion for those who lack it.

How, then, can we honor both Miss Universe and Miss Nobody,

Bill Gates and his garbageman? I believe Lewis would answer such a question by first acknowledging the image of God in every person. "There are no *ordinary* people," Lewis said in a sermon. "You have never talked to a mere mortal. Nations, cultures, arts, civilization—these are mortal, and their life is to ours as the life of a gnat. But it is immortals whom we joke with, work with, marry, snub, and exploit—immortal horrors or everlasting splendours." That startling truth applies equally to a caretaker and a scholar.

Lewis also recognized the qualities we value—talent, beauty, intelligence—as God's gifts, which should prompt a response of humble gratitude. Otherwise, the gift may degenerate into snobbish superiority and an excuse for indulgence. Society rewards naturally gifted people with money, fame, and the opportunity to sample pleasures unavailable to the rest of us—and therein lies a trap. The personalities we elevate in our celebrity culture bear out the danger in their widely publicized episodes of adultery, drug addiction, alcoholism, selfish extravagance, and other forms of overindulgence.

All God's gifts, whether a natural aptitude or an everyday pleasure, come to us with the potential for abuse. Some of you, I'm sure, know personally the power of addiction—perhaps pornography, perhaps alcohol. Pleasures have the raw power to elbow their way out of their intended order and to usurp the Giver who created them. *I must have that, no matter the cost, no matter the morality.*

As Lewis wrote in *The Screwtape Letters*, indulging in pleasure apart from the Creator's intent can lead to a form of slavery. "An ever increasing craving for an ever diminishing pleasure" is the devil's formula. Lewis saw daily proof in the effect of drink on his alcoholic brother and in his own battles with sexual temptation. Old Testament prophets warned of idolatries; our modern prophets, medical scientists, use the word "addiction" for the disorder. The only protection, said Lewis, is to strive to see every natural gift and pleasure as a shaft of God's glory, enjoying it always in its proper place.

Our modern culture exalts absolute freedom of choice. The Christian tradition presents something more like parenting. What expert in child-rearing would recommend always granting children whatever they want? What addiction counselor allows an alcoholic to decide how much to drink? God orders desires for our own sakes because so often we prove unwise in making decisions on our own.

As Christians we are called to embrace the world with gratitude to the Father of all good things, while not letting those pleasures enslave us. At the same time we are called to honor the marginalized—the aged, the disabled, the sick, the unattractive, the poor—who feel deprived of natural gifts and may lack the ability to enjoy certain pleasures. They, too, reflect something of God's image.

✦   ✦   ✦

Finally, C. S. Lewis unifies by bringing together two worlds, the visible and invisible, this life and the next. The suicide bomber sacrifices one for the sake of the other; the Christian ascetic forgoes the pleasures of one for the sake of the next. Lewis believed strongly that the two worlds interpenetrate each other, now and forever.

Lewis felt more at home with the medieval worldview than the modern because at least it recognized meaning and purpose in the universe. Jacques Monod captures the typical modern perspective: Man must learn to live in "an alien world; a world that is deaf to his music, just as indifferent to his hopes as it is to his sufferings or his crimes." He adds, "Man at last knows that he is alone in the universe's unfeeling immensity out of which he emerged only by chance." Writers like Sartre, Heidegger, and Camus amplified that theme of estrangement in Lewis's lifetime.

More recently, environmentalists have pictured human beings as the planet's villains. The novelist Philip Roth concluded his book *The Human Stain* with a telling scene: an ice-covered lake surrounded by trees, the entire landscape covered in newly fallen snow, with only one dark blot to mar the pristine setting, an ice fisherman on the lake, "like the X of an illiterate's signature on a sheet of paper"—the human stain.

Life grinds on. Men and women fall in love and marry and bear children and work at careers, then grow old and die, making room for more blots on planet Earth. Few give thought to whether their lives and choices matter to the cosmos, to eternity. Against that dismal background Lewis affirmed the opposite, that what we do on earth plays a meaningful role in the great dance that will one day heal a fractured universe.

The gods of the Greeks and Romans had little concern for how humans treated each other on earth. The ancients had a conception of life "as above, so below": Zeus's anger in the heavens fell on earth in the form of thunderbolts. Christianity reverses the formula, promising that what we do here matters, ultimately, eternally. When a sinner repents, angels rejoice. A cup of cold water given in Jesus' name, heaven receives as an offering, just like a holy sonnet or a chorus of praise. The biblical story radiates assurance that every moment of life has meaning.

We live, Lewis believed, in evil-occupied territory, which obscures reality and dangerously complicates the journey. As a result the pilgrim's progress toward the heavenly city will involve confusing choices and dreadful falls. In the end, however, we who now see through a glass darkly will see face to face. As Lewis said, "Our first words, on getting to heaven, will be Ohhh..., with an air of Now I understand."

In his anthology of George MacDonald, Lewis included this quote which could serve as an epitaph for his life: "We must refuse, abandon, deny self altogether as a ruling, or determining, or originating element in us. It is to be no longer the regent of our action. We are no more to think 'What should I like to do?' but 'What would the Living One have me to do?'" To answer that question becomes the central focus of a life of faith.

C. S. Lewis answered the question in many forms: in *The Chronicles of Narnia*, in which children lead the decisive battle against evil to regain the cosmos; in the space trilogy, in which other planets brace themselves against the human stain; in his sermons and works of apologetics, all of which trumpet the message that ordinary men and women have a role to play. Most of all, he answered it in his own life, by serving with excellence and humility both—in the classroom, the pulpit, the writing study, and the home.

PART V

BIBLE COLLEGE: STUDENT DAZE

BIBLE COLLEGE:
STUDENT DAZE

10　　Life in a Bubble

The Bible college I attended attracted some weird students. One young man in my dorm said his parents sometimes ground up poison ivy and mixed it with his orange juice so he would develop an immunity to the noxious plant. A classmate who grew up on a farm claimed he used to bury chickens up to their necks and run over them with a lawn mower. After hearing this I tended to avoid him. "You shall know the truth and the truth shall make you odd," said the novelist Flannery O'Connor, who gave us some of the oddest characters in literature.

Another student, a tall, freckled freshman with protruding ears and pale blue eyes, dressed in a box each day lest his pants cuffs touch the dirty floor. Pathologically shy, he walked in a kind of shuffle, with his head down. But if you neglected to speak to him on the sidewalk he would appear at your door hours later asking in a barely controlled stutter, "D-d-d-did I do anything to-to off-off-off-fend you?"

A senior student on my floor proudly limited his showers to one per year. We dorm residents stood at our doors and applauded as he sauntered down the hall with a towel on this landmark day.

The school also included many healthy students, some of whom remain my close friends to this day. At the time, however, I was *un*healthy both emotionally and spiritually, and I viewed the Bible college as a kind of cuckoo's nest. Seeking to overcome the childhood effects of poverty and southern fanaticism, I had looked to college as a springboard to a broader, more sophisticated world. Instead this school seemed an island fortress against the outside world, one with its own private culture.

Social values inverted. Although the student body included a few sexy girls and at least one rich kid who drove a Jaguar and owned a private plane, these individuals ranked low on the new value scale. Other students gossiped about them and prayed for them—though some secretly lusted after the hot girls and envied the rich guy's toys. Students who showed an interest in philosophy, science, or other intellectual pursuits aroused suspicion. The arts barely existed. "Worldly sophistication is the greatest danger to the Christian!" thundered one professor.

The preferred role models were docile, obedient types who spoke in spiritualese. "I missed the bus today…well, the Lord must have a reason for it." *Maybe you should set your alarm next time instead of blaming God.* "Philip, I want you to know that the Lord has put you on my heart. I just have a special love for you." *Right, a special love that wants me to stop being so ornery and end up just like you.*

✦   ✦   ✦

Looking back forty years from the vantage of our belly-baring, pants-drooping, tattooed and lip-ringed society, I find it hard to resurrect the ethos of the late 1960s at a southern Bible college where gentlemen students wore jackets and ties to dinner each evening and all men stood when a female student approached the table.

Female students had a rigid, though annually alterable, dress code. My freshman year, coeds' skirts had to extend below the knee. Over the next three years—the miniskirt era outside the fortress—the acceptable line crept up to mid-knee and then to the top of the knee. Dean's assistants scouted for scofflaws, sometimes requiring them to kneel for a more accurate check with a ruler. The rules forbade slacks, except on some activity such as a hayride, when they were permitted if worn *under a skirt*. If a female student wore slacks in her room (allowed), she had to wear a bathrobe over them just to walk down the hall to the toilet or shower. A friend of mine caught robeless in the hall in the middle of the night challenged this rule. "You never know when you might run into a maintenance worker," the dean of women responded.

The sixties' sexual revolution did not penetrate the Bible college's hermetically sealed environment. "Students must absolutely avoid holding hands, embracing, kissing, and other physical contacts," read the sixty-six-page rule book, which students had to sign each year. To limit temptation, underclassmen were allotted just two dates a week (though not both with the same person)—double-dates, of course, and on Sunday evenings only to church. Freshman women had to apply to the dean of women in advance for each date. Apart from those dates, even students engaged to be married could only "socialize" one hour a day, during the evening meal with the entire student body. Telephone contact was forbidden.

Standing too close to your date in the cafeteria line may subject you to a dean's inquisition. Have you ever held hands? Did you kiss? Why are you flirting with temptation? Eyes were always watching and spies reported infractions of the rules. The bus driver on a school outing confronted a friend of mine: "It's my obligation to talk to you as a Christian. In the rearview mirror I saw you and that girl touching noses. Don't you know the Bible verse, 'It is good for a man not to touch a woman'?"

One revered professor, a bald senior citizen, insisted that in his own car his wife must sit over by the door handle, as far from him as possible, lest someone who didn't know they were married draw the wrong conclusion if they sat too close. He sold his stock in the local Belk Gallant department store because it sold swimsuits, which went against his beliefs on "mixed bathing." "When you wear lipstick," he would balefully warn the virginal girls in his classroom, "you are saying to the world, 'Kiss me! Kiss me!'"

The school's list of forbidden activities included dancing, playing cards, billiards, skating at public rinks, movies, boxing, wrestling, and "the presentation of opera and musical programs which include ballet, dancing, and suggestive songs." In the privacy of their dorm rooms students could play only music "consistent with a Christian testimony," a phrase open to much individual interpretation in the 1960s. Periodically, guilt-ridden students would smash their questionable record albums.

Because I didn't relish most of these activities anyway, I found their prohibition no great loss. The capriciousness and inconsistency of rules grated on me, though. Whereas women had their skirts measured, men had their hair measured: it could not cover the ears and definitely could not grow on the face as a beard or moustache. This seemed strange since our church history textbooks depicted Jesus, the apostles, and most male saints of history with flowing hair and beards. The school banned speaking in tongues, a practice that was plainly biblical. And even though the Bible refers positively to wine scores of times, on that campus alcohol ranked just beneath the unpardonable sin.

In chapel services the deans tried valiantly to anchor each of the college rules to a solid biblical principle, a task made difficult by slight adjustments in the rule book each year. The world outside was changing too fast for the rule-makers to keep up. Billy Graham steered some of his "Jesus people" converts to the school, only to have them met by deans censoring their record albums and steering them to a barber.

Sometimes on a weekend I would catch a ride downtown and wander around a large state university campus. Dormitory lounges—coed dorms, no less—had television sets! Hippie-looking students were making out on the couches in public view. Spray-painted graffiti marred the walls, and psychedelic posters announcing demonstrations and protest marches covered the bulletin boards. Elevators reeked of urine. It seemed like an alternate universe out there, and as I retreated to the bubble environment of the Bible college I appreciated the clean walls, spotless bathrooms, and neat dorm rooms (inspectors checked for made beds and room cleanliness each day). The school had managed to turn frat house values upside down, for on that campus we competed for responsibility, politeness, cleanliness, orderliness, self-control. It all worked.

Still, a part of me rebelled. The philosopher William James wrote after a visit to the Chautauqua camp meetings in 1896, "I stayed for a week, held spell-bound by the charm and ease of everything, by the middle-class paradise, without a victim, without a blot, without a tear. And yet what was my own astonishment, on emerging into the dark and wicked world again, to catch myself...saying 'Ouf, what a relief! Now for something primordial and savage...to set the balance straight.'"

✦ ✦ ✦

Whenever I write about my experience at Bible college, I get one of two reactions from readers. Some scold me for criticizing a godly institution and for distorting reality: "Did you and I attend the same school?!" former students have asked, indignant. Others from a wide variety of backgrounds—Catholic, Pentecostal, Worldwide Church of God, Seventh Day Adventist—recount their own stories of institutions that either shaped or shattered their faith. "Thank you for giving me permission to stop blaming myself for everything," they say.

I write not to demean the sincere people who ran the college (for this reason I avoid using the school's name) but rather to sort through the mixed messages I got there. I had a lively discussion with the man who served as president of the college during my last two years there, someone I greatly respect. "I know all sorts of juicy stories about people in Christian ministry," he said. "But I would never write about them because of the pain it would cause. I go by the Golden Rule: Do unto others as I would have them do to me."

As I thought over his comment I realized that is precisely why I *do* write honestly about my past, even though it may cause others pain. I would hope that readers call me down on my own inconsistencies and exaggerations and theological errors. I know of no more honest book than the Bible, which tells the ugly truth about its main protagonists (think of Moses, David, Peter, Paul) as well as the church established to carry on the tradition (think of James, Galatians, and 1 Corinthians, as well as the letters to the seven churches in Revelation). In contrast, the Pharisees and their kin exhibit one persistent flaw: an inability to take criticism. People and institutions naturally want to present themselves in the best light and thus we rationalize or cover up mistakes. When we do so we move away from authenticity toward the very dangers Jesus warned against, in the process sealing off grace.

I met God at the school I am writing about, a life-changing experience worth twenty years in prison let alone four years in a Bible college. Yet some people, including some whom I love, turned away from God at the same school. I look back on college days with whimsy; they remember mainly the pain of judgment and rejection, a sense of not fitting in. By listening to their stories I better understand Jesus' anger with the Pharisees, a surprising target since they were the most righteous and Bible-believing people of his day.

The Pharisees, accused Jesus, tithed their kitchen spices while neglecting weightier issues like justice. At other colleges students were protesting the Vietnam War and joining the Freedom Riders in Alabama and Mississippi. At our school we were debating such issues as the universal flood, hyperCalvinism, and infant baptism. Yes, we studied the Bible, but selectively. In the words of Marilynne Robinson, "People who insist that the sacredness of Scripture depends on belief in creation in a literal six days seem never to insist on a literal reading of 'to him who asks, give,' or 'sell what you have and give the money to the poor.'"

One year a student shot himself in the face with a pistol. That it was an accident, no one questioned: he was examining the gun when it went off, blasting a bullet through his jawbone. The owner of the gun had to write five hundred times, "I will not have a loaded gun in my room." This being the South, no one raised the larger issue of handgun possession. Another year a student drowned in a nearby river when a dam release upstream unexpectedly raised the water level. His companion, distraught over his best friend's death, had to do a work penalty for swimming on Sunday.

The school's emphasis on the "victorious Christian life" led to another danger Jesus warned the Pharisees about: a two-tiered spirituality. Adolescents who barely perceived themselves as independent moral beings, who had barely lived, competed to "lay it all on the altar," to experience "a deeper walk in the Spirit." If someone lacked the proper zeal—a parent or sibling back home, for instance, or a suspect fellow-student like me—the anxious question arose, "Do they really know the Lord?" The writings of C. S. Lewis, a lifeline of faith for me, were frowned upon because Lewis smoked a pipe and drank beer.

The school held a mandatory chapel service daily, required a personal quiet time of Bible study and prayer each morning—a loudly clanging bell woke us at 6:00 AM—and scheduled quarterly prayer days. Students learned that praying and giving testimonies in public presented the best opportunity to rise in status by displaying one's spiritual intensity. Thus my roommate confessed wild sins I knew he had not committed. One female student lived a double life for seven months, convincing many that she had terminal cancer. The artificial and the authentic became indistinguishable—Jesus' point about the Pharisees, exactly.

A friend of mine got called into the dean's office for wearing a coat hemmed higher than her regulation-length skirt. "Joyce, what are we going to do with you!" she was reprimanded, as if she had broken one of the Ten Commandments. Another time she wore a robe down the hall of the women's dorm with the bottom button undone. The dean shook her head: "Joyce, how can we trust you? If you fail in a thing like this, how can God use you?" Later, that same student was working in the dean of women's office as Valentine's Day approached. She witnessed the bizarre scene of her boss in white gloves censoring one by one the tiny heart-shaped candies to be used as decorations for a party. *You're mine, Friends forever, Be my Valentine* passed muster; *Cutie pie, Hot lips, Love ya* went right into the trash can.

✦ ✦ ✦

Readers who write protesting my unfair caricatures emphasize the wholesome sense of community that such an institution fosters. I agree. What state university imparts such positive values to its students and provides such a supportive community? On holidays we would step outside the bubble and find a world cavorting nude onstage, burning bras and draft cards, bombing campus buildings, tripping on LSD. Assassins killed King, then Kennedy. Ghetto-dwellers rioted. Soldiers shot students at Kent State. Then we returned to a safe, orderly world, a control-based community that measured skirts and hair and debated hyperCalvinism.

Once I tried to explain the rationale for rules at Christian colleges to the author Frederick Buechner, who was encountering a much milder version of them for the first time as a visiting professor at Wheaton College. I began with the moral argument, and had to agree with his response that unlike Wheaton the Bible did not specifically forbid drinking, smoking, card playing, and social dancing. I mentioned the doctrine of *in loco parentis*, in which schools take over responsibility from parents. Bob Jones Sr. used to promote his school as a place "parents can send their children and go to sleep at night knowing their children are safe physically, mentally, and spiritually."

Buechner contemplated this line of reasoning. "Yes, but these kids are twenty, twenty-one, twenty-two," he said at last. "Legally, they're adults." The only rationale that made sense to Buechner was the slippery-slope argument. Had not Harvard, Yale, Princeton, and Oberlin begun with the same commitment as Wheaton? "Everyone shall consider the main end of his life and studies to know God and Jesus Christ which is eternal life," proclaimed the original rule book at Harvard. "Cursed be all learning that is contrary to the cross of Christ," wrote the first president of Princeton. Question the universal flood or the crossing of the Red Sea and before long Jesus' miracles and the Resurrection are under assault. Permit hand-holding and one day they'll demand open dorms.

Shockingly, during my junior year the college hired a sociologist who had been educated at Harvard, and his classes helped me to step outside the bubble and view the Bible college as a subculture. Following the model of "total institutions" described by Erving Goffman, I saw that the school was using tried-and-true control mechanisms to impart to us spiritual values. The dean of men admitted that he favored retaining some irrational rules in order to teach the students to obey. To me, that sounded like the technique Marine sergeants use. Making a bed so tight that coins bounce off it and polishing shoes so bright that they reflect the sergeant's face do not further a recruit's ability to conduct war. They do, however, reinforce an important military principle: "I am boss and you are not, so you must do what I say."

Goffman theorized that total institutions such as military academies and prisons—and Bible colleges? I wondered—gradually enculturate their members so that after a time the insiders think that culture normal. For a sociology project I gave a printed survey form to every freshman and every senior, asking such loaded questions as "Which rule at this school bothers you most?" Sure enough, the seniors defended rules that freshmen thought ridiculous. My project landed me once more on the faculty's suspect list when someone gave the dean a copy of my mimeographed survey. "This is an insurrection!" said one member of the administration. "He can't survey freshmen. They don't know us!"

✦   ✦   ✦

As I admit, I was in a most unhealthy state while a student, especially the first two years. I used chapel as a time to catch up on magazine reading, much to the disgust of more pious students who kept reporting me to the dean. In a sort of reverse-silent-witness, I would sit outdoors and read books like Harvey Cox's *The Secular City* and Bertrand Russell's *Why I Am Not a Christian*. In short, I was the antitype of the ideal Bible college student, and got treated as such. Some called me stiff-necked, some avoided me, some prayed for me. A few, especially the young woman who became my wife, loved me.

Through the grace of God, and also the grace of the college administration, I managed to survive through graduation. I now reflect on my time at Bible college with some shame but much gratitude: for the biblical knowledge I acquired there, for the personal disciplines that I resented at the time but learned to appreciate, and for the essential part the school played in grounding my faith. Ever since, we have had an ambivalent relationship, the school and I. They gave me a Distinguished Alumnus award and nearly asked for it back after I wrote about the school in *What's So Amazing About Grace?*

I have returned to campus as a speaker three times. The first time I delivered a series of talks that became the basic outline for my book on grace. To me, that word *grace* seemed the missing ingredient in acquiring a faith that matters in the world outside the school. The second time, a decade later, the school invited me to deliver a commencement address, at very short notice (prompting me to wonder who had cancelled on them). When I drove on campus and got out of the car, a student came up and asked, "Aren't you Philip Yancey?" I nodded, and he said, "We were told you'd never be invited back here after what you said about grace!"

On that visit administrators and faculty assured me that the school had changed radically in the years since I attended, and from all appearances I had to agree. A few students said to me privately, "Actually, not much has changed. The spirit of mind-control is just the same."

In 2007, I was invited back once again. I agreed, under the condition that I speak on the topic "What I Wish I'd Known as a Student Here."

11   I Wish I'd Known

Bible College, April 2007

Thank you for coming this morning! You don't fool me, though—I know chapel attendance is mandatory, with seats assigned and monitors checking your attendance. I'm looking right now where I used to sit, down front where the administration could keep an eye on me. I sometimes read *Time* magazine during chapel, and the dean called me in to discuss that rude practice. I explained that I had mastered the ability to listen to chapel speakers and read at the same time: multitasking, in other words, before we knew the term.

He mulled over my answer, then asked whether I didn't think it disrespectful to the chapel speaker. "I would be happy to meet with the speakers in advance and explain that I'll be listening to them as I read," I replied. Bible college deans get gray hair and go to early graves because of smart alecks like me.

In my immature state at the time I would have preferred anything to sitting in a chapel service five days a week listening to sermons. Now as an act of penance I find myself *speaking* at college chapels to students who may be just as bored and resistant as I once was. God surely has a sense of humor.

Most speakers, I noticed as a student, address their remarks to the 80 percent of the audience eager to hear what they have to say, not to resentful rebels like me. Today I want to speak primarily to the other 20 percent, those of you who feel like I used to feel, unsure you want to be here. I will tell you what I wish I'd known as a student here some forty years ago. Maybe, just maybe, what I have learned in the time since will save you some trouble while here, or at least give you an idea of what to expect when you leave.

✦   ✦   ✦

I wish I'd known how to appreciate two worlds at once. Christians believe that the world we see outside these windows, a material world of rocks and trees and birds and clouds, is not all that exists, and a Bible college creates an artificial environment to enhance your perception of the invisible world. Many of your classes here focus on *spiritual* disciplines and on mastering the Bible, which Christians believe is our best guidebook in getting to know the Maker of everything, both visible and invisible.

As I review my time on this campus, much of which I spent in a confused and troubled state, everything pales in significance beside the fact that I met God here. Though I grew up in a smothering church environment and knew the Bible as well as some of the faculty here, I had not encountered the living God in a personal and convincing way until I came to this school. That alone makes me eternally grateful for my years at this place. At the same time, though, I believe the school presented an unbalanced picture. An artificial environment geared toward the invisible world makes it easy to devalue the visible, created world. Martin Luther warned, "I fear that Christians who stand with only one leg upon earth also stand with only one leg in heaven."

I once heard Eugene Peterson, known primarily for his paraphrase of the Bible, *The Message*, reminisce about an eccentric woman named Sister Lychen. The Pentecostal church of Peterson's childhood encouraged words of prophecy, and almost every week this frail old woman would stand up and say something like this: "The Lord has revealed that I will not see death before he descends from heaven with a shout and with the sound of trumpets to catch me up with other saints to meet him in the air."

One day to Eugene's dismay his mother asked him to take some homemade cookies to this woman's house. Eugene knocked on the door with fear and trembling and Sister Lychen herself, ninety years old, witchlike with pale, veiny skin and a bony face, invited him in to share those cookies. She served him a glass of milk, and the little boy sat nervously and ate his cookies in near total darkness, for Sister Lychen kept her blinds drawn all day long.

Later, Peterson said, he had a vision of sorts. He saw himself rushing into her house and yanking open all the blinds. "Look outside!" he cried. "See, there's an aspen tree! An osprey on the top branch! And a white-tailed deer. Sister Lychen, there's a whole good world outside!"

It was that "whole good world outside" that helped bring me back to faith, in part by correcting my misconceptions of God. I began to see God as a whimsical artist who invents comical creatures like the porcupine and skunk and naked-nosed wombat, who lavishes the world with desert wildflowers and tropical fish more beautiful than any work displayed in an art museum.

Francis Collins, who supervised the Human Genome Project, sees God's hand in the elegant structure of the DNA double helix. Annie Dillard sees it in the tiny creatures that swim and dive in Tinker Creek, Virginia. From nature writers such as John Muir, Henri Fabre, Loren Eiseley, and Lewis Thomas I gain appreciation for a master Artist they may not even believe in; yet their precise and reverent observations help to raise the blinds for me.

Church historian Mark Noll remarks that the song "Turn Your Eyes Upon Jesus" plainly errs when it says, "And the things of earth will grow strangely dim in the light of his glory and grace." No, the rest of the world grows clearer, not dimmer, in that light. God created the world of matter, set us down in its midst, and entered it in the Incarnation. The least we can do is appreciate it. Helen Keller gave good advice: "Use your eyes as if tomorrow you would be stricken blind; hear the music of voices, the song of a bird, as if you would be stricken deaf tomorrow."

I hope that when you leave this artificial environment—even before you leave it—you will explore the world outside. Cultivate non-Christian friends and demonstrate to them that beauty and longing and curiosity and joy are God's gifts to us, rightly to explore. I hope you embrace the world outside with a sacred sense of gratitude, especially those of you preparing to serve in other countries. I met a pastor in Bahrain who can identify by sight two thousand species of seashells, and a missionary in Costa Rica who has assembled a world-class collection of butterflies and moths. And as you may know, the British pastor and author John Stott has had a lifelong passion for bird-watching, often making his decision to accept a speaking engagement based on whether rare birds nest nearby.

We have biblical models of drawing on the resources of the world outside. For example, the Israelites used the gold of the pagan Egyptians to construct the tabernacle. You may also remember the story told in 2 Kings of what happened when the city of Samaria lay under siege and deadly famine. Desperate, outcasts with leprosy risked their lives by venturing beyond the city walls in search of food. They found an amazing sight, the remnants of an army that had vanished, and so brought the abandoned supplies back to the Israelites cowering inside. Sometimes we must go outside the church to get nourishment—art, beauty, knowledge—which we can then bring inside to appreciate fully.

The church once stood as a steward of culture, its patron as well as its guide. Education, science, art, and music all had their roots in a church community committed to God's will being done "on earth as it is in heaven." When we ignore the world outside the walls we suffer—as does it.

✦   ✦   ✦

I wish I'd known how to nurture the inner life. Do you still have a rule book here? In my day the rules covered sixty-six pages, the number of books in the Bible, and we joked about dividing the rule book into the Old and New Testaments. Actually, the whole scheme had an Old

Testament scent to me. You have doubtless heard stories about rules in "the old days" so let me set the record straight: all those stories are true!

Students, being students, will always push against authority. From this college I went to the graduate school at Wheaton College, where rules barely cover a single page, not sixty-six, and there, too, the students groused about oppression. Strange as it may seem, the *strictness* of rules is not the main issue: West Point and the Air Force Academy have a stricter regimen than you will find at any Bible college, yet thousands of young men and women compete to enter those schools each year.

Here, rules may present a temptation to rely on external behavior rather than cultivating the inner life. Basing your faith on externals has the advantage of letting you know exactly what is expected. On the other hand, it also makes faith easy to cast off. I can exchange one way of behaving for another, like a chameleon changing colors, while nothing really changes on the inside. I know former students who turned completely away from God in reaction against this college's rules, the express opposite of the rule maker's intent.

Some of you plan to work in Islamic countries, and you may know about the backlash against strict rules in some quarters. An Iranian intellectual told a visiting Harvard professor, "These young people may be lost to Islam forever.... They follow the conventions of Islamic dress and custom because they are required to do so by law, but inside their hearts are hollow and cynical. We are losing an entire generation of unbelievers in our zeal to force conformity." You could hardly find better words to express the central danger of legalism in a Christian subculture.

For the Christian, living by strict rules becomes a danger when it quenches the spiritual life rather than expresses it. Do you rely on rules as a way to earn God's approval? Does a rule-based community set up a ranking system of higher and lower spirituality? Do rules distract you from weightier issues? Which do they foster, pride or humility? Do they help nourish the inner life or merely whitewash the outer appearance? These are the questions Jesus raised about the Pharisees, in some of the strongest language he ever used.

I remember spending several months in this bubble environment then heading home for Christmas and summer vacations to encounter the culture shock of a wild world of sex, drugs, and rock and roll. Trust me, that is minor compared to the culture shock you will face if you head to other countries. Some of you will go to Europe, where Christians drink alcohol with every meal save breakfast and women sunbathe topless in public parks. Some will go to Africa, with its child soldiers and rampant corruption, or to Asia with its forced prostitution, or to Islamic countries where your neighbor may have several wives and you'll hear their screams as they are beaten.

How can you prepare for such culture shocks? Jesus gave his disciples plain advice in Mark 7. "Don't you see that nothing that enters a man from the outside can make him 'unclean'? For it doesn't go into his heart but into his stomach, and then out of his body." His Jewish disciples must have scratched their heads, for much of the Old Testament law operates on the contamination principle. Touch an unclean person and you become unclean; eat an unclean animal and you become unclean. Following this principle, the Pharisees worried more about keeping themselves from contamination than about healing the ills around them.

I heard a fascinating sermon on this passage by Dr. Paul Brand, who was speaking in an old stone church in England. "Jesus is giving a lesson in anatomy, and he's entirely accurate," said Dr. Brand. He launched into a description of the marvels of skin, which draws a border between inside and outside. Dangers lurk everywhere on the outside and epithelial cells form a life-saving barrier against those dangers. "I can clean out a muddy gutter with my bare hand, or even reach in to unstop a toilet, encountering millions of bacteria in the process, but my skin cells loyally guard against their entering my body. And, to underscore Jesus' image, epithelial cells line the entire digestive tract so that if you swallow an inert object—a thief swallowing a diamond, for example, or a drug runner swallowing a packet of plastic—the object literally never enters the body, never breaks through that skin barrier before passing back outside."

Dr. Brand then described what happens when skin cells get compromised through injury or, worse, through his own profession of surgery. "We assume the gravest risk by far when we cut through that barrier of skin, exposing the vulnerable insides to hazards from the outside. Surgeons scrub with the strongest disinfectants known before operating, and still we may introduce serious infections into our patients."

Pointing to the stained-glass windows set in the stone walls of the church, he drew a spiritual application. "Have you ever noticed that artists portray saints with their hands together before them, almost in an attitude of prayer? In normal life I rarely see people with their hands together like that—except in the operating room. After I scrub, if the patient is not ready I hold my hands together just like that, fingertip to fingertip, lest I touch anything in the room that might harbor germs. What a terrible image for saints! We should have our hands outstretched, embracing a dirty world because, as Jesus says, nothing on the outside can make us unclean."

In Jesus' own words, "What comes *out of a man* is what makes him 'unclean.' For from within, out of men's hearts, come evil thoughts, sexual immorality, theft, murder, adultery, greed, malice, deceit, lewdness, envy, slander, arrogance and folly. All these evils come from inside and make a man 'unclean.'"

I kept most of the rules as a student here—not all of them, I must admit. Some of us expended a lot of energy resisting them. They seemed so powerful at the time. Later, I saw that their main power was negative: they distracted me from the far more important need to nourish my inner life. That loud bell every morning compelled us to get out of bed and spend time praying and reading our Bibles; periodic checks by the dean enforced that rule. It took years for me to perceive prayer as a privilege and not a duty, to see Bible reading as a source of life and not an obligation.

I wish I had had the maturity as a student here to take my focus off the petty rules and devote my energies to nourishing the inner life. No one but you can accomplish that. If you rely on an external structure for your spiritual life, you can jettison it the day after you leave this campus, as some have. On the other hand, as Jesus told his disciples, if you clean up the inside, nothing on the outside can soil you. You can reach out with loving hands and embrace a world full of violence, abuse, trafficking, injustice, poverty, and promiscuity, all the while remaining clean on the inside.

✦   ✦   ✦

I wish I'd known more humility. I came here as a student because I thought we had The Truth. Later I learned what a small slice of the world evangelicals constitute. Slightly less than a third of the world identifies itself as Christian. Of these, almost two-thirds are Catholic, Orthodox, or near-Catholic. Of the remaining Christians, barely 10 percent of the world's population, many would not accept the label evangelical.

I have learned to appreciate other traditions of the faith. While writing a book about prayer I learned more from Catholics than from any other group; they have, after all, devoted entire orders to the practice. Similarly, I learn mystery and reverence from the Eastern Orthodox. In music, in worship, in theology, they teach me of the *mysterium tremendum* involved when we puny human beings approach the God of the universe—a lesson difficult to learn in evangelical churches where worship is led by guitar players in shorts and sloppy T-shirts who wear their baseball caps backward.

I have concluded that God did not oversee the tortuous process recorded in the Old Testament, and Jesus did not spend his working life among twelve Jews, solely to redeem American evangelicals. Something bigger was afoot, and that something should inspire humility.

Do not misunderstand me. Unlike some of my friends I do not disdain the word evangelical, nor do I confuse it with the media's caricature of evangelicals as right-wing zealots. The word means *good news*, and I have seen that good news broadcast in more than fifty countries where underpaid missionaries and relief workers bring healing, education, justice, and practical help to the disadvantaged because they believe by doing so they are serving God. "You can get evangelicals to do anything," said a friend of mine who recruits them to work in the inner city of Chicago. Then he added the caution, "The challenge is, you've also got to soften their judgmental attitudes before they can be effective."

Langdon Gilkey's classic book *Shantung Compound* describes a community of Christians brought together by force: during World War II Japanese occupiers corralled foreigners including many missionaries into a concentration camp. The evangelicals did not fare so well. They complained about their circumstances, gossiped about the others, and hoarded rather than shared their parcels from the West. By Gilkey's account, of all the groups imprisoned, evangelicals demonstrated the most pettiness, fractiousness, and selfishness. (Trappist monks fared the best. After superiors lifted the rule of silence, the camp seemed to them like a holiday retreat. They had variety in food, they could talk and laugh and swap jokes, and they were around *women*!)

As I survey the history of evangelicalism I see much good. I also see a history of disunity—how many different denominations are represented in this chapel?—and a past that includes shameful lapses in ethics and judgment. Some of the denominations you come from, such as Southern Baptists and Methodists, formed over the issue of slavery: their leaders owned slaves and wanted to continue the practice. Many evangelical denominations, including my own, actively opposed the civil rights movement. Read current surveys and you'll find that evangelicals' marriages end in divorce at a rate similar to everyone else's.

I noted this morning that outside this chapel stands a stone monument to one of the primary values of this school, Victorious Christian Living. Although I certainly do not oppose that ideal, I would simply add, be careful. Be humble. Prepare for a fall.

A few years ago I discussed the victorious Christian life with the professor I most valued as a student here, a professor who lovingly reached out to me and helped salvage my faith. We met not long before his death, and I must say it was a jolt for me to see this man who had been my mentor, a giant of faith, shuffle toward me as an old man in his robe and slippers. "I believe in the victorious Christian life," he said, "because I saw it lived out in the man who founded this school." He went on to describe the sterling character of a great man of God.

"Yes, but can you think of only one?" I could not help asking. We dare not lower the ideal, yet neither should we present the ideal as the norm. D. L. Moody, asked whether he was filled with the Spirit, replied, "Yes. But I leak." Perhaps you should install another stone beside the Victorious Christian Living monument: "Yes, but we leak."

✦ ✦ ✦

I *wish I'd known grace here.* Although I will not expand on this theme, I must mention it for it is "by grace through faith," in Paul's words, that any of us are saved.

I have written that I experienced little grace while attending this school. "Perhaps the grace was there, and you didn't have the receptors to receive it," said the mentor I have just referred to. I objected then and gave him specific examples of ungrace, but he may be right. Perhaps my spiritual numbness caused me to miss the fragrance of grace here—I don't know. I do know, though, that it took some time after graduation for me to realize in my core that the gospel truly is good news; that the heart of the universe is a smile not a frown; that more than any other quality God is love. A verse in 1 John promises, "If your heart condemns you, God is greater than your heart." I wish I had known that while a student here.

I came to this school with a distorted image of God, as a frowning Supercop looking to squash anyone who might be having a good time. How wrong I was. I have come to know a God who has a soft spot for rebels, who recruits people like the adulterer David, the whiner Jeremiah, the traitor Peter, and the human-rights abuser Saul of Tarsus. I have come to know a God whose Son made prodigals the heroes of his stories and the trophies of his ministry.

As you've no doubt noticed, I am wearing a neck brace as a result of a rollover accident a few months ago. For seven hours that day I lay strapped to a gurney unsure whether I would survive the next hour. After all the fire and brimstone sermons I had heard in childhood, I fully expected to smell at least a whiff of sulfur at such a time. To my great relief, I did not. The God I serve is a God I have come to trust, one who scans the horizon for the prodigal and runs to greet him, or her. "God is not unjust," insists the author of the Book of Hebrews in a radical understatement of grace.

The faculty tell me that the complexion of the student body has changed since my days as a student here. Back then many Bible college students saw themselves as the elite, champions marching out to conquer the world for Christ. Along the way, our sick culture caught up with this school. Nowadays far more students come from broken homes and as many as 20 percent of you report sexual abuse in your backgrounds. Some of you have survived alcoholic families, and the scars remain. Even now some of you are sitting here with shameful secrets. I asked faculty to name a burning issue on campus, which in my day might have included hyperCalvinism or women in ministry. Now, they say, it's Internet pornography.

I hold in my hands a letter from a student who graduated from this college a few years before me. "Unlike you," she writes, "I went through Bible college supremely confident. The future looked bright with promise. The reason I was so confident was that I was a quintessential legalist. I was a Pharisee. I thrived on the rules." She goes on to tell of marrying a missionary kid she met here, who over the next twenty-five years betrayed their marriage hundreds of times with both heterosexual and homosexual liaisons. Then she learned that her "godly" father, who conducted family worship every day, had been sexually molesting his granddaughters. A year later her own teenage daughter was raped by an intruder. "Would there be no end to the sorrows?" she asks.

After describing these family tragedies in some detail, she tells of her life-giving discovery of God's grace. "I loved my Christian lifestyle—I didn't love God," she says of her time at this school. But since then "I have been the recipient of the scandalous grace you write about. At a time in my life when I wanted and expected to have hands full of gifts (accomplishments) for God I came to him with *empty* (!) hands." It was only then that she felt the goodness and mercy of God, and a deep contentment and peace settled in amid the pain and sorrow. She found a new life for herself teaching at a tiny mission school in a developing country.

A Bible college is a sort of halfway house on the way to maturity. You will face a world more muddled and mysterious than you can now imagine. What seems perfectly clear now, soon won't. Rules and doctrines alone will not protect you against the surprises you will face, either in yourself or in others around you. You will need to drink often at the fountain of God's grace.

After you graduate no bells will awaken you in the morning and no rule book will instruct you how to behave. This place is temporary. People and experiences vivid to you now, you'll look back on as through a fog. The teachers you sit under every day—trust me, you may not even remember their names. Yet you live in the present; you can only count on *now*. How you spend your time here, who you learn from, who you hang out with will affect you forever. These days matter. They are helping to form you.

Above all else, I leave you this word *grace*, and hope and pray that you will let it soak into you today and the rest of your days. I pray that while here you will not only believe in God, but also know deep in your soul that God believes in you.

PART VI

SOUTH AFRICA: BREAKING DOWN THE WALLS

SOUTH AFRICA:
BREAKING DOWN THE WALLS

COLOUREDS ONLY

12   The Unlikeliest Lot

The letter, addressed to "Pastor Philip," invited me to give the 2003 commencement address for a school in Johannesburg, South Africa. I wrote back, asking for more details and also noting that, since I am not a pastor, "Dear Philip" would suffice. The reply came addressed once again to "Pastor Philip," and communications from Rhema Church have used that salutation ever since.

With a little digging I learned that the charismatic church began in 1979 with thirteen members and has grown to thirty-five thousand; that its pastor Ray McCauley is one of the most recognized figures in South Africa, in part because of his high-profile television ministry and in part because of a headline-making divorce in 2000; that the church's racial makeup has changed from mostly white to 70 percent black. My curiosity aroused, I accepted the invitation. Soon another letter arrived: "Dear Pastor Philip, Before you speak, Pastor Ray and his wife Zelda would like you and your wife to be their guests at a private game reserve."

After a thirty-six-hour journey including a long layover in Germany, we met Ray and Zelda at a Johannesburg hotel. Both were larger-than-life characters. Ray had been a bodybuilder in his youth, finishing second runner-up to Arnold Schwarzenegger in the Mr. Universe contest some thirty years before. Though he gave little evidence of having worked out recently, Ray still remained an imposing physical presence. Incongruously, he came from a family of gamblers and had worked as a nightclub bouncer. After a dramatic conversion he went on to found the church that would become the largest in South Africa with its Sunday services broadcast on all four network TV stations.

Zelda, a striking blonde, had her own rugged history. Abandoned by her parents and reared in an orphanage, she had worked as a model in London and dated rock stars, then returned to South Africa where she bore three children by three different fathers and weathered two divorces before meeting Ray. Zelda was impeccably dressed in an outfit more suited to a shopping expedition than a game park.

We shook hands, stowed our luggage in the trunk, and set off for a weekend with our new acquaintances. It soon became clear that neither Ray nor Zelda had much experience driving—understandable since the church normally provides drivers—and within half an hour we were royally lost. As Zelda pulled into a service station to ask for directions, I got a glimpse of Ray's celebrity status. Instantly several dozen Africans surrounded the car shouting, "It's Pastor Ray! It's Pastor Ray!" One bold woman with a gold-toothed smile came to the window and asked for his blessing. When he held her hand and prayed a short prayer she jumped up and down in delight crying, "He blessed me! Pastor Ray blessed me!" I stole a glance at Janet. Had we signed up for a weekend with the pope for Pentecostal Africans?

Apparently so. Yet over the next few days as we rose before dawn for the early-morning safaris, and spent virtually all our time together, I came to appreciate Ray's spiritual and intellectual journey. He eagerly quizzed me about what books he should be reading and made careful notes of each suggestion. Clearly he had moved beyond the simple "name it and claim it" gospel of his background. As the apartheid government began to crumble, Nelson Mandela and Bishop Desmond Tutu had embraced Ray, no doubt coveting his nationwide television constituency, and in the process Ray's racial attitudes, politics, and fledgling theology underwent a change.

The prosperity gospel has great appeal in developing countries—

for a time. Pastors in places like the Philippines and Brazil have told me of the masses who flock to hear a health-and-wealth message and later leave, disillusioned, when things don't work out as promised. Ray had come to see that the church has a broader mission and could play a crucial role in shaping the culture of the new South Africa. Under his leadership Rhema Church has begun addressing human needs through an AIDS hospital, a housing program, and a farm for rehabilitating addicts.

✦ ✦ ✦

Ray McCauley proved a fascinating raconteur. He knew everyone of note in the country and had participated in key events of recent history. For example, he was once helicoptered into a crisis situation after a massacre. He found himself standing shoulder to shoulder with Bishop Tutu to face down a screaming mob. Ray's heart rate surged when he looked around and noticed that his was the only white face. "I'd never seen anything like it," he said of the tense standoff. "Police helicopters circled overhead. In the bushes, marksmen had guns trained on the crowd, who were out for blood. Desmond took it all in stride. He asked for a glass of Scotch whisky—'Double. No ice.'—sipped it slowly, then stood up and with nothing but the power of his own voice persuaded tens of thousands of angry marchers to disperse."

I heard these behind-the-scenes stories of South African politics in an open-top Land Rover as we navigated the countryside in search of animals. One huge bull elephant fake-charged our vehicle a few times until the guide beat on the fender and stopped him, mere feet away. We watched lions feeding on a fresh kill. We saw bull rhinos, a cluster of giraffes with their babies, a herd of thirty-five elephants, a pod of hippos snorting in a river. In between Ray's stories our zoologically trained guide taught us about animal behavior.

A male hippo, the guide informed us, will not mate unless he first beats up a weaker male hippo. We learned of the tiny capillaries in the nose of the oryx that serve as a cooling mechanism so that its brain doesn't overheat in the desert; of the oxpecker birds that bob unmolested on the backs of rhinos, elephants, and water buffalo, all grateful for the birds' service in removing bugs and ticks; of the small-brained ostriches who lay an egg every other day but often forget where, making the eggs easy to harvest.

In short, we had a delightful and stimulating time, thanks both to our affable companions and to the wild animals. Then we returned to Johannesburg where I would speak at the school's graduation ceremony. "We need to nail down one detail," Ray said on our drive back to the city. "Do you want to give the invitation, or should I?"

I looked at him, puzzled. "I thought this was a graduation service. Give an invitation—you mean an altar call?"

"Yes, you see, many of the graduates will have unbelieving relatives along. We want to give them an opportunity to respond to the message and receive Christ."

I thought for only a second. "You know, Ray, that's kind of a cultural thing. Why don't you do it."

That night after I spoke Ray gave a classic Billy Graham-style altar call and people young and old streamed down the aisles for prayer. To my astonishment the platform I was sitting on started to move. An earthquake? Seeing me startle, the associate pastor next to me whispered that the entire platform was on tracks. "It moves back electronically, like an opera stage, to create more space for those who come forward." Welcome to Rhema Church.

✦ ✦ ✦

Three years later, in 2006, I returned to South Africa, accompanied by British actors from the Saltmine Theatre Company. Again I spoke at Rhema Church, this time as part of a program on the theme of Grace that we were presenting in six cities. On this my second visit instead of touring game parks I went to some of the new museums that had opened to preserve the memory of apartheid days. What might South Africa teach the rest of the world about grace?

South Africans had recently celebrated the tenth anniversary of "the miracle," the changeover of government that abruptly ended apartheid and installed black Africans as the rulers of the country. Everyone had predicted a bloodbath; fourteen thousand people had already died in violence between the time of Nelson Mandela's release from prison in 1990 and his election to the presidency in 1994. Confounding the experts, however, the new regime did not yield to the politics of revenge. Instead, Mandela made peaceful overtures to the white minority and appointed Desmond Tutu to deal with atrocities not through court trials but through an innovative Truth and Reconciliation Commission that would allow the nation to forgive without forgetting.

Bill Clinton tells of a conversation he had with Nelson Mandela. "Didn't you really hate them for what they did?" Clinton asked. Mandela replied, "Oh, yeah, I hated them for a long time. I broke rocks every day in prison, and I stayed alive on hate. They took a lot away from me. They took me away from my wife, and it subsequently destroyed my marriage. They took me away from seeing my children grow up. They abused me mentally and physically. And one day, I realized they could take it all except my mind and my heart. Those things I would have to give to them, and I simply decided not to give them away."

Clinton pressed him. "Well, what about when you were getting out of prison? I got my daughter Chelsea up and we watched you on television as you walked down that dirt road to freedom. Didn't you hate them then?"

Mandela said, "As I felt the anger rising up, I thought to myself, 'They have already had you for twenty-seven years. And if you keep hating them, they'll have you again.' And I said, 'I want to be free.' And so I let it go. I let it go."

With that attitude Mandela set a tone for the entire country. Black leaders urged their followers not to give in to their anger, however merited, but instead to let it go, and to move forward in their newly won freedom. White churches, many of which had supported the oppressive white regime, were taken aback by the new spirit of cooperation. Perhaps they would have a share in the country's future after all.

The Apartheid Museum in Johannesburg attempts to re-create the atmosphere of living under the old system. As our group entered each of us was assigned a racial classification to experience daily life from that perspective. We went in through separate entrances labeled European, Black, Indian, or Coloured (mixed race), and walked through a maze of steel bars on which were mounted actual racial identity cards from the past. Under apartheid, that identity card determined how you were treated. Certain foreign races, such as the Japanese, were designated "honorary whites" and granted the same privileges as normal whites because of their economic importance to the country.

I winced with memory at the segregation laws depicted in the museum, having grown up in Georgia under segregation. Guilt and anger surged up as I moved through the displays documenting racism not so different from my own country's. Blacks and whites had separate schools, restaurants, beaches, swimming pools, restrooms, hospitals. Historical photos showed "Europeans only" signs posted on park benches, escalators, pedestrian bridges, even ambulances.

To further enforce separation, the white government carved out "homelands," much like Indian reservations, into which they began moving blacks, in the process stripping them of South African citizenship. More than three million blacks were forcibly resettled into these homelands or into sprawling new communities outside major cities, including sixty thousand in the township of Soweto (South Western Township). The townships, safely located miles from the cities where blacks held jobs as gardeners and maids, added hours to the workers' daily commute.

Kate, the young white South African who led us through the Apartheid Museum, emerged shaken. For most of her life she had lived under the injustice that required blacks to step off a sidewalk whenever a white person approached—or in some cases banned blacks from the sidewalk altogether. She knew well the reign of indignity and also the violent oppression that kept blacks, who outnumbered whites four to one, "in their place." The museum's video monitors replayed some of the worst massacres. At Sharpeville sixty-nine died at the hands of police and eighteen thousand were arrested in the aftermath; at Soweto the official death total was twenty-three but some suspect that several hundred died.

When we exited the museum, stepping outside into bright sunshine, Kate said bitterly, "In view of what we did and how we treated them, they had the right to take every one of us whites, line us against a wall, and shoot us in the head."

✦ ✦ ✦

But they didn't. Indeed, in the museum cafeteria I saw people of all races mixing together, laughing, sharing meals. At Rhema Church black, white, and Coloured regularly sit next to each other worshiping. Many South Africans have followed Mandela's motto to "let it go," due largely to his extraordinary leadership. In Soweto I visited the tidy home of Mandela, itself now a museum, just down the street from Bishop Tutu's house. A slum made famous by its uprisings boasts the only street in the world that has produced two Nobel Peace Prize winners.

Speaking like an Old Testament prophet, Bishop Tutu gives God the credit for the miracle of reconciliation. "God does have a sense of humor. Who in their right minds could ever have imagined South Africa to be an example of anything but the most awfulness, of how *not* to order a nation's relations and its governance? We South Africans were the unlikeliest lot, and that is precisely why God has chosen us. We cannot really claim much credit ourselves for what we have achieved. We were destined for perdition and were plucked out of total annihilation. We were a hopeless case if there was one."

Grace can live even in such a poisoned environment, and in 2006 I found many signs of its power. Father Michael Lapsley, expelled to a neighboring country for his anti-apartheid activities, one day opened an envelope that exploded in his hands. It was a letter bomb, presumably mailed to him by South African authorities. He lost both hands, but when the government changed he returned to his country and

established an Institute for Healing of Memories. Far from considering his loss a disability, he has used his experience as a platform to
launch a worldwide campaign for victims of violence.

I spoke in St. James Church near Cape Town, the very sanctuary in which four armed blacks broke into a Sunday evening service,
tossed hand grenades covered with six-inch nails, and sprayed the congregation with assault rifles, killing eleven worshipers and wounding
fifty-eight. From some of the survivors I heard that members of the
congregation later met with the perpetrators and publicly forgave them.
St. James Church has since become a beacon of reconciliation. As if
to complete the cycle, as I was signing books in the foyer an elegant
woman came up to me and introduced herself. "You told of Nelson
Mandela inviting his prison warden on the platform at his inauguration. Well, that warden of Pollsmoor Prison was my husband, James
Gregory. He died three years ago. Thank you for mentioning him."

Less dramatic, but just as significant, was a meeting I had with
a man designated to head up the powerful Dutch Reformed Church.
The entire policy of apartheid traces back to a theological doctrine
promoted by that denomination. (In apartheid days a black African
could not legally attend a white church, and in view of the treatment
blacks received from those who brought Christianity to their country,
it's amazing that they have any interest in the faith. Yet today South
Africa has the fourth highest church attendance in the world.)

At our meeting, in the Dutch Reformed stronghold of Stel-
lenbosch, this respected pastor and theologian told me, "I grew up
believing apartheid was biblical for it was, after all, an official church
doctrine and Reformed theologians used the Bible to justify it. I regularly heard it preached from the pulpit. Now my denomination has
formally repented and branded apartheid as heresy. Believe me, that
makes me cautious, very cautious, about making official pronounce-
ments on other issues."

He added, "Now, in large part because of the injustice of apartheid, my denomination has some of the best resources in the country,
with an infrastructure perhaps second only to the government's. We

have large buildings, church kitchens, schools. As an act of penance and also compassion, I would like to lead our denomination toward serving those we have wronged. This country faces immense problems with poverty and AIDS and crime. We can now be a part of the solution."

Grace blooms in South Africa, like the wildflowers that unexpectedly appear in the veld after a summer rain.

✦ ✦ ✦

In 2009 I made my third trip to South Africa. Euphoria over the miracle of the changeover had ebbed, giving way to anxiety over the enormous challenges still facing the country. Whites bemoaned the two thousand white farmers killed in unprovoked attacks and the "reverse discrimination" that had prompted many of their children to emigrate to other countries for better education and jobs. Blacks spoke of relentless poverty and the government's failure to provide housing for millions in the shantytowns. Everyone complained about crime: the odds of being "housebroken" (burglarized), the fear of murder and rape.

One crisis dwarfs others: HIV/AIDS. South Africa has more citizens living with the virus, nearly six million, than any other country, and, until the development of new drugs lowered the rate somewhat, more than a thousand people died from the disease every day. I saw the impact up close at several orphanages—across Africa fifteen million children have lost one or both parents to AIDS. After one such visit my hosts drove me to a nearby cemetery. Several funerals were going on simultaneously, and we could hear the mournful chants and wails from each. Outside the gate a long line of passenger buses stood waiting, such as you would normally see at a sporting event. With the AIDS pandemic, Saturday has become funeral day. One community I visited used to average two funerals per week; now it has seventy-five.

Faced with these multiple challenges, the South African church has stepped in. The government, with its limited resources, welcomes churches into the process of rebuilding society without worrying much about the separation of church and state. As a result the nation has become a laboratory of religious groups who tackle human needs on the front lines.

A hundred thousand non-profit and community organizations, many of them faith-based, are at work, and in the Cape Town area I visited three. Learn to Earn, situated in one of Cape Town's largest slums, teaches young people a range of skills, from cleaning and cooking to online publishing. AIDS affects it too: publishing trainees who once designed wedding invitations now specialize in funeral programs. Another small ministry has had remarkable success rehabilitating gang members in Pollsmoor Prison. The third ministry is perhaps the unlikeliest of all.

John Thomas, a Baptist pastor in the sleepy coastal town of Fish Hoek, heard about the high AIDS infection rate in a nearby shantytown and, investigating further, he was shocked to learn that 70 percent of sixth and seventh graders were sexually active. More, he began to see a direct connection between poverty and AIDS. "A mother may have sex with four or five different men on a regular basis," he told me. "Monday's liaison pays her kids' school fees, Tuesday's pays the utility bills, Wednesday's pays for groceries, and so on. She sees it as survival, not prostitution. If she's infected, and not careful, she may spread the disease to all those partners, who in turn pass it on to others. The kids' stories are even more heartbreaking. I met a thirteen-year-old who sold her virginity to a man in exchange for a meal at McDonald's. I met a fourteen-year-old who said she was having sex as often as she could because that would help her get AIDS so she would die soon. She had no hope of a job or a way out of poverty." Though he must have told these stories many times, Thomas wept in the retelling.

Thomas went on to found a program called Living Hope, which includes a hospice and prevention center as well as outreach programs to AIDS-afflicted homeless and addicts. His church has a budget of $400,000 and a staff of ten; Living Hope has a budget of $1.2 million and a full-time staff of 180. Visitors come from all over the world to see the difference one ordinary church can make. "We didn't really learn about these things in seminary," Thomas says with a laugh. "But I went back and studied all that Jesus had to say about the poor, and I had no choice but to respond."

✦   ✦   ✦

After touring these ministries in Cape Town, I flew north across the country for one more visit to Rhema Church in Johannesburg. Pastor Ray McCauley had made headlines again that week. The presidential candidate Jacob Zuma had spoken at Rhema the previous Sunday, sparking cries of protest from the opposition. And Rhema had released its budget figures, reporting $10 million in income the previous year. When I told my friends in Cape Town where I was headed, they raised their eyebrows in surprise. "How much do you know about Rhema?" one gently asked.

On this visit I stayed with Ray's brother Alan, his opposite in almost every way. Ray is gregarious and outgoing, flamboyant in life-style, always in the spotlight. Alan, a soft-spoken attorney, has chosen a simple life in an intentional community out in the country. He lived with the Jesus People community in Chicago for a time, looks to Jim Wallis of Sojourners as a mentor, and recently hosted Shane Claiborne, founder of a New Monastic community and author of *The Irresistible Revolution: Living as an Ordinary Radical.* Alan and his wife Xana oversee Rhema's ministry to several hundred addicts, unwed mothers, and AIDS orphans.

From the quiet, rather spartan setting in the country, I commuted to the well-kept campus of Rhema Church. First I spoke at a worship service (yes, the platform still moved on tracks). I have little experience with charismatic audiences, but I must admit it's more fun to speak to people who clap, yell "Amen!" and nod enthusiastically throughout.

The following night, our last in South Africa, I spoke to church leaders and students at Rhema's ministry training school. I chose the topic "Growing in Grace" because many of Rhema's leaders, like Ray McCauley himself, first embraced a faith focused on transforming individual lives and now find themselves in a movement to transform society. In some places a church may devote its energies to such internal matters as worship style and building programs. In South Africa increasingly the church is forced to turn outward, to address needs beyond its walls.

Although Rhema once based its appeal on a prosperity-gospel message, Ray told me his vision of the church has changed. "We should be more like a hospital than a hotel," he said. Jesus used the images of a city on a hill, light in darkness, a sprinkling of salt on meat, all of which point to our effect on the world around us. The church as a shaper of culture—could the rainbow congregation at Rhema become an example of that for South Africa?

13   Growing in Grace

South Africa, March 2009

I remember the first time I saw a giraffe in the African bush. It stood serenely next to an acacia tree, its camouflage coat blending with the surroundings. Then this beast taller than a two-story building began to move, loping gracefully through the grass with its small head and endless neck bobbing up and down. I shouted with joy, only to have the safari guide cast a reproving glance my way. Tourists in game preserves should keep their voices down, I was told.

Back at the lodge I read everything I could find about giraffes. They weigh around a ton, I learned, the neck comprising a third of that weight. Surprisingly, they have the same number of neck vertebrae as humans, with oversized joints and anchor muscles to support the stretched length. I studied diagrams of the giraffe's elaborate circulatory system: one-way valves that allow it to bend down for a drink without all the blood rushing to its head; taut skin, like support hose, to keep blood from pooling in the legs; an elongated heart that pumps blood to the extremities at twice the normal pressure. I watched a video of a giraffe giving birth, its baby falling more than six feet to plop on the dust, then within minutes wobbling to its feet to attempt its first steps.

The next day I related arcane facts about the giraffe's lung capacity and thorn-proof tongue to others in our tour group, only to be met with blank stares. They were Africans, you see, and giraffes did not impress. They were hoping to spot a cheetah chasing an antelope, or perhaps happen upon a rare white rhinoceros. Giraffes were for beginners.

As I later reflected on this safari scene, I recognized in it a common pattern: what begins with a burst of excitement often settles into familiarity and ends in disappointment. Falling in love, bringing home a newborn from the hospital, the child's first day of school, the thrill of learning to read—hallmark events in our lives so vivid and flush with promise at the time all too often lose their luster. We flip through photos of that moonstruck young couple now flabby, bored, and middle-aged, or that tiny baby now a troublesome tattooed teenager, and wonder how we ever succumbed to such a surge of emotion.

During my first visit to South Africa, in 2003, people were still talking about "the miracle." Hope abounded. Now, a few years later, political candidates are accusing the government of corruption and incompetence. I hear more talk about crime than about the end of apartheid, more about AIDS than about economic progress.

Those of you training to be pastors and counselors will become well acquainted with this human pattern. The same couple who come enraptured to ask your help with their wedding may return embittered, asking for help in negotiating a divorce. Addicts you bailed out of jail and supported through treatment may slide back down the same path of self-destruction. And new converts whose lives seemed so transformed that they bolstered your own faith will one day announce, "That was just a phase. I'm not into religion anymore."

You at Rhema Church know the initial burst of enthusiasm as people first encounter the good news of the gospel. How can you keep that excitement from fading into familiarity and finally souring as disappointment? More, how can you foster the growth of the kingdom of God so that it heals and transforms the damaged society around you?

✦ ✦ ✦

For the sake of convenience I have labeled three stages of the Christian life: Child, Adult, and Parent. That suggests a progression, of course, yet we have something to learn and retain from each stage. Jesus himself held up children as his models of faith. We dare not stay there, however: the apostle Paul later complained about the Corinthians, "mere infants in Christ," who seemed stuck in the child stage, capable of digesting only spiritual milk and not the solid food they needed.

Each time I come to Africa I experience afresh the rush of excitement that comes with new life, the grasp of the gospel as truly good news. While on this trip I have been reading the history of missions in Africa. A century ago few thought Christianity would take root here, and the great Edinburgh Missionary Conference of 1910 barely made mention of the continent. Not until colonialism fell did the faith take off. Now Africa has more Christians than any other continent, with thirty-two thousand more Africans adding to the church every day. People speak openly and unashamedly about their faith. Christian slogans decorate buses and taxi cabs. Those of us who visit from the West, where Christianity seems more like a corporation than a living movement, need the reminder that the gospel is, at its root, life-transforming good news.

I have a private theory that God is "nicer" to newcomers, reserving the toughest assignments for those more advanced in faith. I interviewed many people while writing a book on prayer, and the most stirring answers to prayer came from new Christians who showed the same childlike faith that impressed Jesus. They took Jesus at his word when he invited disciples to ask whatever they wanted in his name. I sense some of that spirit at Rhema Church, especially as you cheer the many people who respond to Pastor Ray's invitations to follow Christus.

At the same time I must post a warning about two unhealthy

characteristics of the Child stage of the Christian life. The first is *legalism*. It may seem strange to lump together childishness and legalism because we tend to think of legalists as mature, self-disciplined Christians. That is the problem, precisely. Legalism provides a convenient way for some Christians to convey superiority.

On the surface it seems harmless, even comical, this trend toward legalism that surfaces in every religion. Orthodox Jews in Israel have programmed elevators to stop at every floor on the Sabbath because they judge pushing an elevator button as work; for the same reason, some hotels pre-fold toilet paper for their Sabbath guests. The Amish in Pennsylvania ride in buggies rather than automobiles while their neighbors the "black-bumper Mennonites" tolerate cars as long as they are stripped of chrome. What, you may wonder, can be the harm in legalism?

Yet Jesus (see Luke 11 and Matthew 23) and Paul (see the Book of Galatians) both lashed out against it, knowing legalism's tendency to sow dissension and to undermine God's grace. You in South Africa have a perfect example of one danger of legalism—its diversion into petty issues—because the Dutch Reformed Afrikaners were in some ways admirably disciplined people. They banned magazines like *Playboy* and strictly censored unwholesome movies. At the same time they thought nothing of corralling millions of people into homelands. Thirty years ago a South African teenager told me her church would not allow blue jeans in the sanctuary and frowned on chewing gum in the service—the same church that promulgated the racist doctrine of apartheid!

The list of questionable activities changes over time. Many churches have cracked down on smoking even as they grow more tolerant of alcohol—though I hear few sermons on gluttony, perhaps the greatest health danger of all. In our parents' day Hollywood movies, jazz, Halloween, and hairstyles generated heat. In Paul's time Christians fiercely debated such matters as vegetarianism, pagan festival days, meat sacrificed to idols, circumcision, and the worship of angels. Paul did not mince words in his attacks on legalists. In Colossians he rails against those who would judge by how one celebrates a holiday or

Sabbath. He takes on the circumcision crowd in Philippians, calling them "dogs, men who do evil, mutilators of flesh." In 1 Timothy he describes as "hypocritical liars" those who forbid marriage and abstain from certain foods.

Although Paul himself kept a strict code of behavior, he understood the danger of legalism, of substituting rules for a gospel based on grace and forgiveness. Legalism lowers, rather than raises, God's standards. Loving your neighbor as yourself, caring for the poor, bringing about justice, forgiving enemies—none of these reduces to a set of rules. Indeed, any list of rules narrows the breadth of what God wants done in the world. It moves the emphasis away from dispensing God's grace to sinners toward a pointless competition with pseudo-saints. It makes faith petty and irrelevant, not something that urgently matters.

Paul knew firsthand about legalism, having once followed the Pharisaic law in its minutest detail. But he never recovered from the impact of that first great gust of freedom in Christ. Neither should we.

✦ ✦ ✦

I must mention one more unhealthy characteristic of the Child stage of faith, and I do so carefully because I know about your history at Rhema Church. I also know of the progress you have made on this very issue: what is often called the *prosperity gospel* or health-and-wealth theology.

On a trip to Brazil I had a conversation with one of the national church leaders. "No doubt you've heard of the explosive growth of the church in Brazil," he said. "Certainly, it's true. Churches are springing up everywhere. One big reason behind the growth is that preachers promise becoming a Christian will solve all your problems. Need a car or a job? Just pray. Is your child sick? Pray. Naturally, in a poor country like ours that message will attract a crowd. What you don't hear about, though, is what I call the 'back door' of the church in Brazil—the people attracted to that message who discover it doesn't work as they had hoped and who quietly leave."

The New Testament does not contain detailed warnings about the prosperity gospel in the way it does about legalism, for one reason: most of the early Christians weren't prospering. Jesus gave fair warning to his twelve disciples. "I am sending you out like sheep among wolves," he said, and then proceeded to predict floggings, court trials, persecution, and betrayal. Sure enough, ten of the twelve died martyrs' deaths. Paul had to undertake fund-raising campaigns to aid the impoverished Christians in Jerusalem. Given his own biography of shipwreck, prison, beatings, and an unhealed "thorn in the flesh," the concept of a prosperity gospel likely never crossed his mind.

I believe God does want the best for God's people, and that includes health and comfort. We have unconditional promises that one day God will restore this planet to its intended state. Yet the Bible also presents Earth as evil-occupied territory, and Christians get no exemption from the afflictions that plague the planet. My travels to various countries convince me that Christians are as likely as non-Christians to be poor, and in many places they are more subject to oppression. Though I have no statistical proof, I suspect that the same proportion of Christians fall ill as does the rest of the population. I am certain that exactly the same ratio of Christians die as non-Christians: 100 percent.

A church that promises a problem-free life may well fill its auditorium, especially in a time of economic and health challenges. If we over-promise, or misrepresent what the Bible actually says, eventually many of those people will turn away, disappointed and perhaps permanently embittered.

You will often face the delicate task of helping people stuck in the Child stage of spirituality to grow up. No doubt a set of clear rules offers a form of security, and belief in a problem-free life has appeal. Both, like sweet poison, contain grave danger.

✦ ✦ ✦

I am staying at Hands of Compassion, Rhema's ministry to recovering addicts. Even though the ministry has compassion in its very title, the directors have zero tolerance for certain behavior: violence, theft, and possessing drugs or alcohol on the grounds. You cannot use adult-style reasoning with an addict: "Let's consider your problem. What if you drink a pint of alcohol each day rather than a quart—would that help? Ah, I see you're also a kleptomaniac. Could you moderate your behavior so that you steal from your roommates only on weekends?"

The Adult stage of the Christian life does not mean that you abandon all rules and live as you please. To the contrary, when Christians persisted in immoral behavior the apostle Paul reacted like an offended parent scolding a child. To a person stealing he gave the simple rebuke, "Steal no more!" When a man committed incest he urged the Corinthian church to expel him.

The New Testament presents a tricky balance. On the one hand it blasts legalism and its childish insistence on a set of rules. On the other hand it condemns immorality and calls us to holiness. Paul's own life demonstrates how an adult can manage this balance. Even though he fiercely asserted his freedom, he did not flaunt that freedom but used it responsibly. For instance, although Paul had no personal qualms about eating pagans' meat and observing their holidays, he would modify his behavior for the sake of immature Christians who might be offended. "We who are strong ought to bear with the failings of the weak and not to please ourselves," he advised the Romans.

You can almost hear the apostle sigh with relief, however, when he turns from writing cantankerous churches like the one in Corinth to more mature churches like Ephesus and Philippi. No longer need he lecture like a schoolmarm. Rather, he can expound the riches of God's mercy and the depth of Christ's love. Having described these, he can then appeal to higher, adult motives, "to live a life worthy of the calling you have received."

I heard Arun Gandhi, grandson of Mahatma Gandhi, relate an incident from his teenage years that occurred not far from here. As you may know, Arun's father Manilal was a hero in the struggle against apartheid, an activist who spent a total of fourteen years in jail. One day soon after Arun got his driver's license he volunteered to drive his father into Johannesburg, agreeing to meet him at a certain time. Arun went to a double feature movie, and got so engrossed that he was late for the rendezvous. Instead of telling the truth about why he showed up late he invented a story that his father knew was a lie.

As they drove out from the city onto country roads his father asked Arun to pull over. "I am deeply troubled," he said. "What would cause my son to lie to me? How have I failed as a father that my son would not trust me with the truth? I must reflect on this." And so the father got out of the car and proceeded to walk the rest of the way home, with Arun driving behind him to provide light. For *six hours* Arun drove behind his father, his speed never exceeding four miles an hour!

When I heard Arun tell that story, I said, "Man, what a guilt trip your father laid on you." He reacted sharply. "Oh, no! You don't know my father. My father was a great man. More than anything I wanted to please my father, to grow up to be like him. My father was completely sincere when he wondered how he had failed. As for me, I learned a very important lesson. Since that day I have never told another lie." In other words, from then on Arun sought to live as a *worthy* son.

Being an adult does not mean we live irresponsibly. Quite the opposite: it means we live responsibly, fully aware of our freedom yet also aware that we do not live for ourselves alone. We live to please God, who granted us that freedom. Jesus boiled down the essence of pleasing God to two commands: loving God and loving your neighbor as yourself.

The last time I visited Rhema Church I told you about Joanna Flanders-Thomas, a remarkable woman who first worked against apartheid and then turned her attention to a local problem, the most violent prison in South Africa, where Nelson Mandela spent eight years of his confinement. Joanna started visiting prisoners daily, bringing them a simple gospel message of forgiveness and reconciliation. She organized a tiny ministry with the grand name The Centre for Hope and Transformation. The year before her visits began, the prison recorded 279 acts of violence; the next year there were two and the following year eight. Joanna's results attracted the attention of BBC producers, who sent a camera crew from London to film two one-hour documentaries on her work.

I told you how I met Joanna and her husband at a restaurant on the waterfront of Cape Town. "I've seen the BBC documentaries, but I still don't get it," I said. "These guys are monsters—rapists, murderers. And from what I could see you were simply holding Bible studies, playing trust games, having prayer meetings. What really happened to transform Pollsmoor Prison?" Joanna looked up and said, almost without thinking, "Well, of course, Philip, God was already present in the prison. I just had to make him visible."

Joanna's offhand comment became for me a mission statement of how to live as an Adult follower of Jesus. We know God's qualities: justice, righteousness, compassion, mercy, grace, love. For whatever reason, God has chosen to convey those qualities on earth through human beings like us. That can be a daunting task, I assure you, yet I have seen it accomplished through ordinary people here in South Africa.

Let me tell about my next visit with Joanna, right after I left you in 2006. She got me into Pollsmoor Prison—surprisingly difficult, I learned, if you are a foreigner and haven't committed a crime. Along with the actors from England, we put together a worship service for the prisoners. Three hundred men attended and Joanna greeted most of them by name. That one day, at least, they were treated with respect, as human beings and not as numbers. We sang, the actors performed, I spoke, and the prisoners had a time of prayer for all who would be going to court that week. Afterward Joanna invited us to see one of the "Christian cells," a portion of the prison reserved for those who agree to a rigorous program of spiritual training.

We descended dungeonlike concrete corridors below ground. A "Gangsters Only" sign marked some of the cells, the prison's way of isolating gang members from the rest of the population. Men were yelling catcalls at the women in our group, banging their cups on the bars. I could hardly believe the crowded conditions: eight thousand prisoners forced into quarters built for half that number.

When the guard opened the solid steel door to the "Christian cell," I nearly fell over from the stench. Fifty men lived in a space about the size of my living room, sleeping on triple-tier bunks and foam pads on the floor. One toilet served all fifty, hence the smell. Wet laundry hung from the bunks, and the close quarters made it feel like a steam room despite the cool temperature outside.

Some of the prisoners had questions about writing, one of the few activities they could do in the cell. They told us they are locked in the cells all but one hour per day, when they can go to an exercise yard. We answered their questions, the actors did a brief sketch in the crowded room, and then Joanna asked the prisoners if any would like to tell their stories.

Adam spoke first. "I'm in here for life plus thirty-eight years," he said. "I put out a contract to have my wife killed, and the killers squealed on me. I know I did wrong, and through Joanna's restorative justice program I'm trying to reconcile with my in-laws. I'll probably never get out of this place. But you know, I'm actually grateful I'm here, because it was here that I met God, thanks to Joanna and Julian. I want to spend the rest of my life serving God, however I can."

John spoke next: "I'm in the X26 gang. I participated in a gang rape of fourteen-year-old girls. I've got three life sentences, to be served consecutively. Like my brother here, I may never get out either. Like him, I want to commit myself to the Lord and try to redeem the time I have here. I want to live for God."

As they spoke I looked on the walls behind them. Pornography and gang slogans decorated most of the prisons' cells. Here, in neat calligraphy, someone had printed the words to contemporary praise songs. I recognized one by the American singer Andraé Crouch: "Soon and Very Soon," about going to see the King in an eternal place where there will be no more crying and no more dying. It struck me that if you are locked in a concrete cell with forty-nine other men for all but one hour a day for the rest of your life, those words hold a lot of meaning.

Next to that was another praise song and then these words: "Surely the presence of the Lord is in this place." With a start I recalled what Joanna had said three years before: "Well, of course, Philip, God was already present in the prison. I just had to make him visible." Her words had become a kind of prophecy and I was now seeing its fulfillment. Indeed she and Julian did make God visible in Pollsmoor Prison, and now former gang members live and worship together in that most unlikely place. It takes mature adults to accept a ministry call to a place like Pollsmoor, and mature adults to live in a God-pleasing way in such a place.

✦ ✦ ✦

Let me introduce the Parent stage by borrowing an object lesson from Dr. Paul Brand, a mentor of mine whose own life demonstrated the truth he was illustrating. In the middle of a talk in the stately chapel of Wheaton College in Illinois he reached in his pocket and pulled out a cluster of grapes. "Excuse me, I think I need a bit of refreshment," he said, and some in the audience tittered. He plucked a juicy red grape, popped it in his mouth, and chewed it with a smile of satisfaction. Suddenly his face wrinkled into a frown and he loudly spat out the seeds onto the plush carpet, startling the students. After the laughter died down, he went on to make a serious point.

Dr. Brand read a text on the fruit of the Spirit as described by Paul in Galatians 5: love, joy, peace, patience, kindness, goodness, faithfulness, gentleness, and self-control. "These qualities are good for you in every way," he explained. "They are qualities of God, who wants to grow them inside you. Yet as someone who has raised fruit trees, I know that from the fruit's perspective the ultimate goal is reproduction. The fruit is attractive and beautiful so that a bird or perhaps a person will find that grape, or apple, or blackberry, pick it, and do just what I have done: deposit its seed on the ground. If we were meeting outside, rather than in this beautiful chapel, I could come back in ten years or so and find a grape vine growing as a result of my sermon illustration this morning."

I later walked in an orchard with Dr. Brand and heard him explain in more detail. "We think of fruit from our perspective, assuming its appeal is meant for our enjoyment. See this apple? It's colorful, delicious, fragrant. From the viewpoint of the apple, though, our enjoyment is mainly a way to produce more apples. Everything about the fruit is oriented toward reproduction. When it falls to the ground, it makes a slight dent in the soil, and it contains just enough meat to nourish the seeds inside."

The final stage of faith orients us to the world around us. As Paul said to the Galatians, "You were called to be free. But do not use your freedom to indulge the sinful nature; rather, serve one another in love. The entire law is summed up in a single command: 'Love your neighbor as yourself.'"

I've chosen the word Parent for this stage because parenthood forces a person to look beyond his or her needs toward the needs of another. Every young parent marvels at how a tiny creature with no language skills and very limited mobility can turn life upside down. A baby disrupts the family sleep patterns, foils plans and schedules, interrupts careers. You stay up at night cleaning messes and tending a sick child. A few years later you spend hours repeating things you already know well: the alphabet, the multiplication tables, the basics of geography. Yet when children become teenagers, as often as not they act ashamed of you. How many times do you parents hear something like this: "Mom, Dad, I want to thank you for the many selfless sacrifices you've made on my behalf. I'm so grateful."

So why do people become parents? We have an inbuilt desire to perpetuate our genes, say the scientists, just like the animals in the African bush. True, but I believe something more is at work. We also have inbuilt desires to love, to communicate, and even to perpetuate ourselves in another person. Like our creator God, we want to share life in full knowledge of the sacrifices required.

On this trip to South Africa I have made it a point to visit faith-based programs that are spreading seeds of life around your country. I watched tutors in a community center painstakingly teach computer skills to kids who have no electricity in their homes, let alone computers. I visited a Baptist church that runs an AIDS hospice but also a prevention program with seven thousand kids in hopes of keeping them free of the disease. I've seen the staff of Hands of Compassion apply the exquisite blend of toughness and tenderness needed to help addicts break free.

As you know, the rest of the world looks with dismay at Africa with its history of poverty, bad government, corruption, and disease. The relatively peaceful changeover in your government here in South Africa represents one of the few bright spots. With much less fanfare, other signs of hope are burgeoning in this place. I have seen outposts of the kingdom of God during my three visits here. Like the nation itself, the makeup of Rhema Church has changed in the last two decades. I take heart in the fact that you and others in this nation are breaking down the walls of the church and reaching out to the needs around you, that you are looking to transform not just individuals but society itself.

Love is never easy, whether it takes the form of raising children or building houses for the homeless or counseling addicts or adopting AIDS orphans. Jesus did not come and die so that we could live happy and self-indulgent lives to show the rest of the world our self-contentment. No, he came as an example for us to follow in his steps. "I tell you the truth," said Jesus in the original version of Dr. Brand's illustration, "unless a kernel of wheat falls to the ground and dies, it remains only a single seed. But if it dies, it produces many seeds."

Some people are pessimistic about South Africa's future. I am not. I have hope because of the growth in grace I have seen in my three visits to this church, and from the settlements of the kingdom that are sprouting all over this land. The British atheist Matthew Parris wrote in *The Times* of London about Africa's biggest problem, "the crushing passivity of the people's mindset." He concluded, "Missionaries, not aid money, are the solution," and acknowledged "the enormous contribution that Christian evangelism makes...In Africa Christianity changes people's hearts. It brings a spiritual transformation. The rebirth is real. The change is good."

Your great leaders Nelson Mandela and Desmond Tutu would be the first to admit that the change South Africa needs cannot be legislated by government. It will need the concerted effort of all of you who accept Jesus' call to find your lives by giving them away, in the process scattering seeds. That's how the kingdom of God advances: seed by seed.

PART VII

MEMPHIS: AN ALTERNATIVE VISION

MEMPHIS:
AN ALTERNATIVE VISION

14   Out of Ashes

October 2008 was a scary month in the United States, with the nation facing a presidential election and the economy in a state of free fall. Many homeowners found their houses worth far less than their mortgages, and by the end of the year more than two million families would lose their homes to foreclosure. Two of the three large American carmakers teetered toward bankruptcy.

As election day approached, conservative fiscal policies were unraveling. In his final months in office George Bush devised a trillion-dollar rescue plan for the nation's banks and industries. The election of Barack Obama seemed all but certain, and social conservatives wrung their hands in dismay over the implications for such issues as abortion and homosexual rights.

In such a climate of fear this election generated more heat than any in recent memory. I received inflammatory, widely-circulated e-mails about Obama, pointing out that he was a child of Africa: "The dark continent where worship of demonic spirits, bloodshed and violence have been the rule"; a child of Islam, "a religion based upon absolute submission to the god of forces and violence for all infidels"; and "a well documented deceiver/liar who's [sic] tongue is set on fire with the flames of hell."

Earlier in the year I had agreed to speak on November 2 at my church near Denver, Colorado, not realizing I would be speaking just two days before the election. In one month stock values worldwide had shrunk by seven *trillion* dollars, vaporizing retirement plans that had taken years to accumulate. American jobs were disappearing at the rate of half a million a month. Were we headed toward another Great Depression? Fear hung like fog over the congregation, some of whom had recently lost their jobs or their homes, all of whom faced the uncertainty of a truly global crisis.

As I prepared for the weekend three friends came to mind, who together exemplify Christians' varying approaches to politics. Shane Claiborne wears dreadlocks, lives in inner-city Philadelphia, and shortly before the Iraq war put his life on the line by making a Witness for Peace mission to Iraq (the participants camped out by sites the United States might bomb, hoping to deter military action). Tony Campolo has no hair, wears suits, had advised President Bill Clinton, and stirs up controversy wherever he goes. Chuck Colson once worked in the Richard Nixon administration and strongly defends conservative positions while he oversees an outstanding prison ministry.

Campolo and Colson both operate inside the political system, though from opposite directions. Claiborne carves his own path. All three men love their country and follow Jesus, and each can point to a biblical prototype. John the Baptist denounced a ruler's immorality and paid for that prophetic stance with his life. The apostle Paul worked the Roman legal system and testified respectfully before kings and governors. Daniel served in a high position for two different pagan governments, yet committed civil disobedience to continue worshiping his God.

For my text that Sunday I chose Jesus' short parable on "The Wise and Foolish Builders." I could not ignore the economic crisis swirling around us, yet I knew that any sermon touching on politics had the potential to ignite a firestorm. Christians will always disagree on the issues and even on a basic approach to politics; Jesus' parable takes an entirely different tack.

✦ ✦ ✦

The landmark election took place two days later, and I was one of the last people to know the results. That evening I flew to Memphis, Tennessee, to address a group called the Church Health Center. The plane departed at 7:00 PM, just as polling booths closed on the East Coast. When we landed two and a half hours later I had no idea which candidate was winning.

As I deplaned down the steps onto the tarmac I asked the first person I saw, an African-American baggage handler, if he knew how the election was going. "Lookin' good," he said with a broad grin. "Obama has 174 electoral votes in the bag. He got Ohio, Pennsylvania, and Florida, and they ain't even counted California yet!" From a baggage handler who had mastered the intricacies of the electoral college I got a strong clue as to how much this election meant to a people who have been oppressed as well as liberated by democracy. And the next day I got a sobering reminder of the church's mixed record on the issue of race.

My Memphis hosts gave me a choice of touring Elvis Presley's Graceland mansion or the National Civil Rights Museum. Partly because of the historic election I chose the museum, artfully built around the motel where Martin Luther King Jr. was assassinated. For several hours I revisited the scenes I had known as a teenager coming of age in the South. I stood beside the Formica lunch counter salvaged from Greensboro, North Carolina, and watched videos of the black college students who had sat on these vinyl seats as thugs stamped out cigarettes in their hair, squirted mustard and ketchup in their faces, then knocked them off the stools and kicked them while white policemen looked on, laughing. On a nearby screen I saw the eerie scene of black children flying weightless through mist in Birmingham, Alabama, propelled by high-powered fire hoses, as snarling German shepherds lunged toward them.

The museum contained a bus from Montgomery, Alabama, like the one in which Rosa Parks had refused to change seats, its front section demarcated "Whites Only" and the back "Colored." Another room displayed a larger bus charred black, the actual Greyhound burned to a crisp by an Alabama mob intent on chasing away the Freedom Riders, who were trying to integrate transportation. As the bus burned, the mob held its doors shut, hoping to incinerate the young riders inside. With help from highway patrolmen the Freedom Riders escaped, though badly beaten with iron pipes and baseball bats, only to have the local hospital turn them away.

Looking back, it seems incredible to imagine such ferocity directed against people who were seeking the basic ingredients of human dignity: the right to vote, to sit on a bus, to eat in restaurants and sleep in motels, to attend college (two hundred federal troops escorted James Meredith to his first class at the University of Mississippi, and even so scores were injured and two died in the ensuing riots). With shame I recalled cheering with classmates at my all-white high school as Southern sheriffs arrested the "outside agitators" of the civil rights movement.

On the grounds of the museum, the hauntingly prophetic words from King's final "I've Been to the Mountaintop" speech are forged in steel, words that caught in my throat on a sunny day mere hours after Barack Obama got elected: "I may not get there with you but I want you to know that we as a people will get to the Promised Land." The day after he delivered that speech King died in a pool of blood on the very spot where I was standing, on the balcony of the Lorraine Motel.

And what role did the church play in this the central political drama of the 1960s? The civil rights movement had religious roots and was led by ministers like King who challenged social injustice from the outside; in the tradition of biblical prophets they appealed to a higher law than the ones written by legislators. Some white Christians joined the leaders on the front lines in Selma, Alabama, and Jackson, Mississippi, while others worked within the system to overturn unjust laws—but not all did so.

The church I attended while growing up in Atlanta, Georgia, took pride in the purity of its evangelical theology, and yet on this issue most church members came down solidly on the wrong side. Like many white churches in the South, mine stubbornly opposed the civil rights movement. It amazes me that slaves from Africa so readily adopted the religion of their owners and that African-American churches thrive today; surely the whites' gospel must have sounded like bad news at times rather than good.

It took Southern Baptists 150 years to apologize for their support of slavery, and not until November 2008—two weeks after Obama's election—did Bob Jones University admit their error in barring black students before 1971 and banning interracial dating until 2000. "We failed to accurately represent the Lord and to fulfill the commandment to love others as ourselves," said their president Stephen Jones. Those words of apology apply to me and many other evangelicals who opposed the civil rights movement.

I could not help wondering, as I viewed the exhibits at the museum in Memphis, how much of the average Christian's politics gets formed by surrounding culture rather than by the gospel of Jesus. As Stephen Jones further admitted in his apology,

> For almost two centuries American Christianity, including BJU in its early stages, was characterized by the segregationist ethos of American culture. Consequently, for far too long, we allowed institutional policies regarding race to be shaped more directly by that ethos than by the principles and precepts of the Scriptures. We conformed to the culture rather than provide a clear Christian counterpoint to it.

One question lingered as I left the museum: for what will the church be apologizing 150 years from now?

✦   ✦   ✦

My day at the museum left me in a somber mood. To the watching world, God's own reputation rests on the shoulders of the church, and at various times we have soiled that reputation. Critics gleefully blame God for some of the grievous mistakes made by God's followers. Barack Obama ran on a platform of change; shouldn't the church take the lead in change that matters most? Yet in the South I knew, racial injustice began to change not because of a prophetic church but because of forcible intervention by the federal government.

Just as I was despairing over the moral blindness of the church in mirroring rather than shaping culture, a blindness I had shared, I met Dr. Scott Morris in his book-lined office. We had much in common, I learned, for he had grown up in my hometown of Atlanta during the same tumultuous era. A baseball fan, he had mementos of the old Atlanta Crackers minor league team displayed on a shelf. We laughed together about the legend of the longest home run ever: a baseball hit out of the Crackers' ballpark landed in a railroad coal car and traveled all the way to Nashville and back, a 518-mile home run.

As a teenager Morris had attended an exclusive academy on the north side of Atlanta and had few contacts with black people other than the servants who cleaned rooms and mowed lawns. Like me, he was deeply affected by the civil rights movement led by Martin Luther King Jr. After earning a degree from Yale Divinity School, he moved back to Atlanta and studied at Emory University's medical school with a specialty in family practice.

Now an ordained minister and board-certified physician, Morris traveled across the country in search of models for ministering to the whole person, body and soul. He kept running into government restrictions that confounded his goal of bringing holistic health care to poor people who couldn't afford it. Morris decided to pursue an alternative vision by starting his own non-profit program, which he called the Church Health Center. He chose Memphis because of its large population of working poor, the very people on whose behalf King had been protesting when he was killed.

In 1987 Morris opened a clinic offering medical services to people who had jobs but no insurance. He saw twelve patients that first day, and then word began to spread. Now the Church Health Center has a sprawling medical complex that serves fifty thousand patients, all working uninsured or homeless, who pay a sliding scale based on their income, averaging twenty dollars per visit. Morris proudly led me through the facilities housing the various clinics and programs.

Memphis, a medical hub with renowned hospitals, sits in the heart of the Bible Belt South and Morris happily exploits all available resources. From the hospitals he gets donated medical supplies and the volunteer services of some six hundred professionals. He uses the churches as a way to reach people who have more faith in their church than in other institutions. Teams of lay advisors, primarily women from small African-American churches, learn the basics of diet, high blood pressure, diabetes, and prenatal care, then dispense that knowledge to their congregations.

Throughout, Morris has held a position as associate pastor of St. John's United Methodist Church, a downtown church located across the street from the clinic. By creatively combining his faith and medical practice, Dr. Scott Morris has managed to affect an entire community, an example of grassroots justice led by the church. The clinic, largest of its type in the country, accepts no government funding and relies mainly on charitable donations.

The more I learned about the Church Health Center, the more pleased I felt to be addressing its staff and supporters. Out of the ashes in Memphis, site of one of the darkest days of the civil rights movement, a group of Christians is quietly demonstrating another way to address a major problem, in this case by pursuing an alternative vision outside the political system. The church in Memphis is taking the lead in solving locally the health care crisis that so bedevils the federal government.

✦   ✦   ✦

I spoke to supporters of the Church Health Center on the night after the election. As I met people beforehand I sensed much the same spirit of anxiety that I had encountered at my own church in Colorado. Memphis, like the rest of the nation, was still adjusting to the news of a sweeping change in Washington, especially in light of the worst economic crisis in almost a century. What would the future hold?

I heard a radio interview with Dr. Joseph Lowery, a civil rights leader who would give one of the prayers at Obama's inauguration. "How does it feel to see the dreams of the movement realized at last?" he was asked. "Well, I remember when baseball teams chose their first black managers," he replied mischievously. "Seems to me they always got to manage teams that were at the bottom of the pile, nearly bankrupt. That's how I feel about this election—proud we have a black president, of course, but, man, look at the mess he's gonna face."

I turned once again to Jesus' parable that raises sights from the immediate to the eternal.

15   Upon This Rock

Memphis, November 2008

The world watched anxiously yesterday as votes got tallied, resulting in a seismic shift in the U.S. political landscape as well as our first African-American president. If I can judge by appearance, some of you seem happy and full of hope. Others are sad, even frightened about new directions the country may take. We are experiencing an economic upheaval not seen since the Great Depression of the 1930s, and at this point no one knows what the future will look like.

As I thought about what words might be appropriate, one of Jesus' shortest parables came to mind. It goes like this:

> Therefore everyone who hears these words of mine and puts them into practice is like a wise man who built his house on the rock. The rain came down, the streams rose, and the winds blew and beat against that house; yet it did not fall, because it had its foundation on the rock. But everyone who hears these words of mine and does not put them into practice is like a foolish man who built his house on sand. The rain came down, the streams rose, and the winds blew and beat against that house, and it fell with a great crash. *(Matthew 7:24–27)*

I heard a colorful application of this parable from Millard Fuller, the Alabama lawyer who founded Habitat for Humanity. In 1992 a powerful hurricane named Andrew hit near Miami, Florida, destroying or causing major damage to 117,000 houses. Strangely enough, in one devastated area twenty-seven homes stood intact amid a veritable junkyard of lumber, bathroom fixtures, and other housing debris—all twenty-seven, as it happened, built by Habitat for Humanity. "How can you explain this phenomenon?" a CNN reporter asked Fuller, who had flown in to assess the damage. "Your Habitat houses are the only ones still standing."

Millard Fuller never saw a microphone he didn't like. "In the first place," he said in his best Alabama drawl, "as a Christian organization, we build our houses on the Rock!" The reporter stared at him blankly, as if he were speaking in tongues. "Secondly, we put *love* in the mortar joints. And finally, you've got to understand that amateurs build our houses. Professional carpenters put one nail every seventeen inches. Our volunteers may hammer in a nail every inch—not even Hurricane Andrew can blow down a house built like that!"

My question this evening is simple: what are we building our houses on?

Money? In a month in which global stock markets have lost seven trillion dollars in value, money appears a foundation more sand than bedrock. Historians will look at 2008 as a financial tsunami leaving in its wake millions of foreclosed homes, bankruptcies, and lost jobs. Some of us have trusted the financial system with our futures, stashing away enough for retirement, only to see that money vanish like beach sand washed away in a storm. Almost overnight our houses are worth less than we paid for them and twenty or thirty years of savings have disappeared.

If it offers any consolation, let me assure you that conditions could be even worse. This past week Zimbabwe's inflation rate hit a record 231 million percent. If you had saved one million Zimbabwean dollars by Monday, on Tuesday it was worth a few dollars. I received a report from someone in Zimbabwe who described standing in a panicky line for two days to withdraw cash from an ATM machine. When he finally reached the machine he withdrew the maximum allowed, two thousand Zimbabwe dollars, by then worth a mere thousandth of a cent.

Others build houses not on money but on politics. All year we have been hearing Republicans and Democrats present their competing visions for our future. My city of Denver hosted the 2008 Democratic National Convention that nominated Barack Obama and we got a steady dose of grandiose promises. I watched up close as delegates with their funny hats and noisemakers waved flags, released balloons, and loudly cheered each speaker. They seemed truly to believe the politicians' effusive promises to restore U.S. prestige, fix the economy without raising taxes, stop global warming, and provide free health care for all. No pain, all gain.

Forgive me, but having lived through a number of these political conventions by both parties, I don't believe politics will usher in the paradise we long for. Four years from now another party's convention will be pointing out all the failings of this new administration. Regardless, as Martin Luther King Jr. reminded us, politics has its limits. Laws may prevent white people from lynching blacks, but no law can require people of different races to forgive or love one another. Politics can legislate justice but not compassion.

Reading through the Gospels I am struck by Jesus' apparent indifference to politics. Shane Claiborne wrote a book with the catchy title *Jesus for President*, yet I can't imagine Jesus running for any political office. He viewed power politics with mild contempt, calling Herod "that fox" and setting Pontius Pilate in his place with the rebuke, "You would have no power over me if it were not given to you from above."

Jesus placed his trust neither in money ("What good is it for a man to gain the whole world, yet forfeit his soul?") nor in politics ("My kingdom is not of this world"). Rather, the parable of building a house on the rock makes clear where we his followers should place our faith. The wise person is the one "who hears these words of mine and puts them into practice." Since Matthew places this parable as the capstone of the Sermon on the Mount, "these words of mine" refer directly back to that seminal sermon by Jesus.

✦ ✦ ✦

The words of the Sermon on the Mount have become so familiar that they lose their revolutionary sting. From a very different election than the one we just completed, an election that took place halfway around the world in 2004, I gain a striking image of how Jesus' words must have sounded to his original audience.

Have you heard of the Orange Revolution that occurred in the Ukraine in 2004? Let me tell you a little-known story about the unlikely heroes who helped spark that revolution. Like other parts of the Soviet Union, Ukraine moved toward democracy as the Soviet empire collapsed, though in Ukraine democracy advanced at a glacial pace. If you think our elections are dirty, consider that when the Ukrainian reformer Victor Yushchenko dared to challenge the entrenched party, he nearly died from a mysterious case of dioxin poisoning. Against all advice Yushchenko, his body weakened and his face permanently disfigured by the poison, remained in the race. On election day the exit polls showed him with a comfortable 10 percent lead; nevertheless, through outright fraud the government managed to reverse those results.

That evening the state-run television station reported, "Ladies and gentlemen, we announce that the challenger Victor Yushchenko has been decisively defeated." However, government authorities had not taken into account one feature of Ukrainian television, the translation it provides for the hearing-impaired. On the small screen inset in the lower right-hand corner of the television screen a brave woman raised by deaf-mute parents gave a different message in sign language. "I am addressing all the deaf citizens of Ukraine. Don't believe what they [authorities] say. They are lying and I am ashamed to translate these lies. Yushchenko is our President!" No one in the studio understood her radical sign-language message.

Deaf people, inspired by their translator Natalya Dmitruk, led the Orange Revolution. They text-messaged their friends on mobile phones about the fraudulent elections, and soon other journalists took courage from Dmitruk's act of defiance and likewise refused to broadcast the party line. Over the next few weeks as many as a million people wearing orange flooded the capital city of Kiev to demand new elections. The government finally buckled under the pressure, consenting to new elections, and this time Yushchenko emerged as the undisputed winner.

When I heard the story behind the Orange Revolution, the image of a small screen of truth in the corner of the big screen became for me an ideal picture of the church. You see, we in the church do not control the big screen. (When we do, we usually mess it up.) Go to any magazine rack or turn on the television and you will see a consistent message. What matters is how beautiful you are, how much money or power you have. Magazine covers feature shapely supermodels and handsome hunks, even though very few people look like that. You parents know what a devastating impact the relentless big-screen message can have on an unattractive teenager.

Similarly, though the world includes many poor people, they rarely make the magazine covers or the news shows. Instead we focus on the super-rich, names like Bill Gates or Oprah Winfrey. One telling fact symbolizes our celebrity culture: the basketball player Kevin Garnett, who admittedly excels at putting a round ball through a round hoop, will earn more money this year than the entire United States Senate. What kind of society values one person's athletic prowess more than the contributions of its top one hundred legislators?

Our society is hardly unique. Throughout history nations have always glorified winners, not losers. Then, like the sign language translator in the lower-right-hand corner of the screen, along comes a person named Jesus who says in effect, *Don't believe the big screen— they're lying. It's the poor who are blessed, not the rich. Mourners are blessed too, as well as those who hunger and thirst, and the persecuted. Those who go through life thinking they're on top will end up on the bottom. And those who go through life feeling they're at the very bottom will end up on top. After all, what does it profit a person to gain the whole world and lose his soul?*

Putting into practice "these words of mine," said Jesus, will assure a rock-solid foundation for your life. We live out our days in a twisted society that barrages us with the message that worth depends on appearance or income or access to power. Jesus calls us to see the world through God's eyes, to realize that God may care as much about what is happening in Darfur or Haiti right now as on Wall Street, that God may have as much interest in the rundown neighborhood of Memphis 38138 as in Beverly Hills 90210. The prescription for health, for an individual or society, requires attending to the contrarian message of the small screen.

As I travel internationally I see that the kingdom of God, a house built on the rock, can flourish in the most improbable places, often among people who have little access to money or political power. In China I learned of a pastor who went to prison for five years. When he heard his wife was going blind he signed a paper renouncing his faith in order to be with her. He soon felt so guilty, however, that he reported his false confession to the authorities, who promptly put him in prison for an additional thirty years. "Do you pray for a change in government?" I asked the Chinese Christians. "No," they replied, "we assume there will always be persecution. We pray for the strength to bear it." In Eastern Europe I interviewed a young man from Moldova who told me of the days of persecution when he held clandestine prayer meetings in a smelly outhouse, the one place neighbors did not suspect. He said, "Now that we are free, though, the church has lost its passion. Some of us are voting for the Communist Party to return to power, in order to help purify the church."

I hear stories like these and then return to the United States where the news seems to revolve around gun-toting rappers and confused celebrities like Britney Spears and Paris Hilton. I challenge you to watch a television network like MTV four hours straight and then reflect on the fact that we are spreading this big-screen message across the world. The United States, arguably the most blessed nation in history, must confront the sad fact that privilege does not solve everything. We have a stable political system and we have, at least for now, more money than any other nation on earth. And yet with 5 percent of the world's population we house 25 percent of the world's prisoners, more than China and Russia combined. And we consume half of all the world's prescription drugs.

The message of the big screen—Consume! Indulge! Enjoy!— has patently failed. Apart from the damage it does our planet, consider the damage we do to ourselves. Every one of the gravest health concerns in the United States stems from overindulgence: smoking (emphysema, lung cancer); obesity (diabetes, heart problems); stress (heart disease, hypertension); alcohol (fetal damage, violent crime, automobile accidents); drug abuse; sexually transmitted diseases. We smoke too much, eat too much, drink too much, work too much, and sleep around with too many people.

We are quite literally destroying ourselves. In light of that fact, shouldn't we give some thought to the message of the small screen?

✦   ✦   ✦

Let me get specific, with a matter of immediate concern to us all. The economic downturn is affecting everyone in this room, some of us dramatically. How exactly can we put Jesus' words into practice at such a moment? What does "trusting in the rock" look like? I faced that question earlier this week when the religious editor of *Time* magazine called. "I understand you recently wrote a book on prayer," he said. "Tell me, how should a person pray during an economic crisis like this?" In the course of the conversation we came up with a three-stage approach to prayer.

The first stage is simple, an instinctive cry for "Help!" For someone who faces a job cut or health crisis, or watches retirement savings wither away, prayer offers a way to voice fear and anxiety. I've learned to resist the tendency to edit my prayers so that they'll sound sophisticated and mature. I believe God wants us to present ourselves exactly as we are, no matter how childlike we may feel. A God aware of every sparrow that falls surely knows the impact of scary financial times on frail human beings. "Do not worry about tomorrow," said Jesus. The birds still eat, the flowers still bloom. Tomorrow will worry about itself; meanwhile trust in your heavenly Father.

According to the Bible, prayer provides the best possible place to take our fear. "Cast all your anxiety on him because he cares for you," wrote the apostle Peter. As a template for prayers in crisis times, I look at Jesus' night of prayer in Gethsemane. He too felt fear and anxiety: he threw himself on the ground three times, sweat falling from his body like drops of blood, and felt "overwhelmed with sorrow to the point of death." In the midst of that anguish, however, his prayer changed from "Take this cup from me" to "not my will but yours be done." And the trial scenes that follow show Jesus as the calmest character present, even as his disciples succumb to the pressure. Jesus' season of prayer relieved him of anxiety, reaffirmed his trust in a loving Father, and emboldened him to face the ordeal awaiting him.

If I pray with an intent to listen as well as talk, I can enter into a second stage, that of meditation and reflection. OK, my life savings have virtually disappeared. What can I learn from this seeming catastrophe? Last week, as global stock markets tanked, Jesus' parable in the form of the Sunday School song kept running through my mind:

> *The foolish man built his house upon the sand*
> *And the rain came tumbling down . . .*
> *Oh, the rain came down*
> *And the floods came up . . .*
> *And the foolish man's house went splat!*

A crisis helps to unearth the foundation on which I construct my life. If I place my primary trust in financial security, or in the government's ability to solve my problems, I will surely watch the basement flood and the walls crumble. How deeply did the loss of my retirement plan—or the election-day loss of my favorite local politician—affect me? The force of my emotional response gives a strong clue as to the grip the world has on me.

Indeed, the financial crisis has given our entire country a chance to reflect on its moral foundation. As analysts began picking through the ruins of the financial collapse they dusted off old-fashioned words: greed, moderation, integrity, thrift, and trust. When executives pocket huge bonuses at the expense of employees and shareholders, when banks package and resell speculative loans with small likelihood of payback, when borrowers walk away from good-faith contracts, the system breaks apart. A functioning economy holds together by a thin web of trust. If you doubt that, visit a country where you have to pay bribes to get action and must count your change after every purchase.

Two centuries ago John Wesley warned Methodists about the dangers of success and its effect on religious faith:

> I fear, wherever riches have increased, the essence of religion has decreased in the same proportion. Therefore I do not see how it is possible, in the nature of things, for any revival of religion to continue long. For religion must necessarily produce both industry and frugality, and these cannot but produce riches. But as riches increase, so will pride, anger, and love of the world in all its branches.

Conversely, financial setbacks may drive us away from the temptations of the "big screen," back to dependence on God and community. We start paying attention to actual human needs instead of falling for the illusions of a celebrity culture. As a kind of proof, the areas of the world where Christianity is thriving—sub-Saharan Africa, Latin America, rural China, the Philippines—are marked by poverty, not wealth.

The third and perhaps most difficult stage of prayer in crisis times was prompted by the letter from my friend in Zimbabwe. I need God's help in taking my eyes off my own problems in order to look with compassion on the truly desperate.

Jesus taught us to pray, "Your will be done on earth as it is in heaven," and we know that heaven will include no homeless, destitute, and starving people. As the stock market dove to uncharted depths, I couldn't help thinking of mission hospitals, homeless shelters, foreign aid agencies, and other non-profits that depend heavily on the largesse of generous donors.

In the days of a collapsing Roman empire, Christians stood out because they stayed behind to care for plague victims rather than join the flight from afflicted villages, and because platoons of wet nurses would gather up the babies abandoned along the roadside by Romans in their most cruel form of birth control. What a testimony it would be if in the midst of a financial crisis modern Christians resolved to *increase* their giving to build shelters for the homeless, combat AIDS in Africa, provide health care for the poor of Memphis and other cities, and announce kingdom values to a decadent culture.

Such a response defies all logic and common sense—unless we take seriously the moral of Jesus' simple tale about building houses on a sure foundation, unless we believe the message of the small screen.

✦   ✦   ✦

A time of deep crisis presents an opening for Christians to convey our contrarian message by exposing the lies and shallowness of the big screen. You may remember that for brief a time after September 11, 2001, all sporting events, comedy shows, and commercials disappeared from television. This huge industry that entertains us and tempts us to indulge in material things had to confront its own irrelevance in the face of a national tragedy. People spontaneously turned to the church for comfort and for answers. Those next few weeks church attendance went up by 25 percent, until the industries cranked up again and reclaimed our attention.

Even more important, a time of crisis offers the church the opportunity to present an alternative vision. Borrowing an image from the kitchen, Jesus likened his kingdom to salt, a preservative so effective that a mere sprinkling can forestall decay in a slab of meat. Jesus never encouraged his followers to take on the commendable task of cleaning up the Roman Empire. Neither he nor the apostle Paul even mentioned such practices as lethal gladiator games or Roman orgies or the abandonment of infants. Rather, both exhorted followers to demonstrate a different way of living, one contrary to the culture around them. Visit Rome today and you can see still standing the Colosseum where Christians were once fed to lions and wild beasts—an amphitheater eventually purged of its games and topped with a cross. Against all odds, that tiny alternative society prevailed.

We in twentieth-century America need not obsessively wring our hands over what offends us in the broader culture. Instead, like the orange-clad resisters gathered in the square of Kiev, we can refuse to believe the lies broadcast on the big screen. We can insist that a person's worth is not determined by his appearance or her income, or by ethnic background or even citizenship status, but rather is a sacred, inviolable gift of God. And that compassion and justice—our care for "the least of these," in Jesus' phrase—are not arbitrary values agreed on by politicians and sociologists but holy commands from the One who created us.

On my trips overseas I have seen inspiring examples of a church that does just that. A woman in the Philippines began inviting street children into her home and now provides food and shelter for more than three dozen. A couple in Guatemala City set up schools and housing for the eleven thousand people who support themselves by combing through Central America's largest garbage dump. Volunteers in Africa bring pots of soup and trays of bread to prisoners each day, the only prison food available in those cash-strapped countries.

I must add that I also take heart from what I've seen today here in Memphis. Dr. Scott Morris, with a divinity degree from Yale and a medical degree from Emory, could have had his pick of jobs with perks and lavish rewards. Instead he listened to the message of the small screen and with no reliance on the government developed a program that cares for the health needs of "the least of these" in Memphis.

Today Dr. Morris led me through your facilities. Like a happy father he showed me his pride and joy, the Hope and Healing Center. There I saw wealthy clients using the state-of-the-art fitness center, their membership fees subsidizing the programs for the poor. Attorneys and businesswomen were working out on exercise machines right next to clients referred here by doctors to work on their diabetes. Age, class, and race mix freely in that center, something unheard of in the Memphis of my youth.

Most of you in this room have a stake in this alternative society, whether you volunteer as lay advisers, stuff envelopes, treat patients, or write donation checks. Together, you have created something virtually without precedent, and visitors from other cities and other countries travel to Memphis to marvel and to learn. Memphis has Graceland, a monument to our celebrity culture; the Civil Rights Museum, a monument to a shameful chapter in our region's history; and the Church Health Center, a living monument to the alternative vision of the gospel. God bless all of you who have contributed.

✦   ✦   ✦

Yesterday we had an election, one in which the winner based his appeal on the word *change*. Without doubt we need change. Yet I believe that no matter who gets elected, for a healthy society to work we need help that politics alone cannot supply. As the contemporary German philosopher Jürgen Habermas expressed it, "Democracy requires of its citizens qualities that it cannot provide." Politicians may conjure an exalted vision of a prosperous, healthy, and free society, but no government can supply the qualities of honesty, compassion, and personal responsibility that must undergird it.

We need a new vision in which we see ourselves not as owners but as stewards of a planet, not as masters of one another but as servants of a God of love and also justice. We need to blot out the seductive message of the big screen and start paying attention to that small screen in the lower right hand corner. We need to build our house on the rock: to hear the words of Jesus and put them into practice. If we do so, no matter what happens with the stock market, no matter what happens with Iran or North Korea or China or any other threat, when the rains come down and the streams rise up, our house will stand.

PART VIII

MIDDLE EAST: CHURCH AT RISK

MIDDLE EAST:

CHURCH AT RISK

16

Sand Dunes and Skyscrapers

Early in 2009 I went on a speaking tour of the Middle East, primarily in the United Arab Emirates and other small countries along the Arabian (or Persian) Gulf. Only two generations ago the locals were Bedouins traipsing across the desert in camel caravans, and you can still see wild camels ranging over the wavy sand dunes—as you now zoom past on six-lane superhighways. The world has come to the Middle East, setting in motion a breathtaking pace of change fueled by the modern thirst for oil.

The West needs oil from the Gulf as badly as that region needs the markets and expertise of Western nations, and in a classic case of codependency the two regions have a love/hate relationship. Every day a new skirmish breaks out in "the clash of civilizations" between Islam and the Christian West, with the Middle East positioned directly in the line of fire. A recent book, *The Geopolitics of Emotion*, describes the clash as a collision of humiliation and fear: the humiliations of recent history inflame Islamic extremism which in turn heightens the West's anxiety and fear of the other.

I flew to the Middle East with some apprehension, aware that the media portray that part of the world mostly in stereotypes. To my surprise I saw relatively few local Arabs in the Gulf countries. As few as 10 to 20 percent of the population are native citizens; the vast majority migrate from places like India and the Philippines in search of work, joining the well-heeled business managers and tourists from Europe and the United States. This unusual mixture offers up some strange sights. A woman in a head-to-toe black robe speaks through her veil on an iPhone while stepping around bikini-clad sunbathers on a beach. An Arab man in a headdress walks slowly and proudly through a modern shopping mall trailed by his four wives, who follow as if in formation a few steps behind.

The religion of Islam dominates life in the region and imams, not politicians, set the rules. An arrow in every hotel room points the way to Mecca and the newspaper prints the precise five times a day (they vary with the moon) in which the call to prayer will resound from omnipresent mosques. Freedom has limits: once while checking a fact on the British Museum Web site I got the message, "Blocked under the Prohibited Content Categories of U.A.E.'s Internet Access Management Policy."

For a newcomer, the treatment of women in traditional Islamic countries stands out glaringly. Some husbands never allow their wives to set foot outside their homes. Restaurants in the Gulf partition off separate sections with screens so that women can lift or remove their veils in order to eat without exposing their faces in mixed company. Even mosques have separate entrances and prayer halls for women. The most conservative Muslim country, Saudi Arabia, still does not allow women to drive, and a woman caught in a taxi unaccompanied by her husband risks a beating by club-wielding morals police. Adultery may result in a death sentence.

At the same time, the massive infusion of oil money has transformed Gulf countries into some of the most modern places on the planet. The skyline of Dubai looks like Las Vegas on steroids, as if the rulers had given a group of leading architects a billion dollars each and turned them loose to design skyscrapers. One amazing sail-shaped hotel—it has featured ads of Roger Federer playing tennis on its grass-carpeted helipad and Tiger Woods hitting golf balls into the ocean—rents its luxury rooms for $5,000 per night, complete with a private butler. Down the road the world's tallest building, the Burj Khalifa, soars almost twice the height of the Empire State Building. Locals joke about the national bird of the Emirates, the construction crane, and honor crane operator Babu Sassi, who during construction slept in a cab half a mile high atop the Burj Khalifa because it would take him too long to come to the ground each night.

Every country in the region has its own flavor. "The drivers in Kuwait are crazy," we heard, and indeed Kuwaiti pedestrians take their lives in their hands to cross a street. Qatar hosts the progressive television network Al Jazeera, ubiquitous in Arab homes. Bahrain serves up movie theaters, alcohol, and prostitutes to the repressed folks from Saudi Arabia, who create traffic jams on a long causeway to spend weekends there. (Muslim men get around the rule against prostitution by "weekend marriages," agreeing to marriage with a prostitute for a designated time period, then divorcing her when time expires.)

On the surface, however, the Gulf countries increasingly resemble the West, with American food franchises in abundance: KFC, Cinnabon, Chili's, Applebee's, Pizza Hut, Ben & Jerry's. A clash of civilizations is occurring not only between Arab countries and the West, but also within the Arab countries themselves as tradition and modernity collide.

✦ ✦ ✦

Mention the word *Christian* to the average Muslim in the Gulf, and David Beckham or Madonna may come to mind. For most Arabs I talked to, Christian means non-Muslim, and they draw their images of Christianity from Western movies and television. In general, Muslims are surprised and pleased to meet Christians who take their faith seriously. Even in a brief visit I found that, despite a history of religious conflicts, conversations about faith occur far more readily in Arab lands than in the West.

Muslims respect Jesus as an esteemed prophet, though not on the same level as Mohammed. Arabs still name children *Isa*, their word for Jesus, and a revered local sheikh in Bahrain had that name, leading to such unexpected monuments as "King Jesus Bridge" and "King Jesus Library." When Mel Gibson's movie *Passion of the Christ* was released, Qatar broke ranks with other Arab countries by allowing it in and soon the movie was showing a hundred times a day in the region to customers jetting in from other Arab countries, their curiosity no doubt piqued by rumors of its anti-Semitism. Arab speakers could understand much of the Aramaic used in the film, and for many it served as their first introduction to the facts of Jesus' life.

Jesus may command respect, but conversion to Christianity is illegal and can be dangerous. I asked our hosts how many native Arab Christians lived in the Gulf region and they went through the list country by country, counting by hand, in some places able to name every known convert. Nonetheless, the early missionaries from just over a century ago left a good impression, and strict Muslim countries still permit some Christian-based agencies. For example, in Bahrain the medical clinic founded by American missionary Samuel Zwemer in 1903 holds the address "Post Office Box 1."

Another Christian cared for the mother of a ruling sheikh, and the grateful sheikh granted her the right to establish a network of schools across his territory.

I participated in a worship service at Oasis Hospital, founded by missionaries in 1960, where doctors and midwives have safely delivered seventeen members of the royal family, some despite medical complications. Thanks largely to the hospital, infant mortality rates in the area plummeted from 50 percent to less than 1 percent. When the hospital staff applied for a $2 million expansion project, the ruler of Abu Dhabi rejected their proposal. "Too modest," he said, and countered with a $100 million expansion plan funded by the government. "If it weren't for Oasis Hospital, I wouldn't be here," he explained. Health workers from thirty-four countries now live in the oasis community and work in the hospital. Each patient gets a DVD of the *Jesus* film and a gift copy of the Arabic Gospel of Luke bound in elegant maroon leather with gold lettering.

Most Arab governments allow churches to serve the international community as long as they don't try to proselytize locals. Usually the rulers assign one plot of land for Christian worship, and all denominations must share the facilities—sometimes along with Mormons, Sikhs, and other varieties of religion. In Kuwait we held our meeting in a building shared by seventy-five separate congregations: on weekends five different Filipino congregations and seven Indian-language services alternate with Korean Presbyterians, Anglicans, Southern Baptists, Pentecostals, and several score other groups. I could not miss the irony of the elusive goal of Christian unity finally being achieved—at the insistence of an Islamic government. One national group, however, is conspicuously missing from every congregation: Kuwaitis.

Barred from working with locals, churches in the area often shift their focus to the expatriate workers. A typical Gulf country may host several hundred thousand Filipinos, Nepalis, Pakistanis, and Indians to do the labor, while the Bahrainis or Qataris or Kuwaitis collect a monthly government subsidy and enjoy the spoils. The foreigners often find conditions appalling, and a construction worker from Nepal explained the system to me. A simple villager mortgages everything of value to pay a huge fee of $3,000 to an agent who promises him a job in a luxurious labor camp in the Gulf. He leaves his family and emigrates, only to find surroundings very different from what he expected. He sleeps in an ovenlike dorm room with a dozen other men, shares a single toilet, and works long hours for the equivalent of $100 to $200 per month, barely enough to cover rent, food, and the interest payment on his debt. If he complains or causes any trouble whatsoever, the host country will revoke his work permit and deport him back to Nepal.

The churches visit foreign workers in their camps and distribute phone cards, music, and food from their countries of origin, along with perhaps a soccer ball and native-language Bibles. One church operates a shelter home for Filipino maids, who are notoriously abused by their Arab employers. Another visits expatriates held in prison, who have virtually no legal rights. In such ways Christians who live in the

Gulf region find opportunity for ministry, though strictly among people who hail from elsewhere. As a result of this outreach, the groups I spoke to presented an exotic mix of nationalities and backgrounds.

I gained great respect for the Christian workers who choose this part of the world. In one Gulf country we stayed in a guest house frequented by Christians who use it as a retreat place. I ate breakfast with a lovely young couple visiting from a Muslim country marked by violence from the Taliban. In that culture, men and women simply do not appear in public together, so they can't go out on a "date," and would have nowhere to go regardless. They hear cries from a wife being beaten next door, and can do nothing except tend to her wounds the next day since wife beating is no crime there. Meanwhile they try to teach basic education to a country with a minority of literates, very few of whom are women. That kind of daily challenge, both social and spiritual, tests the most stalwart faith.

✦ ✦ ✦

The most intriguing event of our Gulf visit brought together local converts or "Muslim Background Believers," as they call themselves. We met a small group rather secretively in a conference room. Most spoke in passable English, though an interpreter jumped in if needed.

One middle-aged woman told of reading the Koran and finding the prophet Jesus mysteriously attractive, even more so than Mohammed. The more she read about Jesus, the more she wanted to know him. She would hear strange words at night in her sleep: Messiah, child of God, lamb, sheep. *Why is God talking about sheep?* she wondered. Then she heard the words, "The truth will set you free," unaware that they came from the Christian Bible. One night she experienced a vision of Jesus beckoning her to follow. After several more such visions over the course of fourteen years, she declared herself openly as one of Jesus' followers. She spoke darkly of persecution from her family, but choked up before she could elaborate. She did not need to, as her face bore telltale scars.

A man with abundant brown hair and bushy eyebrows traveled

a different path to faith. "As a Muslim, I had many questions," he said. "Who is right, Shiite, Sunni, Sufi? A friend invited me to study with him, and every day for two hours we studied the Koran together. Then I found out he was a Christian, a convert from Islam. I was furious. I wanted to kill him. Instead, I simply stopped seeing him or talking to him. Later I went on a pilgrimage to Saudi Arabia, and while there I asked questions of imams on the bus as we toured the religious sites. They had no interest in questions and scolded me for my lack of faith. The more I read the Koran, I began to see flaws. I wanted a true relationship with God, not just a repetition of prayers somebody wrote. I prayed the Lord's Prayer, my first true prayer and the beginning of my relationship with God."

After a series of dreams the man's wife also came to faith. She had spent a full year angry at her husband for converting. In one dream she saw herself coming to her husband to get a key; in another she saw herself on a beach, her skin peeling from sunburn, "like a snake changing its skin." Finally, Jesus himself appeared to her in a dream and she decided to follow the same risky path as her husband.

Their daughter, a beautiful young university graduate, avoided talking to her parents about religion for many months, afraid of the social consequences of changing religion. Gradually, though, she saw positive changes in her parents and began to view Islam as authoritarian and negative. *Why is it illegal to convert to Christianity in Islamic countries?* she wondered. *Why does the imam rebuke me when I talk to him about my questions and doubts?* Eventually she too became a Christian.

Most of the converts told of dreams and visions, and all described rejection by family members horrified by their "apostasy" from Islam. Christians who convert from Islam differ in their approach. Some make a clean break with the past and publicly identify with the new faith. Others pursue an in-between state as "Muslim followers of Jesus," in which they continue to attend mosque, worship on Friday, read the Koran, and pray Muslim prayers, all the while studying the Bible and following Jesus. The Muslim Background Believers I interviewed clearly prefer the clean break, though they admit that huge barriers confront any Muslim who considers converting to Christianity.

I later learned that one Muslim convert had left the country after being beaten by his family, imprisoned, and stripped of his children. And several former Muslims brought up the case of Fatima al-Mutayri, a twenty-six-year-old poet killed by her brother in Saudi Arabia a few months before my visit. After he discovered some of her meditations about Christian faith on the Internet, he cut out her tongue and burned her to death.

✦ ✦ ✦

Visiting the Middle East today, where local Christians must meet secretively and run the risk of arrest, it is easy to forget that Jesus himself lived here, the birthplace of Christian faith. As recently as 1948, at the time of modern Israel's birth, 40 percent of Palestinians in the Middle East were Christians, proudly tracing their lineage back to the earliest days of the apostles. Now only 2 percent identify themselves as Christian, the rest having fled the region. More recently, the war in Iraq disrupted one of the few stable Christian communities in Arab lands, chasing out half the country's 1.4 million Christians.

Nowadays no part of the world has more resistance to Christian faith and influence. I got a taste of that resistance in one of the Gulf countries we visited where locals had rented a downtown hall and widely promoted the evening meeting. First, authorities demanded $5,000 for the use of audio equipment. Then, the day before the meeting, a fax came canceling permission to use the hall "because of the nature of the meeting." The local committee scrambled to find an alternate venue and to notify hundreds of people of the new location. Some weeks later, the government revoked the visas of many key Christians in the country.

After our tour of Gulf countries we stopped off in Cairo, Egypt, where the underlying tensions of the Middle East broke into the open. One of the members of the church I was visiting, a Wheaton College graduate, was kidnapped by secret police and underwent harsh interrogation until his case got the attention of Amnesty International and the *New York Times*. And exactly one week after I dined with friends at a famous Cairo teahouse, a bomb exploded there, killing one tourist and injuring many others.

Yet in Cairo I also visited a unique community of faith. Unlike the Gulf countries, Egypt has a historic population of Christians, some 10 percent of the population, who trace their origins back to the apostle Mark. They have legal rights, but face many roadblocks in their activities, as well as a ban on proselytism. On Sunday we went to a place called Mokkattam on the outskirts of Cairo.

A sprawling slum of thirty thousand people has grown up around the profession of garbage picking. Cairo lacks an organized garbage industry, and so individuals roam the streets and collect garbage in plastic bags which they transport to this slum, where residents spread the garbage on rooftops and sort out recyclable plastic, textiles, glass, and metal. A cloud of stench hangs over the slum, especially in summer months. Because they feed the organic garbage to pigs, which are disdained by Muslims, this community has an unusually high Christian population.*

Led by a priest in the Coptic Orthodox church, the community built houses, schools, a sports field, and a clinic at the foot of a mountain in an abandoned quarry. Around thirty years ago one of the slum dwellers stumbled across a large cave, and over time Coptic Christians moved one hundred forty thousand tons of rock out of the cave to form a three-thousand-seat auditorium. They worked mostly at

---

* Shortly after our visit the entire community was shaken by a side effect of the HINI flu outbreak (incorrectly termed "swine flu"). Egypt's Muslim-dominated parliament made a rash decision to slaughter all 350,000 pigs in Egypt, even though there were no confirmed cases of the flu in the country. Since Muslims do not eat pork and shun pigs, this decision only affected the minority Christian community. Garbage pickers no longer had the use of pigs in sorting out organic matter from recyclable garbage, and as a result rotting garbage piled up in the streets of Cairo, attracting rats and spreading disease. Many of the poorer families who sorted garbage, consumed pork, and sold pigs for income found their livelihoods destroyed.

night during Muslim fast periods, when the guards who might harass them went home to eat.

The church outgrew that facility and now meets in a thirteen-thousand-seat amphitheater likewise hewn out of rock, the largest church in the Middle East by far. A Polish sculptor has carved biblical scenes in the sandstone cliffs all around. The charity World Vision contributed to the project (before getting evicted from Egypt) and the grounds are lushly planted, an oasis of beauty in a desert of poverty. When we visited, on a weekday, hundreds of people were milling about the grounds, enjoying the shade, looking at the sculptures, lining up to talk to the priests. Just over the edge of a cliff we could see thousands of rooftops covered in garbage, with scavenger birds circling overhead.

On my last stop in the Middle East I went to Jordan. From Mt. Nebo I looked down on Israel from the very spot where, according to tradition, Moses gazed on the Promised Land many years before. I saw the site of Jesus' baptism at the very beginning of his ministry. That day at the Jordan River a seed took root that has never stopped growing, despite many setbacks and much opposition. In far-flung places around the world, as well as in its original soil, the faith of Jesus' followers continues to spread. Like a plant among rocks, it sprouts in the least likely places—an underground church in Afghanistan, a house church in the Arabian Gulf, a garbage pit in Cairo.

✦   ✦   ✦

Looking back on the tour, in some ways it seemed strange that the Christian faith meets such resistance in the very area which gave it birth. In other ways, perhaps our meetings resembled the scene some two millennia ago when the new movement faced hostility from both Jewish and Roman authorities. Each time before speaking I thought of the contrast between Christians in my own country, who live in freedom and comfort, and those who live under what must feel like a state of siege. I remembered the Muslim Background Believers I had interviewed earlier, and the cloud of fear they live under. Churches in the U.S. debate such matters as a new Web site and whether to pave the parking lot; in some parts of the Middle East they look for safe houses to meet in and worry about informants.

Human rights organizations claim that more Christians were martyred in the twentieth century than in all the rest of history combined. Today in places like Pakistan, India, Yemen, and Indonesia, as well as some of the Gulf countries, Christians risk arrest and torture simply for what they believe. I felt a sense of shyness, even shame, to be speaking to people who live in such a climate.

In addition to the larger gatherings in Middle Eastern cities, in each place I also met with a group of pastors and local Christian leaders, sharing a meal and listening to their stories before I spoke. They represented many denominations and came from such places as India, South Africa, the Philippines, South Korea, and Egypt, as well as the U.K. and the U.S.

In Bahrain we met in a backyard and thirty people joined us from Saudi Arabia, all expatriates. Most of them live on compounds built by the oil companies, and all had chilling stories about life in this the most conservative Muslim country. Our hosts asked the caterers to step inside as I talked, for fear of being reported to the Saudi authorities. What words of encouragement could I bring to Christians who feel so beleaguered and discouraged? How could I remind them of God's goodness even in circumstances like these?

17 Stream in the Desert

Bahrain, January 2009

If someone had stood here in Julius Caesar's day and predicted the decline of the mighty Roman Empire and the triumph of an upstart religion founded by a Galilean peasant, he would have been judged a lunatic. As would anyone who stood in the Middle East five centuries later and predicted the downfall of Christianity, by then dominant in places like Iraq, Syria, and Turkey. Yet here we are in the twenty-first century meeting rather furtively in a backyard in an Islamic state, hoping that none of the hired help are eavesdropping. As a visitor I cannot help wondering why this part of the world, the birthplace and once the center of the Christian faith, became the region most resistant to it.

I get one possible clue from the French sociologist Jacques Ellul who, looking around him at the modern world, noted a paradoxical trend: as the Christian faith permeates society, it tends to produce values that contradict the gospel. I sometimes test his theory while traveling by asking foreigners, "When I say the words *United States,* what first comes to mind?" Invariably, I get one of three responses: wealth, power, or decadence.

- *Wealth*. Representing only 5 percent of the world's population, the United States generates almost a fourth of the world's economic output and still dominates global finance.

- *Military power.* The United States, as the media regularly remind us, is "the world's only superpower." The U.S. military budget exceeds that of the next twenty-three nations combined, including China, Russia, Iran, and North Korea.
- *Decadence.* Most people in other countries get their notion of the United States from Hollywood movies, which seem to them obsessed with sex and crime.

Rightly or wrongly, these qualities come to mind when people think of the United States, at least in my unscientific survey. Each contradicts the teachings and example of Jesus, whose life was marked by poverty, self-sacrifice, and purity. No wonder followers of Islam puzzle over Christianity, a robust faith that somehow produces the opposite of its ideals in society at large.

American soldiers stationed here know the pattern: while fighting in two Gulf wars they had to get by without alcohol and *Playboy* in deference to the strict Islamic code in the staging nations. One Muslim mentioned to me the *Baywatch* syndrome, alluding to the titillating television program that some years ago replaced *Dallas* as the most popular U.S. television export overseas. "We are attracted to what we most fear," he said. "Imagine what decadent American culture represents to a young Muslim who, outside of his family, has never seen a woman's knee, or even her face."

For our part, Americans react with confusion and dismay as mobs of screaming Muslims call for "death to the Great Satan," and burn our leaders in effigy. Most Americans do not know what to make of these scenes. The label "Great Satan" especially rankles, for we think of the United States as a Christian nation, far more devout than, say, most European countries. At least we still go to church. How can anyone consider us diabolical?

All of you understand the difference between a committed Christian who accepts Jesus as a model for living and a "cultural Christian" who happens to live in a nation with a Christian heritage. Most of your Muslim neighbors do not. (Similarly, many Americans paint the Middle East with a broad brush, judging all Muslims as radicals and terrorists.) One reason for their confusion, I believe, relates to the total-society approach to religion typical of Islam and the laissez-faire approach more common in Christian societies.

Several years ago a Muslim man said to me, "I have read the entire Koran and can find no guidance in it on how Muslims should live as a *minority* in a society. I have read the entire New Testament and can find no guidance in it on how Christians should live as a *majority*." He put his finger on a central difference between the two faiths. Muslim societies tend to unify religion, culture, law, and politics. Whereas U.S. courts debate the legality of nonsectarian prayers at football games and public monuments to the Ten Commandments, here even the airlines broadcast the call to prayer five times a day. And in countries with a mix of religions, like Nigeria, as the Muslim population increases they seek to impose the religious Sharia law on all citizens.

The top-down approach has a certain ruthless efficiency. At one point Islam conquered three-fourths of all Christian territory, including the Middle East, North Africa, and much of Europe. Of course, we Christians have had our own experiments with moral coercion—Spain's Inquisition, Calvin's Geneva, Cromwell's England, New England's Puritans—which we look back upon with some regret. Over time, though, the Christian West moved toward a separation of church and state and a respect for religious freedom.

Much of the misgiving that Muslims feel for the West stems from our strong emphasis on freedom, always a risky enterprise. I've heard some of you say you would rather rear your children in a closely guarded Islamic society than in the United States, where freedom so often leads to decadence. An Egyptian Christian told me he cannot check into a hotel room with a woman until they show evidence that she is his wife—a policy he appreciates, as does his wife. We could also learn from the Islamic emphasis on family. Middle Eastern émigrés to the West are shocked to find us shuttling preschoolers off to day care and elderly parents to nursing homes.

Although there may be advantages to living in this part of the world, all of you face the daily challenge of practicing your Christian faith as a small minority in a culture that may sometimes seem hostile. How can you stay true to your beliefs and present a different picture of Christianity to your Muslim neighbors? Fortunately, you have a good model to follow: the original Christians who came from this region.

Recently I have been reading a historical study by Rodney Stark, *The Rise of Christianity*. A sociologist of religion, Stark investigated the success of the early Christian movement which, starting from a few thousand followers, grew to encompass half the population of the Roman Empire in three centuries. In the midst of a hostile environment, the Christians simply acted on their beliefs. Going against the majority culture, they treated slaves as human beings, often liberating them, and elevated women to positions of leadership. When an epidemic hit their towns, they stayed behind to nurse the sick. They refused to participate in such common practices as abortion and infanticide. They responded to persecution as martyrs, not as terrorists. And when Roman social networks disintegrated, the church stepped in. Even one of their pagan critics had to acknowledge that early Christians loved their neighbors "as if they were our own family."

In the long run, the compassionate work that many of you are doing among the laborers from other countries may have more impact on Middle Eastern society than all the billions of dollars being poured into oil exploration and construction projects. I have seen the long-term results of a few early missionaries who sacrificially brought education and medical care to neglected groups here. People instinctively know the difference between something done with a profit motive and something done with a love motive.

Some in the United States judge our nation's success by such measures as gross national product, military might, and global dominance. The kingdom of God measures such things as care for the downtrodden and love for enemies. In the final reckoning described in Matthew 25, God will judge nations by how they treat the poor, the sick, the hungry, the alien, and the prisoner. How differently would the world view my country if it associated the U.S. with the "Jesus syndrome" rather than with weapons, wealth, and the "*Baywatch* syndrome"?

✦ ✦ ✦

I once attended a weekend retreat sponsored by the late psychiatrist M. Scott Peck, author of *The Road Less Traveled*, that brought together ten Jews, ten Christians, and ten Muslims. Peck had the idea that in order to solve human problems we should first work to create a spirit of community, and only then try to resolve differences on issues— precisely the opposite of the normal approach in diplomacy. I regret to say that the weekend mainly accentuated conflict between the Jews and Muslims as the Christians sat silent on the sidelines.

One of the attendees was Dr. Hanan Ashrawi, a prominent Palestinian legislator, activist, and scholar. She introduced herself by saying, "I am quadruply marginalized. I am a feminist woman in a male-dominated society. I am a Christian from a predominantly Muslim society. I am a Palestinian, a people without a country. And here in the United States I am part of a racial and cultural minority."

Shortly after that retreat I came across the writings of René Girard, a French philosopher and anthropologist whose brilliant career culminated in a position at Stanford University. Girard became fascinated with the fact that in modern times a "marginalized" person assumes a moral authority. In our group, for example, Dr. Ashrawi's introduction gained her respect. Girard noted that a cavalcade of liberation movements—abolition of slavery, women's suffrage, the civil rights movement, animal rights, gay rights, women's rights, minority rights, human rights—had gathered speed in the twentieth century.

The trend mystified Girard because he found nothing comparable in his readings of ancient literature. Victors, not the marginalized, wrote history, and the myths from Babylon, Greece, and elsewhere celebrated strong heroes, not pitiable victims. In his further research, Girard traced the phenomenon back to the historical figure of Jesus. It struck Girard that Jesus' story cuts against the grain of every heroic story from its time. Indeed, Jesus chose poverty and disgrace, spent his infancy as a refugee, lived in a minority race under a harsh regime, and died as a prisoner. From the very beginning Jesus took the side of the underdog: the poor, the oppressed, the sick, the "marginalized." His crucifixion, Girard concluded, introduced a new plot to history: the victim becomes a hero by being a victim. To the consternation of his secular colleagues, Girard converted to Christianity.

When Jesus died as an innocent victim, it introduced what one of Girard's disciples has called "the most sweeping historical revolution in the world, namely, the emergence of an empathy for victims." Today the victim occupies the moral high ground everywhere in the Western world: consider how the media portray the plight of AIDS orphans in Africa or Tibetan refugees or uprooted Palestinians. Girard contends that Jesus' life and death brought forth a new stream in history, one that undermines injustice. It may take centuries for that stream to erode a hard bank of oppression, as it did with slavery, but the stream of liberation flows on.

Sometimes Jesus' own followers join the stream, and sometimes they stand on the bank and watch. Yet over time the gospel works its liberating effect. (You can see the contrast clearly in societies that have experienced little Christian influence.) Women, minorities, the disabled, human rights activists—all these draw their moral force from the power of the gospel unleashed at the cross, when God took the side of the victim. In a great irony, the "politically correct" movement defending these rights often positions itself as an enemy of Christianity, when in fact the gospel has contributed the very underpinnings that make possible such a movement. And those who condemn the church for its episodes of violence, slavery, sexism, and racism do so by gospel principles. The gospel continues to leaven a culture even when the church takes the wrong side on an issue.

I have seen the stream flowing here in the Middle East as many of you reach out to help victims of injustice. Some countries in this region have a pecking order based on gender, race, and religion as rigid in its own way as the caste system in India. By your own examples you are showing your neighbors another way to treat women, aliens, servants, and other races. In the process you are also showing a new Christian face to a region that tends to judge us by stereotypes.

You may feel like a beleaguered minority here, with good reason. Yet again and again in human history a minority of Christians who simply express the spirit of Jesus can have a potent subversive influence. It has happened in this part of the world before, and it can happen anew.

✦ ✦ ✦

Faith, like history, runs in cycles. I learned a key insight from Gordon Cosby, the founding pastor of Church of the Saviour in Washington, D.C., who noted a pattern as he studied the history of religious orders. First, an idealist attracts people with a strong sense of devotion. The devotees then form a community, which requires discipline—hence the strict rules of founders like Benedict and Ignatius. Disciplined groups tend to prosper, and ultimately that very success undermines the group's commitment and leads to self-indulgence. The movement begins to fall apart. Then someone comes along to revive the spirit of idealism and the cycle starts over again.

Cosby termed this pattern the "monastic cycle," and the movements led by such idealists as Ignatius of Loyola, Francis of Assisi, and Benedict of Nursia demonstrate the sequence. Early Benedictines worked hard to clear forests and cultivate land, investing their earnings in drainage, livestock, and seed. A few centuries later they were hiring people to do the work while they sat back to enjoy the fruits of their labors, such as Benedictine brandy. At times half the order's revenue went to maintain the abbots' luxurious lifestyles. Every so often a reformer would arise, remind the order of the original Rule of Benedict, and start a revival, only to see the same downward spiral eventually repeat itself.

Perhaps we should call this trend the human cycle rather than the monastic cycle. Beginning with Adam and Eve's brief sojourn in paradise, human beings have shown a remarkable inability to handle prosperity and success. In Old Testament days, whenever the economy boomed and peace prevailed the Israelites attended less and less to spiritual matters and looked instead to military power and alliances for their security. In the prophets' telling phrase, they forgot God. We turn to God out of need and forget God when things go well.

I worry about the prospects for my own country in light of this cycle. Several years ago I spent a most revealing, if not to say bizarre, day in Orlando, Florida. My publisher was producing a video series on one of my books and did not have the budget to send a film crew to a variety of settings so instead they went to Orlando, which has a fake version of every setting. Early in the morning they rented the Universal Studios lot and filmed a scene at a fake subway stop on a fake street of New York in front of the fake New York Public Library. That same day we filmed another scene at the Holy Land Experience, a theme park reconstruction of ancient Jerusalem; I descended the steps of a fake temple and stood in front of a fake cross and tomb as I talked. ("Don't miss the crucifixion at twelve and three today," the public-address system announced at one point.) In between we filmed a segment at the Ripley's Believe It or Not! Museum.

We made one more stop, at a high-tech animation school renowned for training future designers of video games and animation. Students pay tuition fees rivaling those charged by Harvard and Princeton in order to study at this school. I watched as bright young minds worked their magic on-screen to produce video games along the lines of *Grand Theft Auto* and *Sims*, the virtual-reality games that now generate more income than all sporting events and all Hollywood movies. I have nothing against video games, would likely have been attracted to them if they had existed thirty years ago (I did, after all, play *Galaxy Quest* and *Pac-Man* back then). On the other hand, I could not help wondering about a society that steers its best and brightest toward producing ever new versions of artificial reality—the same young minds that could be working in laboratories to find a cure for real-life problems such as AIDS and malaria.

While I was waiting for the film crew to set up, I watched tourists file through Universal Studios and Ripley's Museum and the Holy Land Experience. Mostly I saw overweight Americans in shorts, sloppy T-shirts, and flip-flops wandering from exhibit to exhibit, gazing at the fake displays. No doubt a lack of sleep and glut of coffee contributed to my gloomy attitude, yet I could not help thinking back to the monastic cycle. This is how a free, prosperous, blessed society spends its energy and its resources?

The Middle East, it seems to me, is following headlong down the same path. The desert kingdom of Dubai has an indoor ski hill to rival some of the slopes I ski in Colorado. Desalination plants pump water to golf course fairways that flourish incongruously in the sand. Your shopping malls recreate scenes from Venice, the Taj Mahal, and the Great Wall of China. Prosperity abounds here, even as the workers who construct such marvels live in squalor.

Oddly enough, that very disparity gives me hope, for it was in exactly such a setting that the kingdom of God first took root. Although laws may prohibit you from sharing your faith with the locals, you can devote your energies to those workers who help create but do not share in the wealth. Local Arabs may draw their image of Christians from Western movies and television shows, yet they also turn to mission hospitals and clinics for their medical needs. Some of the strictest Islamic governments turn a blind eye to you who visit prisoners, because they have seen your compassionate care for the internationals locked inside. Like the early Christians who faced a hostile Rome, you are called simply to act out what you believe. Some seeds may fall on dry ground, but others will bear fruit.

Every generation of Christians puzzles over how to sustain the revolutionary character of the gospel. Can our faith indeed transform a society from the bottom up? You in this place have an opportunity to demonstrate just that.

✦ ✦ ✦

I close with a true story from Afghanistan that took place in the early 1970s, before the Russian occupation or the Taliban regime or the NATO intervention. At the time the government allowed a small Christian church to service internationals who worked there, though no Afghans could attend. (A sterner government later revoked permission and destroyed the church, bulldozing a large hole in the ground because they had heard rumors of an "underground church.")

A friend of mine named Len organized a musical team of young people to tour countries in the Middle East. With some trepidation he also accepted an invitation to extend the trip to Afghanistan for a concert in downtown Kabul. Len made the teenagers write out exactly what they would say, subject to his approval. "This is a strict Muslim government," he warned them. "If you say the wrong thing, you could end up in prison and at the same time jeopardize every Christian who lives in this country. Memorize these words, and don't dare stray from them when you perform." The teenagers listened wide-eyed as he described the ominous consequence of a slight misstep.

In a warm-up the team gave an abbreviated program at a UN-sponsored school and then a restaurant, singing folk tunes and songs about God's love. The night of the official concert in Kabul, almost a thousand Afghans filled the hall and spilled outside the open doors to listen. All went well until one teenager on the team put down his guitar and started improvising: "I'd like to tell you about my best friend, a man named Jesus, and the difference he has made in my life." From the side of the stage, Len motioned wildly for him to stop, drawing his finger across his neck. Ignoring him, the teenager proceeded to give a detailed account of how God had transformed his life.

"I was practically beside myself," Len told me. "I knew the consequences, and I sat with my head in my hands waiting for the sword to drop. Instead, the most amazing thing happened. The Minister of Cultural Affairs for Afghanistan stood and walked to the stage to respond.

"'We have seen many American young people come through this country,' he said. 'Most of them come for drugs, and most look like hippies. We have not seen nor heard from young people like you. God's love is a message my country needs. How thrilled I am to hear you! You are a prototype for the youth of Afghanistan to follow in the future. I would like to invite you to expand your tour so that you visit every college and faculty and also give this same message on Kabul Radio. I will make it happen.'"

Len was dumbfounded. That night he gathered the musical group together. "Did you hear what the man said? We're changing our tickets, of course, to lengthen our visit. And he wants you to give this same message—you'd better not change a word!"

Over the next few days the musical team held other performances. After each event Afghan young people crowded around with questions. *Tell me more about this Jesus—we know of him through the Koran. You speak of a personal relationship with God, can you describe it? How does your faith change you?* Some asked to pray with the teenagers. Nothing like it had ever happened in Afghanistan.

On the last day, after a triumphant tour, the teenagers met Dr. J. Christy Wilson, a revered figure in Afghanistan. Born of missionary parents in Iran, he earned a degree from Princeton University and a PhD in Oriental Studies from the University of Edinburgh, Scotland. He then spent twenty-two years in Afghanistan, serving as principal of a government high school and teaching English to the Crown Prince and Afghan diplomats. He also led the Community Christian Church and founded the School for the Blind in Kabul.

Wilson drove the teenagers to an unusual tourist site, the only cemetery in Afghanistan where "infidels" could be buried. He walked to the first, ancient gravestone, pitted with age. "This man worked here thirty years, and translated the Bible into the Afghan language," he said. "Not a single convert. And in this grave next to him lies the man who replaced him, along with his children who died here. He toiled for twenty-five years, and baptized the first Afghan Christian." As they strolled among the gravestones, he recounted the stories of early missionaries and their fates.

At the end of the row he stopped, turned, and looked the teenagers straight in the eye. "For thirty years, one man moved rocks. That's all he did, move rocks. Then came his replacement, who did nothing but dig furrows. There came another who planted seeds, and another who watered. And now you kids—*you kids*—are bringing in the harvest."

"It was one of the great moments of my life," Len recalls. "I watched their faces as it suddenly dawned on these exuberant American teenagers that the amazing spiritual awakening they had witnessed was but the last step in a long line of faithful service stretching back over many decades. I'll never forget that scene."

Those of you who work and pray in this hostile part of the world may sometimes feel as if you do nothing but move rocks, or dig furrows. Maybe so. God alone controls the harvest. We have no idea what the future will hold for the Middle East. Most of the Westerners who come here represent something other than Jesus. Some bring in military equipment. Some come to exploit the resources and invest their dollars. But you have a different calling: to make known the spirit of Jesus and to join the stream of liberation that broke free two thousand years ago. That image, of course, comes not just from René Girard but from the prophet Amos who said, "Let justice roll on like a river, righteousness like a never-failing stream!" May that stream gather momentum in this place.

PART IX

CHICAGO: A PLACE FOR MISFITS

CHICAGO:
A PLACE FOR MISFITS

18   The Comedy and the Tragedy

As I scanned the newspaper an advertisement for "Comedy Addiction Tour" caught my eye, the headline itself an oxymoron. Professional comedians would appear together in Denver to do stand-up routines on their respective addictions. I glanced at the date, one week after I was scheduled for minor abdominal surgery, and set the page aside for a later decision.

The afternoon of the performance snow began to fall, clogging streets and making driving treacherous. Having spent the day downtown, my wife and I debated heading back to our home in the foothills. Just in case some tickets remained, though, I drove past the performing arts theater to check. Yes, seats were available. With some misgivings ("Remember your surgery," Janet said, "you're not supposed to laugh.") I parked the car and we made our way inside.

Unlike the typical audience for a play or concert, this one drew from every social group. Ragged street people sat next to sharply dressed business types; teenagers mingled with senior citizens; straights with gays. More than a thousand people showed up that snowy evening, and they all seemed to know each other—by first name only. It dawned on me that for most of the audience this event represented a citywide reunion of 12-step groups. Rather insensitively, the theater had not closed the lobby's cash bar, though it seemed to be attracting little business.

Janet and I found seats toward the back of the hall and started reading the quotes projected on the stage curtain. Mark Twain: "Giving up smoking is easy. I've done it hundreds of times." Tallulah Bankhead: "Marijuana is not addictive. I ought to know, I've been using it for years." Robin Williams: "Cocaine is God's way of saying you're making too much money."

The lead performer, a regular on Broadway and on television comedy networks, came onstage about fifteen minutes late and tried to start his routine. The microphone crackled, buzzed, then quit altogether. The comedian shrugged and disappeared behind the curtain. I turned to Janet: "I thought these things only happened in church. Maybe we should have just gone home."

More time passed as stagehands got the sound system working. And then a series of comedians took turns telling their stories. They walked to the microphone, with no props or PowerPoint displays to back them up, and talked in ten- to twenty-minute segments. Poignant, funny, sad, happy, gutsy, profane, sacred—the stories kept us on the edge of our seats and caused tears to flow in the midst of deep laughter. It was Sunday evening and I found myself wishing the church service I had attended that morning had just a fraction of the *reality* I was hearing.

A woman in the group told of growing up as the daughter of a Holocaust survivor. Her father had scores of electric shock treatments for his subsequent mental condition and she spent many hours sitting in hospital lobbies waiting to take him home. "I had dozens of different sex partners between ages fifteen and nineteen," she said. "It was a perfect storm: the chaos at home, my poor self-image, and older men's interest in my body. You know those 1,000-piece jigsaw puzzles? I felt like I was trying to fit together the pieces of my life into some sort of design that made sense, only the pieces didn't seem to match and, besides, I had no photo on the box to go by."

Following her, a middle-aged man talked about his addictions. "I also attended those sex addiction groups—well, sort of. Most of the time I sat in my car out in the parking lot hoping some of the chicks would relapse. I wasted a good decade of my life looking for more: more sex, more alcohol, more drugs. To get anywhere south or west from South Carolina I had to drive around the entire state of Georgia, which had a drunk-driving arrest warrant out for me. I went through binges, arrests, a divorce, you name it, before learning the hard lesson that more is never enough. Now I live by the 'First thought wrong' principle. Almost every first thought I have is wrong. What a babe! *No, man, you're married.* I need a drink. *Don't do it. You know where that leads.* That jerk just cut me off! *Maybe he's as messed up as I am.* Years of therapy and hundreds of support-group meetings with people just like you have given me new voices to listen to. I can't silence the first thoughts but I can correct them. Along the way I've learned some second thoughts."

The most poignant moment came after a hilarious young man had given colorful accounts of his drunken adventures. Just as he had the audience where he wanted them he paused and changed tone. "So then I woke up one night and found myself sprawled on the median strip of a highway, thrown out of my car, which was lying wrecked and upside-down beside me. I had no memories of the evening or the drinking or the crash, but I knew I had to get out of there before the cops came. I walked home, almost two miles, and my mother answered the doorbell. She looked at the blood and bruises, she smelled the alcohol on my breath, and still she smothered me in her arms. That was the last drink I ever took. And, ladies and gentlemen, I want to introduce you to my mom. She hasn't seen me perform until this evening. She flew in from Portland and she's seated on the second row." We applauded her wildly and he tried a couple of times to continue his routine, but could not, so he blew his nose and hurried off the stage.

✦ ✦ ✦

Growing up I believed a person could commit no greater sin than drinking alcohol. I knew some Christians who smoked cigarettes—they lit up on the steps of Methodist and Presbyterian churches on Sunday mornings—but none who drank. My rambunctious brother decided to try wine (in a McDonald's cup, with ice) as a Bible college student, and then felt so guilty that he confessed to the dean. While pondering the appropriate punishment the college authorities discovered that their sixty-six-page rule book did not mention alcohol. The sin was so obvious and heinous that, as with murder or sex with animals, no one had thought of specifying a rule against it.

The fundamentalism of my childhood paid scant attention to institutional sins like racism and injustice and ignored the private sins of pride and legalism that Jesus railed against. Alcohol, though, surely greased the road to hell. Such sentiments had a long history for, long before the issues of abortion and homosexual rights captured headlines, the "Noble Experiment" of Prohibition galvanized conservative Christians into politics. Two amendments to the U.S. Constitution center on alcohol: the Eighteenth Amendment prohibited its sale and fourteen years later the Twenty-first Amendment reversed the ban.

To my shock I later learned that some denominations saw no problem with alcohol and even served real wine, not grape juice, for Holy Communion. I also learned the Bible mentions wine some 231 times, often positively. During the Middle Ages, with Europe's polluted water supplies, people drank a lot of beer, and some historians report that the Protestants' 11:00 AM Sunday worship time traces back to that practice: Martin Luther, who liked to sleep in after Saturday night beer benders, scheduled Sunday services for the last hour still considered morning.

Nowadays doctors extol the health benefits of a moderate intake of wine and sociologists note that teetotal families are more likely to produce alcoholics than families who drink in moderation. That word *moderation* is the key. In colonial times Americans drank three times as much alcohol per capita as they do today. In some areas of nineteenth-century London one in five buildings housed a pub, and children as young as five would seek out their fathers on a mission to bring them home before they drank up all the day's earnings; the fathers would pull up a stool and order a round of gin for their sons and daughters. (William Booth founded the Salvation Army in direct response to these conditions.)

I did not need to attend a Comedy Addiction Tour to learn the tragic consequences of addiction. I have relatives who ruined their lives through unquenchable cravings and friends whose teenagers wear court-ordered ankle bracelets and report daily for urine tests. I've served meals in rescue missions to former executives and physicians who now hang out on street corners and beg for loose change. I have attended A.A. meetings with friends and heard sorrowful stories of broken marriages and lost careers and drunk-driving accidents.

Once, after I used Alcoholics Anonymous as an example in a talk, a woman came up to me and shook my hand. "Do you know Bill Wilson?" she asked. I searched my memory bank for an instant and said I couldn't recall anyone by that name. She nodded and moved away. Later, I realized she was using a code for A.A. members, something like a Christian asking, "Do you know Jesus?" Bill Wilson was one of the two founders of A.A., the man Aldous Huxley called "the greatest social architect of the twentieth century."

✦   ✦   ✦

The story of A.A.'s founding has achieved almost mythical status. In 1934 Bill Wilson, a gregarious New York entrepreneur, met an old friend named Ebby who told him he had found the cure to alcoholism through religion. Already that year Bill had spent four sessions in a hospital drying-out facility. Clinically depressed, he slept on the ground floor of his home to avoid the temptation of throwing himself out an upstairs window. With his doctor threatening to commit him to an asylum, Bill listened to his friend, who actually had spent time in an asylum. Ebby was now sober—he turned down the drink Bill offered—and seemingly at peace. He did not force his faith on Bill, but somehow one alcoholic talking openly with another broke through the barriers Bill usually put up against people who tried to help him. Ebby had a simple formula: "Realize you are licked, admit it, and get willing to turn your life over to the care of God."

Bill Wilson went on one more alcoholic binge that lasted three days, but he did attend a meeting at a local rescue mission sponsored by the Oxford Group of Christian reformers. Then, while recovering in a hospital he had an authentic conversion experience. *So this is the God of the preachers!* he thought to himself. "A great peace stole over me and I thought, 'No matter how wrong things seem to be, they are all right. Things are all right with God and His world.' "

For five months Bill did not drink. Then, after failing to wrap up a business deal in Akron, Ohio, he sank again into depression and called a clergyman for help in locating another member of the Oxford Group. The woman who fielded his phone call put him in touch with Dr. Bob Smith, a proctologist who had never found a cure for his own alcoholism. The two became fast friends. Over the next few months Dr. Bob got sober and together the two men devised the basic principles of the 12-step program. Today more than two million people worldwide attend Alcoholics Anonymous meetings and many more have joined the spin-off programs that provide support groups and treat addictions to food, drugs, tobacco, sex, work, pain, even chocolate—some 250 variations in all.

Early in the process the founders faced a crossroads. The Oxford Group had a clear Christian commitment and strove to practice the "Four Absolutes": absolute honesty, absolute purity, absolute unselfishness, and absolute love. To Bill Wilson these absolutes smacked of perfectionism and fed the alcoholic's tendency toward all-or-nothing. His friend Ebby's formula had stressed just the opposite, an admission of helplessness and surrender. Bill wanted to offer something more practical and workable, a plan that held up the ideal of progress rather than perfection. "These ideas had to be fed with teaspoons rather than by buckets," he said. Too many times he had seen an alcoholic become convinced of a total cure, only to watch that person fall off the wagon. Too many times he too had taken the tumble.

Eventually the group that became Alcoholics Anonymous broke with the Oxford Group. Having initially shied away from religion himself, Bill believed that others did not want to get too good too soon. The Four Absolutes were too absolute, and not every alcoholic would assent to a Christian creed. His group started with a dependence on grace, acknowledging that its members would never achieve perfection. Absolutes, said Wilson, either discouraged alcoholics or gave them a dangerous feeling of "spiritual inflation." Over time the perfectionist group shriveled up and disappeared; grace-based A.A. has never stopped expanding.

The same issue continues to divide Christians who join A.A. Its generic spirituality grates on some members: the use of "Higher Power" rather than God, the omission of Jesus or conversion, the references to spirituality rather than religion. I once rode in a taxi driven by a red-haired woman who wore a tongue ring and had a flower tattooed on her neck. Within minutes she told me of her addiction to crack, her wasted years, and her recovery through the Teen Challenge program. "Crack isn't for people to feel good," she said, "it's for people to feel nothing. Crack is only for people whose wounds are so great that it alone can numb them. When you come down you feel terrible shame and self-hatred, so you go for it again and again." I asked her about A.A. "Ah, that's a waste of time. All those 12-steps are a waste of time without repentance. You gotta repent to God first."

Many addicts would rise up to refute her. Yet most would agree that a spiritual component is essential. Addicts direly need God on their side in the struggle. Before psychiatrists began to take seriously the spiritual aspect of alcoholism they had little success in treating it. Now the most effective treatment programs use a three-pronged approach, addressing the physical, psychological, and spiritual aspects of addiction.

Bill Wilson stripped Christian principles to their basics—helplessness, honesty, repentance, restitution, dependence, prayer, community—and set them loose with a minimum of doctrine and a maximum of love. Jesus likened the kingdom of God to a tiny mustard seed which ultimately grows into a tree in which the birds of the air take refuge; as with the movement that became A.A., the gospel can work itself into the soil of culture, then germinate in ways that benefit the world outside the walls of church.

Wilson always insisted, though, that neglecting Step Eleven ("Sought through prayer and meditation to improve our conscious contact with God, as we understood Him, praying only for knowledge of His will for us and the power to carry that out") was the worst mistake an alcoholic could make. His New York group had only half the success rate of early groups in Ohio until he began to emphasize the spiritual. In a letter he spelled out his belief:

> During the past 12 months we have had quite a number who felt that the fellowship, the helpful attitude toward others, the warming of the heart at social gatherings, was going to be sufficient to overcome the alcoholic's obsession. Taking stock at the year's end, we find that this school of thought has few survivors, for the bottled heat treatment has persuaded them that we must find some sort of spiritual basis for living, else we die. A few, who have worked ardently with other alcoholics on the philosophical, rather than the spiritual plane, now say of themselves "We believed that faith without works was dead, but we have now conclusively proved that works without Faith is dead also." *(The Spirit of Imperfection)*

✦ ✦ ✦

For years I met with a friend in Chicago who invited me to A.A. meetings, shared every step of his long journey to recovery, and reflected on all aspects of his addiction. At one of his annual parties he gave me his ten-year sobriety medal, still one of my most precious possessions. Almost every day George went to an A.A. meeting in a building called the Mustard Seed, which sponsors fifty meetings a week.

George freely admitted that for him A.A. had largely replaced the church, which sometimes troubled him. He called it "the Christological question" of A.A. "It has no theology to speak of. You rarely hear about Christ. A.A. groups borrow the sociology of the church, along with a few of the words and concepts, but they have no underlying doctrine. I miss that, but mainly I'm trying to survive, and A.A. helps me in that struggle far better than any local church." The church—steeples loom within sight of the Mustard Seed building—seemed vapid and gutless to him.

When George did attend church, often he would go to mine. An inner city church, it served a free breakfast to senior citizens on Sunday morning. Sometimes drunks would wander in for breakfast, then head upstairs into the warm sanctuary where they would stretch out on a pew and snore loudly through the service. Not all the eccentrics slept through the service. One man liked to throw things: once he threw a spiral football pass at the pastor just as he was praying over trays of three hundred little communion glasses. (He missed.) Somehow that church found a place for these unbalanced characters, a haven of grace stretched to the limits.

Yet I had to admit that visiting the Mustard Seed with George gave me a different model of what the church could be. There, members greet each other with hugs and smiles. They sit around and confess their sins and tell their stories—the Comedy Addiction Tour without the comedy. Many, raised in "don't talk" families of denial, find the chance to speak both inspiring and moving, much like the old-fashioned testimony meetings in some churches. They also pledge to help each other with any problem at any time. If you are tempted to drink at four o'clock in the morning, all you need do is call another A.A. member and he or she will come to you right away. And A.A. insists that all members, regardless of status or background, be treated on the same level, hence the use of first names only.

Every week the Mustard Seed group recites the Twelve Steps together, and as I listened they seemed to boil down to two big steps. One is radical honesty. These alcoholics and drug addicts can smell a deception a mile away and have learned to be brutally honest about their flaws and failures. The second step is radical dependence. They know they cannot make it through another day without the help of their friends and without the help of God. After confessing their faults they pray for help. It occurred to me, as I listened to the alcoholics and drug addicts, that my own church could use a refresher course on those very two steps. People can fake it in church. *How's it going?* "Oh, fine, fine"—when in truth a marriage is falling apart, a teenager has run away. *Need any help?* "No, no, everything's fine. The Lord is good."

I asked George why most of his friends in A.A. avoid church. He told me about people who have experienced rejection and who see church as a place to underscore their failures. "When I invite friends, they feel uncomfortable in church. They feel like misfits. Church people are so *together*, they think. They dress nice and have families and jobs. Their lives work out. Our lives are a mess. We'd rather sit in our blue jeans and T-shirts and smoke cigarettes or drink coffee and be totally honest with each other."

George then made a shrewd observation. He said that in church if someone comes in late, people turn and look at the latecomer. Some scowl, some smile a self-satisfied smile—*See, that person's not as responsible as I am.* In A.A., though, if a person shows up late, the meeting comes to a halt and everyone jumps up to greet the late-comer, aware that the tardiness may be a sign that the addict almost didn't make it. As George put it, "When I show up late, it proves that my desperate need for them won out over my desperate need for alcohol."

Ultimately George did find his way back to church, an Episcopal church very different from his low-church Mennonite background. The words from the *Book of Common Prayer* filled in what had been missing in A.A., his "Christological question." Sometime later he also stumbled upon a group that sought to put both parts together.

One day, ten years after I had moved away from Chicago, I received an invitation to speak at a convention of overtly Christian 12-step groups. George gave me the background: "A warning: it's a disorganized, down-home bunch of folks and the 'convention' will be held in a church basement. This is not the kind of speaking assignment you'll want to put on your résumé. We'd be pleased if you could come, though."

I accepted, and as I thought through what to say, I decided on the title "Why I Wish I Was an Alcoholic." I chose the title not to be witty, rather to convey the truth that alcoholics and other addicts have taught me lessons about life that I might not have learned in any other way.

Much later, when I decided to rework that talk as a chapter in this book, an editor asked me if I should change the title to "Why I Wish I *Were* an Alcoholic." I checked the grammar books, and the subjunctive mood applies depending on how likely or unlikely the scenario is. I concluded it would be best to identify with alcoholics by using *was*, which puts me on their side. From George I had learned that we are all vulnerable to addictions of one sort or another, for an addiction is simply a form of idolatry, something that supplants God as the center of our lives.

19 Why I Wish I Was an Alcoholic

Chicago, August 2003

Let me begin with a paragraph from Herman Melville's novel *Moby-Dick*:

> He had been an artisan of famed excellence, and with plenty to do; owned a house and garden; embraced a youthful, daughter-like, loving wife, and three blithe, ruddy children; every Sunday went to a cheerful-looking church, planted in a grove. But one night, under cover of darkness, and further concealed in a most cunning disguisement, a desperate burglar slid into his happy home, and robbed them all of everything. And darker yet to tell, the blacksmith himself did ignorantly conduct this burglar into his family's heart. It was the Bottle Conjuror! Upon the opening of that fatal cork, forth flew the fiend, and shrivelled up his home.

All of you know something of the conjuror Melville described some 150 years ago, and some of you know, too, of the ruin that may creep in under cover of darkness and shrivel a heart as well as a home. You need no lectures about the dangers of addiction and the wreckage it can cause, so I will take a different approach altogether.

Don't think my title treats lightly or diminishes your struggle; rather, I want to commend you who have gathered here in an effort to redeem that struggle. I take on personally the issues I am writing about. When I write about pain I suffer emotionally if not physically, and when I write about doubt I begin to question what before had seemed certain. A writer vicariously takes the stance of the reader or the audience, and that is why I chose the title "Why I Wish I Was an Alcoholic." As I prepared for this evening it struck me that recovering addicts must daily affirm spiritual truths that the rest of us either neglect or encounter as stumbling blocks.

A friend of mine once told me, "I prayed every day that God would take away my thirst for drink, and every day when I woke up my first thought was Jack Daniel's whiskey. Then one day I realized my craving for drink was the very reason I pray every day. My weakness drives me to God." That simple statement contains profound theology, and with your permission I want to unpack some of the theology underlying the recovery movement.

✦   ✦   ✦

The word *sin* rarely comes up in polite society anymore, and even your recovery groups may avoid the word with its slithery connotations. Nevertheless, alcoholics and other addicts have taught me about the nature of sin. When you met in groups this morning you introduced yourselves by saying, "Hi, I'm John and I'm an alcoholic," and "Hi, I'm Maria and I'm a cocaine addict." If someone had said, "I'm John and I used to be an alcoholic but I've been cured," the group would have jumped all over him. Twelve-step groups insist on the perilous use of the present tense. Alcoholics are not "cured," they simply stop drinking; addicts are recovering, not recovered. Always an alcoholic remains one drink away from sliding back toward ruin, one lurch away from falling off the wagon.

You have a sympathizer in the apostle Paul, who wrote Timothy, "Here is a trustworthy saying that deserves full acceptance: Christ Jesus came into the world to save sinners—of whom I am the worst."

Note the present tense, employed by someone who knew Greek grammar. Paul, the world's best missionary and author of a fair portion of the New Testament, knew that he too stood on the edge of a moral precipice. He battled his own set of temptations—boastful pride, an impatience with slow learners, a sense of moral superiority—which we tend to view with more tolerance. After all, Paul was brilliant and demanding and high-principled, and those very qualities helped him change the world. Unlike the blacksmith in *Moby-Dick*, he didn't ruin his life and betray his family.

As Paul makes clear in his letter to the Romans, however, the more "respectable" sins may cause more damage than the ones that society disdains. Remember, moral superiority led him to assist in the stoning of Stephen, a memory that may have weighed on him as he wrote to Timothy. Recovery groups cut apart our artificial grouping of sins and force us to, in the words of Step Five, "admit to God, to ourselves, and to another human being the exact nature of our wrongs."

Six of the Twelve Steps you recited this morning mention God or a Higher Power, because Bill W. and Dr. Bob had the insight to see that all sin constitutes an act against God. "Against you, you only, have I sinned," David prayed after committing murder and adultery. At its root, sin disrupts the moral order of the universe established by God.

Saint Augustine observed that evil has no power to create, can only bend and twist the good that God has created. The apostle Paul's intelligence and high principles, good things in themselves, could nonetheless be twisted to the service of evil. The juice of the grape, pharmaceuticals, sex, food, work—all good things—can likewise be used in the wrong way, which counselors aptly term "substance abuse." Once corrupted, these otherwise good things can enslave and destroy.

I know a lifelong bachelor who has a pornography addiction. Due to diabetes he has lost all vision in one eye and 90 percent in the other. He lives in a cluttered, filthy house and rarely ventures outdoors. With his few remaining teeth he eats whatever the Meals on Wheels social program delivers to his house each day. To save money on fuel bills in the winter, he bundles up in a down jacket and pulls a stocking cap over his head. Despite his poverty he spends much of his Social Security check on X-rated pornography. Every night he drags a chair very close to the television monitor, fumbles to insert a DVD, and holds up a large magnifying glass to scrutinize the naked bodies on-screen. I am quite sure that is not what God had in mind when he bestowed the subtle gift of human sexuality.

We need more than our own wisdom to manage the gifts God has given. We need a Higher Power to re-order our desires. The pixels of paid actors digitized on-screen, the temporary escape of an alcoholic blackout, the momentary high of a cocaine party—all these disrupt the order of a good world given us to steward.

Augustine went on to say that evil passes your door first as a stranger, then enters as a guest, and finally installs itself as master. You in this room know that downward spiral, and each of you could tell a story of the harm that results. This dark knowledge gives you a peculiar advantage, I believe, because many sincere church members live in a state of denial. Unlike you, they believe themselves immune to the destructive power of sin. Unlike Paul, they think of sin in the past tense.

I received a letter from an alcoholic who had learned the hard truth:

> I know that I can go out and start drinking today and begin one heck of a riotous life. I can have all the sex I want with all the women I want and live in a state of continued drunkenness for quite some time. BUT, there is a catch. I know firsthand all the misery and guilt that comes along with it. And, that is something I want no part of. I have experienced guilt and misery so extreme that I didn't want to live anymore at all—and that, my friend, is why I would rather not have to take advantage of God's generosity in being willing to forgive me once again should I go that route.... Plus, in my present life, every now and then I

think I do manage to do God's will. And, when I do, then the rewards are so tremendous and satisfying, that I get kind of addicted to that closeness to God.

There is a common saying in A.A.: "Religion is for people who believe in Hell. Spirituality is for people who have been there."

People do not decide one day, "I think I'll become an addict." No, you feel pain or rejection or loneliness and seek something to provide relief. As one of Tennessee Williams's characters put it, "I have to hear that little click in my head that makes me peaceful." At first the substance seems to work because it dulls the negative feelings and gives a euphoric high. But then the addiction keeps enlarging the very void it was meant to fill. It brings less relief and only a little pleasure.

Eventually addiction begins to work actual harm: on the lungs, on the liver, on the brain, and also on relationships. A teenager discovers his dad's computer files of child pornography. A wife stumbles upon an e-mail from her husband's lover. A mother comes out of a drunken haze to see the reddening imprint of her hand on her daughter's face. A squad car pulls into the driveway to examine a car after a hit-and-run accident. The downward spiral ends—at the very bottom. Sin has taken its toll.

✦ ✦ ✦

Immediately after admitting to Timothy that he is the worst of sinners, Paul adds these words: "But for that very reason I was shown mercy so that in me, the worst of sinners, Christ Jesus might display his unlimited patience as an example for those who would believe on him and receive eternal life." He can't resist inserting a quick prayer of thanksgiving, "Now to the King eternal, immortal, invisible, the only God, be honor and glory for ever and ever. Amen."

Addicts not only teach me the nature and consequences of sin, they also demonstrate our permanent need for grace. I received another letter from an alcoholic who spelled out the number 901,800,000,000,000: he had calculated the total number of sins if everyone on earth lived for seventy years and sinned only one time each and every day of their lives. (I came up with a different figure, still one impressively large.) He did this not as a morbid exercise, rather as a mathematical celebration of God's amazing grace. Following the Twelve Steps, daily he asks God to remove his own wrongs, shortcomings, and defects of character, and then exults in forgiveness.

Some churches lead their members through prayers of repentance and many celebrate communion or the Eucharist or mass as a sacrament of confession and forgiveness. In my experience, though, few churches achieve the kind of contrition practiced by those of you who attend addiction groups. Instead, many Christians emerge from church with a feeling of self-satisfied pride: *Look at us. We got up and went to church today instead of mowing the lawn or watching sporting events.* In contrast, addicts leave their 12-step group mindful of their wrongs and also emboldened by an overpowering sense of God's grace. The sayings posted on the wall express it well. *One day at a time. Spiritual progress, not perfection. Came, came to, came to believe. Let go and let God. Turn it over. There but for the grace of God go I.*

In this conference I have heard heart-rending stories of shame and failure, accounts of what led you to seek help. They carried me back to the days of my childhood church when I heard "testimonies" of men and women who found God after a life of degradation. I sense an important difference here, though. Church testimonies graphically described the past but tended to end with conversion. You proceed to describe the continuing struggle, an ongoing need for God's grace. Like my friend who thinks of Jack Daniel's the second he wakes up, you cannot escape awareness of that need. You lack the luxury of denial.

"If I go up to the heavens, you are there," writes the psalmist, who quickly adds, "If I make my bed in the depths, you are there." You have learned that we cannot fall out of range of God's grace. No matter how low we plunge, God's grace goes lower still. The beauty of grace is that it does not leave us there.

I heard a professional comedian describe the "first thought wrong" principle. On the path to recovery he started distrusting his first thoughts. "I need a drink." *Don't do it. You know where that leads.* I happened to be studying the Book of Romans at the time, and in Romans 7 Paul gives an eloquent description of that same principle. Note that again he uses the present tense: "I do not understand what I do. For what I want to do I do not do, but what I hate I do." His language eerily resembles what I heard today as you described your struggles with addiction. "What a wretched man I am!" Paul concludes.

Then, as if someone switched channels, the tone abruptly changes. Paul corrects the first-thought-wrong formula with a dose of grace-reality: "Therefore, there is now no condemnation for those who are in Christ Jesus." I know no better corrective to wrong thinking, and no better reminder of God's grace, than reading Romans 7 and 8 back to back. God wants to alter our first thoughts so that they reflect our true state, as God's forgiven, beloved children.

Not long ago I sat by the bedside of a relative who had suffered a progressive stroke. One day while playing golf he began to experience blurry vision. A few days later his speech became garbled. Then he lost use of his right hand and arm. The next day he could no longer walk. When I arrived at the hospital and sat by his bedside he lay immobile with a vacant, unfocused stare. Bit by bit his brain had shut down parts of his body, like a pilot shutting down the systems of an airplane. The MRI revealed three dead spots in his brain and a large at-risk section that covered almost a third of its surface. A neurosurgeon elected to perform a delicate procedure in which he removed a section of skull and redirected an artery from close to the scalp down into the deeper brain. The post-surgery MRI revealed that the at-risk area was now perfused with blood, and functioning started to return. I could see a clear difference in his alertness within hours after the surgery. Over the next few weeks he gradually regained speech, as well as some use of his right leg and arm.

Watching my relative gave me a vivid metaphor of sin and grace. That musty word *sin* simply labels those actions that bring us physical and spiritual harm; by abusing God's good gifts we introduce something toxic into our souls. Allow sin to become an addiction and it will work serious damage, shutting down the potential for which we were made. Repentance removes the blockage and restores nourishment to the at-risk areas, releasing the vital, cleansing flow of God's grace.

✦   ✦   ✦

Addicts have helped me understand some of the deepest mysteries of the Christian life. After reading John Calvin's *Institutes of the Christian Religion* and Martin Luther's *The Bondage of the Will*, I came away with more questions than answers. Are we truly free? How can I be held responsible for some original sin passed down from Adam or even from a dysfunctional family? Does God know my future by predestination or by foresight?

Then I began meeting with a friend here in Chicago who grappled with the same issues in a more personal way. "For me the hardest step toward recovery was the first step, to admit I was powerless, my life unmanageable," he said. "A.A. insists my alcoholism is a disease, and I agree. I can trace the genetic history in my family as well as my own chemical imbalances. Most of the time while drinking I felt I had no choice, no freedom. I could not go on without the addiction, I had to yield. At the time I blamed depression, employment failure, sexual rejection, whatever. Yet I must also admit that each time I took a drink there was a split second in which I made a free choice, in full knowledge of the consequences. Now I make the choice against drinking."

I interrupted, "But you said alcoholism was a disease..."

"I know, I know. It seems like a contradiction. Even so, to make any progress at all I had to take full and complete responsibility for *all* my behavior, even what happened during blackouts when I had no conscious awareness. My A.A. buddies made me stop blaming anyone but myself. In fact, although many Christians balk at the doctrine, original sin makes perfect sense to the average A.A. person. We don't have to choose to drink, but we can't help it. We'll never escape that cycle unless we admit that we're powerless and need outside help. And even when we ask for God's help, we still have to work like crazy to stay sober."

In the Gospel accounts, Jesus shows great compassion toward people who have fallen to the very bottom. He more than anyone understood institutional sins like racism and injustice, as well as the challenges faced by the disabled. Consistently, however, Jesus emphasizes freedom, throwing responsibility back on the individual. "Do you want to be healed?" he asks, and only when a person answers yes does healing take place. God offers us not only the insight to see our true, forgiven state but also the power to realize that state.

My friend went on to say that he has heard this comment in A.A. meetings, and has made it himself: "I know I have another drunk left in me. The problem is that I am afraid I don't have another 'sobering up' left in me." That image, a drunk and a sober person wrestling inside, summons up images of the Christian life I heard in childhood. Sunday school illustrations portrayed a hairy, scowling, Turkish-looking wrestler grappling with a clean-cut, Nordic blond wrestler inside a human heart. Sometimes the "carnal Christian" won, with the Turk pinning the Scandinavian to the mat, and sometimes the "spiritual Christian" ended up on top. That, said the teacher, represented the spiritual battles that take place inside each believer.

Despite its ethnic crudity, the illustration reflects something of reality. The human person is complex and rarely does behavior reduce to a single cause or explanation. As the civil rights leader W. E. B. DuBois said about his race, in a formula that applies to all of us, "We are more than we seem." I think I'm in control and then emotions surge up and catch me off guard. Therapy may help me identify some hidden parts of my personality, but other parts will always remain inaccessible: I may be unwittingly playing out unresolved issues from childhood, or acting out of a chemical imbalance.

A business consultant I know describes what he calls the "person-as-company" model of human personality. "I operate much like the president of a company. My 'company' (my self) comprises many different 'employees'—meaning my feelings, impulses, genetic disposition, rational choices—who share the same facility, my body. As president, I may be responsible for the company, but I do not always have direct control over all the employees. In fact, not infrequently one of them surprises me by taking over. I have an emotional outburst or make an impulsive decision and wonder how in the world that could have happened."

Just when I think I have myself—the company—under control, some employee spills coffee, shows up late for meetings, misses deadlines, and generally undermines what "I" work so hard to achieve. The company veers out of control, its very existence threatened. "I have another drunk in me, but do I have a sobering up?" the alcoholic asks. "I do not understand what I do," says Paul. "For what I want to do I do not do, but what I hate I do." We are more than we seem.

As Paul explains elsewhere, the Christian can tap in to additional resources. "I will not boast about myself, except about my weaknesses," he tells the Corinthians. "I will boast all the more gladly about my weaknesses, so that Christ's power may rest on me." Following the analogy, you might say conversion invites a new director into the bankrupt company. With a large infusion of fresh capital he moves it onto a stable foundation and begins the long, slow work of creating unity and corporate health. Like any director, he succeeds not by imposing his will but by mobilizing the members to join in a team effort. As the Twelve Steps express so well, that process involves a constant reliance on God and on others. Paradoxically, we best realize our freedom through dependence.

✦ ✦ ✦

Finally, I wish I was an alcoholic because I believe you have much to teach us about what the church can and should be. Some of the most spiritual addicts I know avoid church because they view it as a place for people who already have it together. Oh, my! I can think of far more entertaining ways to spend my Sunday mornings if I already have it together. I go to church as an expression of my need for God and for God's family—the same reason you go to 12-step groups. So often, however, I leave with an empty feeling because church covers reality with a veneer of respectability. What have we done that we communicate church as a place for well people rather than a place to get well?

Dorothy Day, founder of the Catholic Worker movement, spent her life ministering to addicts and broken people and in her diary she admitted the temptation to give up on them. Immediately, she followed with the reason that kept her from doing so:

> Yes, I see only too clearly how bad people are. I wish I did not see it so. It is my own sins that give me such clarity. If I did not bear the scars of so many sins to dim my sight and dull my capacity for love and joy, then I would see Christ more clearly in you all. I cannot worry much about your sins and miseries when I have so many of my own. I can only love you all, poor fellow travelers, fellow sufferers. I do not want to add one least straw to the burden you already carry. My prayer from day to day is that God will so enlarge my heart that I will see you all, and live with you all, in His love.

It was Dorothy Day's brutal honesty about herself—her unwed pregnancy, her biting tongue, her quick temper—that allowed her to show grace toward others. I yearn for a grace-abounding church that rewards rather than punishes honesty, and that, in Jesus' words, exists for the sinners and not the righteous, the sick and not the healthy. We are all sick, we are all unwell, and your 12-step groups make acknowledgment of that fact a prerequisite of membership. Not everyone appreciates this emphasis. Whenever I speak on the topic of grace and follow my talk with a time for questions, inevitably someone brings up the issue of "grace abuse." What about people who take advantage of forgiveness? What about rules and responsibility? What about accountability?

They have a point. You may know the novel *Leaving Las Vegas* by John O'Brien, made into a movie starring Nicolas Cage. In it Sera, a prostitute, falls in love with a man named Ben who is quite obviously drinking himself to death. "I know that you'll never change," she says, and vows to accept him as he is. In a tragic display of codependency, she gives him a silver flask for his birthday. In the end, both Sera and Ben self-destruct (as did John O'Brien, who committed suicide at the age of thirty-four, two weeks after selling the film rights to his novel). The two lovers die of grace abuse.

Many of you could tell similar stories of codependency. Yet your 12-step groups help supply the very accountability that prevents grace abuse. You bore in on anyone who seems fake or in denial about their addiction. With your buddy system you make grace visible by caring and supporting one another in the most practical ways: cleaning up vomit, sitting up all night with a detoxing friend. You focus on one human failing, addiction, and like a true community you hold each other accountable for that failing. As one alcoholic told me, "If I walked into A.A. and said, 'I just shot my wife,' someone would ask, 'Well, are you going to drink?'" No church I know of provides that kind of round-the-clock accountability.

Ernest Kurtz, the historian of Alcoholics Anonymous, remarks, "What unites alcoholics, what makes it possible for one alcoholic to learn from another, is that the foundation that they share is not a strength but a *weakness*; each knows what he or she *cannot* do." The church needs that reminder—a reminder, not a novelty, for the apostle Paul spoke of his own weakness more than three dozen times. Christian leaders may publicly apologize after some major transgression, but how many openly discuss their doubts, their mistaken predictions, their biases and exaggerations? You remind us of the danger posed by the small but nagging temptations, the careless cover-ups and prevarications. Like icy spots on a mountain trail, they slick the way to a disastrous fall.

I have a hunch that if the watching world saw the church as a place that welcomes broken people for healing, it might have a greater impact than all our sophisticated outreach programs put together. One of the seven Trappist monks martyred by terrorists in Algeria in 1996 described his calling in a way that can stand as a definition of the church: "A monk is simply a sinner who joins a community of sinners who are confident in God's mercy and who strive to recognize their weaknesses in the presence of their brothers."

That could also stand as a description of your groups, as you seek to re-anchor the Twelve Steps in the biblical framework they came from. Acknowledging a broken relationship with God, accepting moral responsibility for failures, admitting powerlessness and the need for outside help, asking God to remove defects of character, committing to make amends to all who have been harmed, seeking through prayer to improve contact with God, carrying this message of healing to others—the formula for 12-step groups comes straight from the pages of the Bible.

Thanks to people like you, the rest of us need not become alcoholics or addicts to learn these lessons. We can look to you as our mentors in brokenness and apply what you have learned to our own lives.

Several times in my writing I've referred to my alcoholic friend George, who happens to be here tonight. He told me that when he first stumbled into an A.A. meeting on a bitterly cold night some twenty years ago a group of total strangers welcomed him with open arms and told him to "keep coming back." George had hit bottom, his life was a mess, and since nobody else was telling him that in those days, he accepted their invitation.

George sometimes gets a different response from his church friends. "Aren't you done with that issue yet?" they ask. And this is what George says: "I realize that for the rest of my life, I can go to A.A. meetings and nobody will ask me, 'Aren't you finished with all this talk about your alcoholism?' They will just say, 'Keep coming back—glad you could make it.'"

May the church learn.

PART X

MUMBAI: A MARATHON OF HORROR

MUMBAI:

A MARATHON OF HORROR

20 Tour, Interrupted

I first visited India in 1982 and again in 1990 while doing research for books with Dr. Paul Brand, the British orthopedic surgeon who had founded a renowned leprosy hospital in southern India. Dr. Brand felt more at home in India than in England or in his new home, a leprosarium in Louisiana. He preferred bathing the Indian way, by ladling water over his head, rather than using a more wasteful shower or tub. He needed no eating utensils, having mastered the Indian style of forming a ball of rice with one hand to dip into the meat or vegetable dish. He went barefoot whenever possible, quick to extol the advantages for feet and posture as he complained about the "No shoes, no shirt, no service" signs posted in U.S. shops and restaurants. (Traveling with him, I tried all three techniques and came away favoring showers, cutlery, and shoes.)

More important, Dr. Brand loved the Indian people and he conveyed that love to me. First-time visitors are shocked by the poverty in Calcutta, where half a million people sleep on the streets each night, or by the sprawling slums of Mumbai (formerly Bombay) depicted in the movie *Slumdog Millionaire*. On my first trip the plane circled the Madras (Chennai) airport as a jeep with floodlights drove up and down the runway to clear it of people bedded down on the warm tarmac. Dr. Brand had treated the poorest of the poor, for many of his patients came from the Dalits (Untouchable caste), yet he knew them not as a class but as individuals. Sometimes he wept as he told me their stories of hardship and rejection. Through his eyes I saw the grace and resilience that make it possible for a billion people to share an overtaxed land.

I got a sore neck on that first visit, turning this way and that to take in the sights of the five-ring circus that is India. A brightly painted elephant walking unaccompanied down the street among the roaming cows. A snake charmer with his wily mongoose and basketful of cobras. Rickshaw pullers, some on bicycles and some on foot, perilously making their way through impossible traffic. Women in colorful silk saris, no two alike, exotic as tropical birds. A monkey dressed in an embroidered jacket and fez sitting on a dog and smoking a cigarette as his master tries to hawk photos. A Hindu temple covered with erotic stone carvings adjacent to a severe Muslim mosque devoid of images.

I sat unmoving for three hours watching the sunrise and the play of light on the pearly Taj Mahal. I walked among the burning ghats of Varanasi, smelling the sickly scent of human flesh as crackling fires reduced dead bodies to ashes to be dumped into the Ganges River. I bounced up and down on potholed roads in the countryside, watching platoons of farmers plant rice by hand while my driver swerved to avoid the animals, people, and vehicles swarming the roads. I dodged beggars in Calcutta after learning that many of the children with blinded eyes and twisted limbs had been deformed by syndicates who used them to rake in profits.

✦ ✦ ✦

India has changed," I heard as I prepared for yet another visit in late 2008. "You won't recognize it. It's the New India, with high-tech companies, fancy shopping malls, and skyscrapers." Sure enough, I saw obvious changes right away. Since my first visit India's population had increased by a number greater than the total population of the United States, which made cities and streets far more crowded. The newspaper reported that India adds four thousand new cars to its roads every day, so now Mercedes, Audis, and the occasional Jaguar rule the roads, with motorbikes and three-wheel taxis weaving through the snarl of traffic like small fish cutting through a school of larger ones.

Nothing in India goes away, though; the layers simply accumulate. Exotic cars still have to share the highways with bullock carts, horses, and perhaps an elephant or camel. The electric wires now crisscrossing the major cities serve as convenient highways for the resident monkeys. Modern buildings may tower in the cities, yet leave the urban areas and the old India surges back: women walk the road with brass pots and pans balanced on their heads; water buffalo pull hand-hewn plows to till the ground; irrigation workers stand all day dipping water from one channel to another; bent-over old women sweep the streets with handleless brooms of straw. More Indians own a mobile phone, I am told, than have access to clean water.

The social realities of India boggle the mind. One hundred and sixty million Dalits, formerly known as Untouchables, live at the bottom of the caste ladder. Though nominally Hindu, they are barred from Hindu temples and in recent years have increasingly turned toward other religions, including Christianity. I traveled to India two weeks after Barack Obama's election, and one Dalit scholar said to me, "You Americans are celebrating the election of a black man only 250 years after slavery. We are still waiting for liberation after four thousand years of living under Hindu caste."

Just above Dalits are the Other Backward Castes which make up more than half of India's population: six hundred million people. Activists from these castes regard Hinduism as an oppressive social structure designed to keep them in an inferior state. Of course, any sign of resistance prompts an outburst from fundamentalist Hindus, which partly explains a 2008 riot in the province of Orissa which chased fifty thousand Christians out of their homes into the forest, their churches and houses burned.

As an Indian friend told me, "My country is so diverse, with so many castes and subcultures and more than fifteen hundred languages, that I have more in common with you than with people from other parts of India." Newcomers see the strife, the class divisions, the apparent chaos of a billion people with competing loyalties. Under the surface, however, you find many signs of compassion and come away amazed by the nation's fortitude. Longsuffering, magical, baffling, mysterious—any adjective you can think of applies to India.

✦ ✦ ✦

In Hyderabad I spent a day touring Good Shepherd schools, a project targeting the Dalits which has built a hundred schools across India. Our host Joseph D'souza explained, "Early missionaries directed their efforts toward the Brahmins, the upper castes, hoping the liberating message of the gospel would trickle down to the oppressed. It didn't happen. Now we are working in the other direction, starting with the lower castes."

At one such school in the countryside four hundred students were standing at attention in precise rows awaiting our arrival. They gave speeches, read aloud a summary of the day's news, sang the national anthem and a few hymns, then recited Psalm 23 before marching off to class. In the classrooms they proudly displayed their knowledge to the visitors, shouting out the multiplication tables and ABCs as if to get extra credit for loud volume: "Capital A, small a! Capital B, small b! Capital C, small c!..." I was struck by the absence of cynicism such as you would find in a comparable school in the United States. No one wore sloppy clothes or slouched at the desk with an "I dare you to teach me" attitude. These kids are the first generation of Dalits in four thousand years to get an education, and they're getting it in English, which assures them of better job possibilities. As a bonus they also receive a nutritious lunch, health care, and two school uniforms, by far the best clothes they own. The pride they bring home each day elevates the spirit of the entire community.

In the afternoon we visited a "pipe village" where some of the students live, a ramshackle community located next to a factory that makes the large concrete culvert pipes used to control sewage and flood waters. For years the factory discarded defective pipes in an open field and in time the workers' families moved in. They now live inside these scattered concrete pipes, five or six feet in diameter, with no running water or electricity. All day long the concrete absorbs the sun's heat, so when I stooped to enter the tiny pipe-homes I had the sensation of entering an oven.

Kids in ragged clothes were chasing each other along the dirt paths, posing for photos and singing songs for the foreign guests, and I recognized some of the very same students who had lined up in smart uniforms at school earlier that day. One young girl announced proudly that she planned to become a doctor. "What kind?" I asked. "A cardiologist!" I could only imagine the quantum leap in ambition for these Dalit children who previously faced a life of sweeping streets or emptying the latrines of higher castes.

Indians are unfailingly hospitable. As we traveled from city to city, at every airport a group welcomed us with large photo banners, floral leis and bouquets, and sometimes a choir of uniformed school children singing greetings. The welcome underscored what for me was the biggest change of all: my new role. In the three decades since my first visit to India, much has happened in my life. In 1982 I was a young journalist with frizzy hair following around a man I esteemed and admired. I took notes, interviewed his friends and colleagues, searched for ways to capture Paul Brand's life and thoughts. In 2008 I was on a six-city speaking tour sponsored by the publisher of my own books. In each city I found myself thrust up on a platform with lights in my eyes. I must confess I feel more comfortable with the older role than the newer. And I am amazed that what I write in my Colorado office can strike a responsive chord in people who live as a religious minority in a hot, crowded country halfway around the globe.

My Indian hosts had asked me to speak on grace, a fitting topic for such a diverse and divided country. As the speaking tour unfolded, each city presented unique challenges. The first night, in New Delhi, I learned as I arrived at the venue that several hundred Dalits would attend, requiring the talk to be translated—which meant I quickly had to cut my speech in half because translation doubles the time. A crowd of three thousand was sitting outdoors, and I contended with car horns and alarms as well as a balky computer that projected my PowerPoint slides at all the wrong times. In Bangalore the power kept cutting off the sound system as the soloist performed. (No one blinks at a power cut in India, despite its reputation as the high-tech capital of the world.) In Hyderabad I was the victim: in the middle of my talk the large auditorium went completely dark. I stood there awkwardly for a few minutes not knowing what to do until someone yelled, "We can still hear you!" and so I shouted into the darkness until lights and power came back on.

To me it felt like combat speaking, but Indians are patient people and nothing seemed to rattle them. The meetings started at 5:30 or 6:00 PM, and I usually got up to speak around 8:00 PM after much music, long introductions, and endless thank-yous to the staff and volunteers. Afterward Janet and I sat at a book table for an hour to greet people and sign books, with Indians crowding around to shove not only books but also cameras and cell phone cameras in our faces. Apparently the British did not manage to pass on their tradition of orderly queues.

This was my first visit to India without Dr. Brand, who had introduced me to this country. I acknowledged him each time I spoke and inevitably someone mentioned a connection. In Hyderabad, for instance, an elderly woman in a purple sari told of traveling by train for twelve hours to attend the night's meeting. In 1980 she read *Fearfully and Wonderfully Made* just after it came out and began praying for her son to follow in Paul Brand's footsteps as a doctor. She didn't tell him about her prayer since children often do the opposite of their parents' wishes, yet he chose to study at the Christian Medical College in Vellore where Dr. Brand taught, and today he works as a hand surgeon in a department named for Dr. Brand. The legacy continues.

✦ ✦ ✦

The tour, now approaching its end, has gone well. We will leave here inspired by people who practice their faith in a way that is transforming society, especially among the Dalits. We have one remaining engagement, tomorrow night, an event in downtown Mumbai. Tonight we are staying at the home of Dr. Stephen Alfred in a suburb some twenty miles from the city center. Our hosts apologize for putting us in a private home rather than a tourist hotel downtown; they want us to see the remarkable hospital and AIDS clinic built by this doctor.

Around the dinner table we hear some of Stephen Alfred's story. He had studied in England, married an English woman, and built up a thriving surgery practice until one night he had a kind of vision. He heard God ask him three questions: *Why did I make you Indian? Why did I make you good? What are you doing about it?* Haunted by those questions, he left his practice, moved his family to India, and opened a hospital that focuses on serving the poor.

The next morning I awake in the dark, dress in running clothes, and quietly undo the locks on the front door. The Alfreds live in a gated community, and I playfully salute the guard as I exit. I have a habit of getting lost on these early morning runs, so I head for a nearby lake which I can run around and around rather than trying to negotiate the winding streets.

Vendors are selling chai on every street corner. A few people stare at the skinny foreigner with pale legs, but no one hassles me. I keep my head down, looking to avoid the droppings of dogs, cows, goats, pigs, and other animals. The morning is cool, and coming from the altitude of Colorado to a town near sea level, I feel fresh and invigorated on this run. I've made it through this trip with no intestinal problems, a first for me in India.

Strangely, as I return the Alfreds are standing at the door, waiting. "Are you all right?" Stephen asks in a concerned tone. "We were about to send a search party after you. Better get inside. It seems they're targeting foreigners."

And now I hear the news. Last night as were sitting around the table swapping stories, terrorists from Pakistan landed in downtown Mumbai and attacked ten different sites, including the main train station, several tourist hotels, a hospital, a café, a cinema, a college, and a Jewish community center. Mumbai is under police lockdown as pitched battles still rage at the Jewish center and the Taj Mahal Hotel. There will be no meeting downtown tonight. The Alfreds have also canceled our planned hotel reservations by the airport and opened their home to us until things calm down.

We gather around a small television in the living room and watch the news. Eleven policemen have died, including the head of state security. The civilian death toll rises by the hour: at least seventy, perhaps a hundred, but with uncounted bodies in Mumbai's two leading hotels, both of which are billowing smoke. (The final tally will reach 172 dead and 380 wounded.) A few guests on upper floors are leaning out of windows waving towels. Tanks and armored cars surround the scene, along with several thousand onlookers.

We sit down for breakfast, and as we say grace I remember that later today, some thirteen time zones away, Americans will celebrate Thanksgiving. We have much to be thankful for, beginning with safety. We would have been staying at a downtown hotel near the planned venue were it not for this "detour" on the itinerary.

As we begin eating the phone rings and a minute later to my surprise Stephen says, "It's for you." Who knows where we are? After multiple Internet searches and phone calls to our Indian sponsors, Janet's family, gathered together for the holiday, has managed to track us down. "Are you OK?" her sister asks. "Over here the news looks awful, and we've been so worried."

Thus begins a marathon of horror. I keep flashing back to September 11, 2001, when our entire country sat glued to television. A *plane hit the World Trade Center—no, two planes. Not small planes, either, large passenger jets. There's a report of another one at the Pentagon. And an explosion in rural Pennsylvania. We're under attack. Wait, one of the towers is shaking. It's starting to buckle. My God, it's falling! Some 50,000 people work in those towers...*

Most terrorist events hit suddenly and end just as suddenly; this one drags on nearly three days. Indian television provides nonstop coverage and it becomes clear that the terrorists themselves are following media reports, adjusting their positions as they watch real-time images of commandos dropping from helicopters onto the rooftops of buildings they are holding. The first night, local policemen charged into the invaded hotels with 9 mm automatic pistols, only to meet terrorists wielding grenades and AK-47s. It took a full day for well-armed federal commandos to arrive.

Normal life ceases, just as it did in the United States after 9/11. In homes, restaurants, airports, and train stations all over India people sit quietly in front of television sets. Banners run across the bottom of the screen with poignant messages: "Veneeta, we are praying for you...Vijay, please call home—we are so concerned."

✦ ✦ ✦

Each day the Indian newspapers recount stories of the ongoing drama. A well-known female journalist held hostage in her hotel room text-messages a half-page article that describes gunshots in the corridor and smoke licking under her door from the grenade blasts. She barricades the door with furniture, but still feels vulnerable. She's a good writer, and reading her account we share her fright. The next day the newspaper prints her final message, written from under her bed— "They are in my bathroom. This is the end for me..."—with an editor's note that commandos have found her body.

A man who has just made a champagne toast in celebration of a business deal spends the next two days lying in shattered glass feigning death, his arm covering his face so they won't notice he is a foreigner. A Muslim couple hears a noise that sounds like firecrackers. They go to the window overlooking a popular café and are killed in a hail of bullets as their young son watches. Rumors spread like weeds: of corpses showing marks of torture and disfigurement, of scores of bodies floating in the hotel swimming pool, of explosives set to destroy entire buildings. (Five days after the drama ends police find a huge unexploded bomb smack in the middle of the train station.)

As for the Taj Hotel, one Indian tells me, "You cannot imagine what the Taj Mahal Palace Hotel means to the Indian people. It's a great source of national pride, an icon, like the Statue of Liberty is to you." A wealthy Indian constructed the stately building in 1903 after being refused entrance to a whites-only British hotel. The ornate railway station under siege also dates from the Victorian era; once called Victoria Terminus, it is listed as a World Heritage Site.

Just as in 9/11, tales of luck and heroism also surface amid the tragedy. The twelve-year-old son of a British couple dining in the Taj Hotel restaurant goes to the bathroom minutes before the terrorists attack. For thirty-six hours his parents are pinned down, not knowing if their son has escaped. All survive, and are reunited. The manager of the Taj Hotel helps hide guests in a basement food locker even as, unbeknown to him, his wife and two children burn to death in their suite several floors above. A British lawyer, barricaded in his room and hiding under the bed, sets up an impromptu network with other hostages who have BlackBerry phones. The Indian nanny caring for the two-year-old son of a rabbi smuggles him out of the Jewish center, saving him from the torture and death that await his parents. (Israel has since named her a "righteous Gentile" and granted her citizenship.)

Looking for some good news, the media feature interviews with an alert railroad employee at the attacked train station. After noticing a terrorist on the steps with a machine gun, he calmly announced over the loudspeaker, "The stairway from platform one is closed, please do not use it," thus diverting crowds of passengers and saving an estimated five hundred lives. Even so, more than fifty people died in that station.

✦ ✦ ✦

There is no question of holding the scheduled meeting tonight, especially not in an auditorium close to the ongoing action. I feel bad for the local organizers who have worked for months planning a program, printing tickets, designing banners, stocking books. As we talk throughout the day, another idea comes to mind. What if we hold an impromptu meeting in a local church, so that at least people who live in the suburbs on our side of Mumbai can attend? I remember the night of September 11, 2001, in my hometown when my church spontaneously filled with hundreds of people. No one announced or planned a meeting. Stunned, grieving, afraid, we went by instinct to church, to join with fellow believers in prayer. If our faith matters at all, it must matter at such a time of crisis, and inadvertently I have just found myself in the midst of another faith-testing crisis.

As we talk through the possibilities, the doorbell rings. Somehow Dayanidhi Rao, the energetic young singer who has shared the platform in all five cities, has made it to the doctor's home. We now have music and a speaker. Stephen Alfred gets on the phone, calls a few friends and a local pastor, and by midafternoon the service has taken shape. By the time the service starts, around 250 people have gathered. We sing. We pray. We tell stories of our day. We weep for the dead and wounded. We pray some more. And now it's my turn to speak—on grace.

21   Grace Under Fire

Mumbai, November 2008

All day I have been reliving a tragic day in my own nation's history: September 11, 2001. Like you, we were attacked by fanatics from another country, partly due to differences in belief and partly due to sheer hatred. Like you, we sat dazed by news reports so harrowing that we could hardly keep listening yet so gripping that we could not stop. And, like you, we spontaneously gathered that fateful night in an unscheduled church service to share our grief, our questions, and our prayers.

The weekend after September 11 my wife and I headed to a beautiful part of our state, Colorado, and attempted to climb a mountain. Fall had arrived, gilding the aspen leaves, and morning snow coated them with a rim of white—the same snow that ultimately forced us off the peak. We found it restorative to get away from television and, yes, away from the human race that can treat its fellow members with such cruelty. That brief respite reminded us that life goes on and beauty goes on, even in the midst of great tragedy.

A week later I flew to Washington, D.C., and then New York on a promotional tour for a new book. Each interviewer ignored the book I was supposed to promote and asked instead about one I had written twenty-five years earlier, *Where Is God When It Hurts?*, for that was the question still uppermost in all minds. As the plane took off from

Washington, the pilot came on with a pre-flight announcement unlike any I had ever heard. "All of you know what recently happened," he said. "As a precaution, I recommend you keep an eye on the passenger sitting next to you. If that person acts in a threatening manner, I suggest that the rest of you use pillows and blankets to overpower that passenger until the crew arrives with restraints." Startled, I snuck a look at the overweight bald man by the window, who quickly averted his eyes, and in that moment I realized that a single act of terror had torn the fabric of trust that holds a society together. Now anyone was a potential enemy.

As we neared New York the pilot spoke on the intercom again. "Just today the flight path has changed, permitting us to fly over Manhattan," he said. "We're one of the first planes to do so, and on your left you can see Ground Zero." He tilted the plane slightly and there, where a few weeks ago had stood two of the world's tallest buildings, gaped an ugly black hole with tiny yellow bulldozers crawling over the still smoldering ruins.

"India's September 11," read one newspaper headline this morning. And of course the United Kingdom has already had theirs, as has Spain. When will it end, this cycle of hatred in which people who disagree express their opinions by flying planes into office buildings or blowing up trains and buses or spraying hotel lobbies with machine gun fire?

As you know, I was scheduled to speak on grace this evening in downtown Mumbai at a location close to where battles are raging right now. I want to thank the pastor of this church for opening the doors to us on such short notice as well as all of you who helped make this service possible. I will indeed speak on grace, for I know of nothing that India needs more at this moment. Before I do so, though, I want to assure you that you are not alone.

Today is Thanksgiving Day in the United States, perhaps our only religious holiday not smothered in commercialism. Schools and businesses have closed and millions of families have gathered together. Most will be following closely the news from Mumbai and many will be praying for you. Already today I have answered several dozen e-mails and phone calls from Americans who care deeply about what is happening in India. The world grieves with you and stands in solidarity with you.

Some of you know of my work with Dr. Paul Brand, who taught at the Christian Medical College in Vellore and founded a leprosy hospital. From him I learned the value of pain as the body's unifier. Dr. Brand once told me of an old man with leprosy in New Guinea who would reach into a bed of hot coals with his bare hands to turn a roasting potato. After observing scenes like that, Dr. Brand went on to discover that virtually all the disfigurement that makes leprosy such a dreaded disease results from a single cause: the person with leprosy cannot feel pain. The old man no longer treated his fingers as something worth preserving, as part of *self*, because his fingers felt no pain.

Dr. Brand said, in a comment that has always stayed with me, "A healthy body attends to the pain of the weakest part." Today, I assure you, the world is attending to the pain of India. We in the West suffered with you some months ago when we heard about the thousands made homeless in Orissa, and we suffer with you in the midst of this act of terror that drags on not far from us tonight.

✦ ✦ ✦

What is transpiring in downtown Mumbai gives a vivid picture of a world that does not operate by the rule of grace. Instead it operates by something akin to Newton's third law of motion: every action produces an equal and opposite reaction. If you hit me, I'll hit you back. Bomb my country and I'll bomb you back. Certainly that was my country's response after 9/11 and years later we are still dealing with the repercussions in far-flung places like Afghanistan and Iraq. Today leaders around the world are pleading for India not to follow that course.

The world operates by set rules. Politicians speak of justice, of individuals' rights and criminals getting what they deserve. Banks operate that way: they will loan you money to buy a motorcycle or even a house, but if you fall behind in payments they will repossess it. Empires operate that way, as you in India know well; offend the ruling power, and you pay a price.

Moreover, religions operate by similar rules. Need I point that out in a land that gave us the very term *karma*? Though it may take six or seven million reincarnations, say the Hindu scholars, eventually every person on earth will get exactly what he or she deserves.

Into that world Jesus spoke a radically different message. We get not what we deserve but the very opposite. We deserve punishment and get forgiveness; we deserve God's wrath and get God's love. In a world divided by race, culture, class, language, and religion, Jesus set loose the most powerful force in the universe, the force of grace. That counterforce brings a new message of hope to a world marked by violence and division.

I know no better research laboratory for grace than here in India, the most volatile mixture of caste, language, race, and religion on earth. We know what the alternative to grace looks like: step outside and you can almost see the smoke rising from hotels under siege in Mumbai. My question is, do we know what *grace* would look like in this place?

It requires no grace to get along with someone who looks like you and wholly agrees with you. Grace meets its test in the context of difference: a Dalit thrust next to a Brahmin, an abortionist or homosexual activist who thinks you bigoted and narrow-minded, a neighbor who hails from Pakistan. Realistically, how can grace work in such a setting? For clues, I turn to scenes from the life of Jesus, who turned loose this elusive counterforce.

In his public debut Jesus went to the synagogue in his home town and read aloud this passage from the prophet Isaiah:

> *The Spirit of the Lord is on me,*
>   *because he has anointed me*
>   *to preach good news to the poor.*

He has sent me to proclaim freedom for the prisoners
and recovery of sight for the blind,
to release the oppressed,
to proclaim the year of the Lord's favor. (Luke 4:18–19)

With the eyes of everyone fastened on him, he then made the dramatic announcement, "Today this scripture is fulfilled in your hearing." The congregation would have recognized the passage as one of Isaiah's Servant Songs predicting the Messiah, and yet Luke notes that no one took offense at Jesus' sensational claim. "All spoke well of him and were amazed at the gracious words that came from his lips."

A few minutes later, however, the fawning crowd turned into a lynch mob intent on pushing Jesus off a cliff. Why? Because he had the audacity to bring up incidents from the Old Testament in which God showed grace to two of Israel's enemies, a famished Phoenician widow and a leprous Syrian general. In doing so Jesus exposed the very human tendency of ranking one group above another. The Jewish audience welcomed Jesus' words as long as they assumed *themselves* to be the prisoners who needed freeing and the oppressed who needed releasing from the grinding rule of Rome. They clung to their privileged status as God's chosen people and resented any implication that others might dilute it. In effect, they wanted John 3:16 to read, "For God so loved the Jews" not "God so loved the world."

In Jesus' day everyone knew the ranking order: a pious Jewish man gave thanks every day that he had not been born a slave, a woman, or a Gentile. Likewise, in modern India you are born with a ranking that brands you throughout life. Though the caste system has softened over the years, every Dalit faces discrimination that a Brahmin will never encounter. Although Brahmin children may have Dalit playmates, they shy away from physical contact, a holdover from the "Untouchable" days. Here, as in my own country, everyone with dark skin confronts obstacles that do not apply to a lighter-skinned person.

To our shame we in the church often perpetuate the tendency to rank, sometimes by mimicking the prejudices of society and sometimes by adding our own. By last report there are thirty-eight thousand different Christian denominations in the world. There used to be 37,999 until one person decided he or she had a corner on truth that made his church more "pure" than all the rest and formed a new denomination or cult. I have a friend who, unable to find a church pure enough in the United States, moved to Australia where he still couldn't find a church with a theology that satisfied him. So he started his own church. Last I heard there were three people left in the church, after numerous splits and divisions: an old man with Parkinson's disease, my friend, and my friend's wife. The two men take turns preaching at each other (women aren't allowed to speak in this church).

Jesus came to us "full of grace and truth," John wrote in the prologue to his Gospel. The existence of thirty-eight thousand denominations, not to mention a history of creeds and councils and wars of religion, demonstrates the length to which churches go to compete for truth. I only wish churches expended equal energy competing to dispense grace.

Even the rare church that manages to bring together people of different races and social classes may create a new ranking system based on spirituality. Those with theological training look down on those who lack it. Spiritual gifts and healthy disciplines such as prayer and Bible study lapse into a form of unhealthy competition. Legalism creeps in, allowing the more "spiritual" to view others with mild contempt.

Jesus' final prayer with his disciples, in John 17, was an urgent plea for unity: "that they may be one as we are one." So far that prayer has gone grievously unanswered.

A few years ago I agreed to speak at a World Vision conference in your neighboring country Myanmar, or Burma. "You should know that almost all of the pastors who will attend have spent time in prison for their faith," said the man who invited me. "This is a very oppressive regime."

"Then should I speak on pain and suffering?" I asked.

"No, no, they expect that," he quickly replied. "They're used to it. We'd like you to speak on grace. You see, the various groups of Christians here can't get along with each other."

The unity of the church, Jesus' last request, is a miracle the world still awaits. What better place than India? I once heard an Indian church leader say that other religions here can replicate every reported Christian miracle except one. Christians claim physical healings, and so do Hindus and Muslims. Christians claim changed lives, and so do Buddhists. Only one miracle by the Christians causes other Indians to marvel: when people of different genders, races, castes, and social classes come together in a true spirit of unity.

Paul, a good Jew who had daily thanked God that he was no slave, woman, or Gentile, changed his prayer after experiencing the liberating power of grace. In an amazing turnabout he told the fractious Galatians, "There is neither Jew nor Greek, slave nor free, male nor female, for you are all one in Christ Jesus." May you in the church in India take the lead in showing a divided world at last the power of grace to overcome the human instinct to rank and disunite.

✦ ✦ ✦

The poor, prisoners, the blind, the oppressed—groups mentioned in Jesus' first sermon give a strong clue to his upside-down way of looking at the world. The poor are truly blessed, he would say in the Beatitudes, and also the meek, the persecuted, and those who mourn. These words should provide some hope and solace to India on this dark day. As if to underscore the point, many of Jesus' stories featured the least likely person—the *slumdog*, you might say—as the hero.

Jesus told of two men, one rich and successful, the other a beggar covered with sores. Lazarus the beggar stands out as the obvious hero; Jesus doesn't bother to give the rich man a name. In another story, two pedigreed religious professionals ignore the victim of a crime; a mixed-race heretic, the Good *Samaritan,* emerges as the hero. In perhaps his most famous story, Jesus commends not the obedient, responsible, parent-respecting brother but the rebellious profligate, the *Prodigal* Son.

Not only Jesus' stories, but also his personal contacts show that same pattern of reversal. I have actually gone through the Gospels and placed Jesus' contacts on a homemade graph. With few exceptions, the more upright, conscientious, even righteous a person is, the more Jesus threatens that person. The more immoral, irresponsible, social outcast a person is—in other words, most unlike Jesus himself—the more Jesus attracts that person. (How is it that Jesus' followers usually do the opposite?) The free gift of grace descends to whoever will receive it, and sometimes those who have nowhere else to turn are most eager to hold out open hands.

In one clear example, recorded in John 4, a woman has virtually nothing in common with Jesus. A despised Samaritan accustomed to racial prejudice, she feels surprise that a Jewish rabbi would deign to speak to her, much less drink from her "unclean" jar. Jesus' disciples seem more shocked that he would go against cultural mores by conversing with a woman. If any villagers were watching, they would no doubt question Jesus' prudence in conversing with *this* woman, for it soon comes out that she has a history of five failed marriages and is living with a man not her husband. Some scholars speculate that Jesus found her alone at a well under a blazing noonday sun because of shunning by other women, who would normally draw water in a group in the cool of the morning.

The woman represents huge differences from Jesus: racial, social, moral, and religious. In their conversation Jesus cuts right through those differences. He deflects her diversionary remarks about famous ancestors and where to worship and instead bores in on a most basic human need which she has in common with everyone else: thirst. He is speaking both literally and figuratively, for every sexual compulsion, every addiction eventually reveals itself as a false god incapable of satisfying our deepest thirst. Then Jesus proceeds to tell her of a living water that can quench thirst.

In all four Gospels only here do we find Jesus introducing himself to someone as the Messiah. This woman, whose background would disqualify her from most ministries I know of, Jesus taps as his first missionary. He chooses well, for many Samaritans become Jesus-followers as a result of this most unlikely witness. "This man really is the Savior of the world," they soon exclaim to the woman. Thanks to her they too encounter one who sees them as objects of God's transforming love and not God's judgment, and who envisions not what they have been but what they could be.

No doubt Jesus gave us these stories and embraced the outcasts to undercut what he knew was our basic human tendency to rank and to divide. As the Sermon on the Mount makes clear, the people in most danger are the ones who think they have arrived, for in doing so they miss out on grace. Only those aware of thirst ask for living water.

✦ ✦ ✦

Grace, which has the power to overcome differences in class and race and even theology, and power to quench the thirst of moral and social outcasts, offers hope both to the oppressed and the oppressor. Luke shrewdly brings together the two contrasting groups in his account of Jesus' visit to Jericho (Luke 18-19).

One could hardly find a better poster child for the oppressed than Bartimaeus. Like so many disabled and impoverished people here in India, he subsisted by begging. Blind, he had few options in that day. To make matters worse, his very name in Hebrew meant "son of garbage" or "son of filth," so that everytime someone called his name it deepened the insult. Bartimaeus stands for the underclass all over the world, those who for whatever reason cannot live without outside help.

"Son of David, have mercy on me!" Bartimaeus cried as Jesus approached, and the throng of Jesus' admirers quickly tried to shut him up. Beggars like Bartimaeus embarrassed the locals. Plus, Jesus was passing through Jericho at the height of his popularity and no doubt had a busy agenda. *Leave the famous rabbi alone—he has impor-tant work to do!* Yet to Jesus, what work could be more important than showing mercy to a blind beggar? He stopped, summoned the noisy Bartimaeus, and promptly healed him. Of all the people healed by Jesus, Bartimaeus is the only one whose name the Gospels record.

The church has done remarkably well at following Jesus' exam-ple of extending grace to the oppressed. Wherever I travel in the world I see this, from the church groups rebuilding houses after Hurricane Katrina in my country, to the relief agencies caring for AIDS orphans in Africa, to the mission hospitals and schools in the most remote parts of the world. In the last few weeks I have seen many inspiring examples here in India.

I have mentioned Dr. Paul Brand's work with leprosy. Most of the advances in the understanding and treatment of that feared dis-ease came from missionaries: not always because they were the best doctors and scientists, but because they alone were willing to serve and touch people with leprosy. This very morning I saw the AIDS work that developed out of Dr. Stephen Alfred's hospital as my wife and I accompanied two social workers on their visits to clients in a slum area. When a person is first diagnosed with the disease, these social workers visit the family *every day*, counseling other family mem-bers on safe practices and monitoring the medication. No government agency could afford to pay for the kind of personal care the church provides.

The church in India has a proud tradition of education and medical care. Even though Christians represent only 2 or 3 percent of the population, they manage a fifth of the country's health care. They run some of the best schools and now are extending that education for the first time to Dalits. I have watched some schools and hospitals founded for the poor gradually shift their emphasis in order to attract students and patients who can afford their services. I pray that you resist that trend, that you stay faithful to the example shown by Jesus with blind Bartimaeus, the son of garbage.

According to Luke, Jesus had not planned to spend time in Jericho and the incident with Bartimaeus merely delayed his passage through the town. His schedule changed, however, when he encountered a notorious oppressor named Zacchaeus. The chief of the region's tax collectors, Zacchaeus worked on commission and the townsfolk rightly viewed him as a collaborator with Rome. After all, he took good Jewish money and gave it to the very occupiers who enforced their rule with armed legions.

Luke mentions that Zacchaeus climbed a tree because, being short, he could not see over the crowd. Given his reputation he probably felt safer high up in a tree. Jesus soon exposed his vantage point, however, stopping the procession dead in its tracks and calling out to the little man perched among the sycamore leaves. "Zacchaeus, come down immediately. I must stay at your house today," he said, much to the dismay of the crowd who would never think of setting foot in the house of a publican. What follows demonstrates one key to bringing about more justice: convert the oppressors. So moved was Zacchaeus by Jesus' gesture that he immediately pledged to give half his holdings to the poor and restore fourfold to anyone he had cheated.

The muttering of the crowd against Jesus betrays an important truth: it is far harder to show grace to the oppressor than to the oppressed.

In a deed that shocked this nation, in 1999 a mob of Hindu fanatics attacked Graham Staines, an Australian missionary who was working among leprosy patients in the state of Orissa. They burned alive Graham and his two sons, aged ten and eight, inside their station wagon. Everyone expected his widow Gladys to retreat to Australia, but instead she stayed for five more years, continuing her husband's work. "I have forgiven the killers," she said of the attackers, after appealing in court for clemency. "I...have no bitterness because forgiveness brings healing and our land needs healing from hatred and violence." Before her retirement she oversaw the construction of a new leprosy center, the Graham Staines Memorial Hospital. In recognition, the

Indian government awarded Gladys Staines, a foreigner, the nation's second highest civilian honor.

Last year five young Islamic extremists infiltrated a Bible study in Turkey, pretending interest in Christianity. In a planned attack they turned on the Christian workers, torturing and killing three of them. One of the victims, a German missionary, had 150 stab wounds in his body. His widow responded exactly like Gladys Staines, forgiving the men who had so cruelly killed her husband. She quoted Jesus' words from the cross, "Father forgive them, for they know not what they do," which made front-page news in Turkey, a shining example of grace in a nation burdened with a long chain of violence toward Armenians and Kurds.

When the world sees grace in action toward undeserving oppressors, it falls silent. Nelson Mandela taught the world a lesson in grace when, after emerging from prison after twenty-seven years and being elected president of South Africa, he asked his jailer to join him at the inauguration and recruited white Afrikaner policemen as his bodyguards. He then appointed Archbishop Desmund Tutu to head the Truth and Reconciliation Commission, a creative way of bringing to light the ugly truth of oppression without exacting revenge.

According to the Commission's rules, if an oppressor faced his accusers and fully confessed his crime, he could not be prosecuted for that crime. Some in South Africa protested the injustice of letting criminals go free, but Mandela insisted the country needed healing even more than it needed justice. I have told the story of one such hearing before the TRC:

> A policeman named van de Broek recounted an incident when he and other officers shot an eighteen-year-old boy and burned the body, turning it on the fire like a piece of barbecue meat in order to destroy the evidence. Eight years later van de Broek returned to the same house and seized the boy's father. The wife was forced to watch as policemen

bound her husband on a woodpile, poured gasoline over his body, and ignited it.

The courtroom grew hushed as the elderly woman who had lost first her son and then her husband was given a chance to respond. "What do you want from Mr. van de Broek?" the judge asked. She said she wanted van de Broek to go to the place where they burned her husband's body and gather up the dust so she could give him a decent burial. His head down, the policeman nodded agreement.

Then she added a further request, "Mr. van de Broek took all my family away from me, and I still have a lot of love to give. Twice a month, I would like for him to come to the ghetto and spend a day with me so I can be a mother to him. And I would like Mr. van de Broek to know that he is forgiven by God, and that I forgive him, too. I would like to embrace him so he can know my forgiveness is real."

Some in the courtroom spontaneously began singing "Amazing Grace" as the elderly woman made her way to the witness stand, but van de Broek did not hear the hymn. He had fainted, physically overwhelmed by grace.

Justice was not done in South Africa that day, nor in the entire country as the TRC exposed atrocities to public view. Something beyond justice took place, the first step toward reconciliation.

Nations rightly pursue justice, as they will in the case of the Mumbai massacre. There comes a point, however, when justice reaches a dead end. Your revered leader Mahatma Gandhi said it well: "An eye for an eye and a tooth for a tooth, and the whole world would soon be blind and toothless."

In his life and death Jesus set forth another way, of otherworldly grace, and we his followers are commanded to follow in his steps. "Do not be overcome by evil, but overcome evil with good," said Paul. Evil is overcome by good only if the injured party absorbs it, refusing to allow it to go any further. And that is the pattern Jesus showed us in his life and death, a pattern repeated in Orissa as well as in Turkey and South Africa.

We who follow Jesus are called to be dispensers of God's grace, setting loose this powerful force on a weary, violent planet. May the church be known as a place where grace flows on tap: to sinners, to rich and poor alike, to those who need more light, to outcasts, to those who disagree, to oppressed and oppressors both.

Afterthoughts:
What Good Is God?

How do I get myself into these predicaments? I asked myself as the plane left the chaos of India and sped toward my Colorado home. *Why do I travel anyway?* It's a good question, one I reflect on after each grueling trip.

In partial answer, I travel for the same reasons anyone travels. We experience beauty and adventure, expand horizons, gain a new perspective on our own culture. And as a journalist I depend on a fresh supply of such experiences. I have watched the first rays of sun hit the Taj Mahal, and followed an endless line of wildebeest as they snaked across the Serengeti; I've jogged through Moscow's Red Square in winter's biting cold, and snorkeled the warm waters of Australia's Great Barrier Reef. From Japan I learn about courtesy and civility: even the gas station attendants wear white gloves, bow to your car as you drive in, and wash your windshield without expecting a tip. The Middle East could give lessons to the rest of us on gracious hospitality.

Eventually, though, the glamour of travel wears off, especially after 9/11: long security lines, the hassle of removing shoes, belt, watch, and change, then extracting phone, laptop, gels, and liquids from hand luggage. International travel may also take a toll on health. On plane trips beyond twelve hours I sometimes feel a sore throat developing cell by cell. Unable to sleep on flights, I try to sit quietly and read even as scum grows over my teeth and my eyes dry out.

I have toured in developing-world countries where traffic and pollution are oppressive, the food suspect. During meetings the air-conditioning and the sound system may malfunction, and afterward people crowd around suffocatingly at book signings. Just as I'm feeling sorry for myself, ready to swear off trips forever, I meet some nurse who runs an AIDS program in remote villages and rides a motorbike on muddy roads four to five hours every day. At that point I remind myself of a second, deeper reason why I travel, the true origin of this book. I go in search of a faith that matters.

As I look back over the ten trips recounted in this book, what have I found?

On the somber campus of Virginia Tech and in the shell-shocked city of Mumbai I saw the church as a haven of comfort for those who grieve. Scientific studies of the effect of prayer on physical healing yield mixed results, but every study verifies that wounded people heal best and live best in a supportive community. We are not designed to bear pain alone, and in Blacksburg, Virginia, and Mumbai, India, the church opened wide its doors at a time of profound suffering. More, I also saw that the church can offer a place to confront the reality of evil without giving in to revenge. A world marked by acts of terrorism and madness desperately needs the church to show another way to cope with differences in culture, race, and caste.

Admittedly, the church has at times contributed more to the problem than to the solution, something I learned while growing up in a Bible Belt subculture that clung to segregation with one hand and biblical inerrancy with the other. I sometimes joke about being "in recovery" from a toxic local church, and in my writing I bend over backwards to acknowledge rather than deny the historical flaws of the broader church. It struck me, as I returned to a Bible college campus I described as "Life in a Bubble," that Christian faith may sour when lived in isolation from the rest of the world. When I review Jesus' loud complaints against the Pharisees, they seem to reduce to a single implicit accusation: Pharisees spend too much time around other Pharisees. As a result Pharisees (whether the Jewish or Christian variety) neglect wider issues, narrow their vision, and compete to achieve an artificial piety.

I emerged from the Bible college bubble with enduring gratitude for certain things I learned there: personal discipline, a sense of life's ultimacy, a commitment to the Jesus way. In the days since, I have seen Christians draw on those very qualities to help transform the world around them. Scott Morris of the Church Health Center in Memphis provides a sterling example, by setting out an alternative vision to solve a huge social problem and then attracting volunteers to put their faith into action. To be fair to the school I attended, I also know classmates who are now working with flood victims in the Philippines, teaching English in China, flying supplies to schools and clinics in Peru, and visiting prisons in South Africa. Bubble institutions can serve a healthy purpose as long as they prepare for life outside.

In my interviews with addicts and prostitutes I heard several dozen wrenching accounts of the power of evil to control and destroy lives—and the power of God to overcome that evil. I wish skeptics like Christopher Hitchens and Richard Dawkins had the same chance to hear stories of transformation from social outcasts who hit the very bottom and now credit God for the strong grace that saved them in the most literal sense. *What good is God? He rescued me from sex slavery and drug addiction. God brought me back to life.* No doubt the skeptics would have a different, psychosocial explanation for the life changes, but hearing a dozen such stories in an afternoon tends to overwhelm rational argument. Jesus himself rarely offered theological proofs; he simply went around transforming lives.

At the other end of the spectrum, the scholar C. S. Lewis worked in a sophisticated academic environment that bred its own form of evil: contention, snobbery, arrogance, backbiting. Though Lewis did indeed offer logical arguments in support of what he believed, those who knew him before and after conversion point to his own life as the strongest proof. "He's the most thoroughly converted man I have ever met," said one acquaintance.

China gave me snapshots of transformation of another kind, one that percolates through society. Jesus likened the kingdom to small things—salt on meat, yeast in bread, a tiny seed in the garden—as if to emphasize we dare not judge the gospel's impact by numbers. Visitors to communist countries, with their doctrinaire atheism, might ask an opposite question than the one of this book: what good is no-God? Chairman Mao still stares out from photos on the walls of most Chinese homes, but most would reckon his attempt to displace God a failure. Mao redirected the universal human instinct to worship toward his own personality cult, yet in the process he severed morality and virtue from their roots. Does faith matter? One need only consider the last century to see grim proof that, at the least, no-faith matters. Stalin and Mao, ardent enemies of religion, together caused the deaths of one hundred million of their own citizens. Meanwhile, Christians carrying candles and singing hymns marched through the streets of Eastern Europe until the Iron Curtain fell in a heap. And below the radar screen of media attention a religious revival broke out in Mao's China that may yet change the history of Asia and the world.

Western powers have learned a related and painful lesson in Iraq and Afghanistan: change imposed by force rarely produces the desired results. Likewise, a faith that matters grows best from the ground up, working its way through society gradually, without coercion. Christianity first spread by this route along the eastern frontier of the Roman empire, and after a period of triumphalism Christians in that Middle East region find themselves once again as a beleaguered minority. Their example of compassion for social outcasts and respect for women's rights may, in the long term, do more to advance democratic values than any imposed political solution.

Of all the places I visited, South Africa presented at once the most excitement and the most daunting challenge. Nelson Mandela may well have asked "What good is God?" as he spent twenty-seven years in prison under a regime that quoted the Bible to support its racist doctrine. Yet Mandela's faith held strong, and with a moral authority backed by Bishop Desmond Tutu he led his nation through a peaceful transition when nearly everyone was predicting a bloodbath. Today South Africa has a flourishing church and people of all races are working to tackle the enormous problems of poverty, AIDS, crime, and corruption.

Often when people pose a question like "What good is God?" they are asking why God doesn't intervene more directly and with more force. Why did God let Hitler do so much damage, or Stalin and Mao? Why doesn't God take a more active role in human history? I can think of several possible reasons. According to the Old Testament, God did take an active and forceful role in the past, yet it failed to produce lasting faith among the Israelites. And, as earthly powers have learned, force and freedom make uneasy partners and an emphasis on one always diminishes the other; God consistently tilts toward human freedom. In the end, though, we have no sure answer and only fleeting glimpses of God's ultimate plan.

For whatever reason, God chooses to make himself known primarily through ordinary people like us. Yet again, I recall my friend Joanna's clear statement to explain the transformation that took place in Pollsmoor Prison: "Well, of course, Philip, God was already present in the prison. I just had to make him visible." The question "What good is God?" is an open question whose answer God has invested in us his followers. We are the ones called to demonstrate a faith that matters to a watching world. I have reported on ten places where I have seen that question answered—incompletely as it must be when entrusted to ordinary people, yet in a way that assuredly releases the fragrance of hope and transformation. May that fragrance continue to spread.